P9-AEU-346

AUDUBON

by the same author

AMERICAN HUMOR
DAVY CROCKETT
TROUPERS OF THE GOLD COAST
TRUMPETS OF JUBILEE

PAINTED BUNTING. *PLATE NO. LIII*

AUDUBON

BY

Constance Rourke

With 12 colored plates from original Audubon prints

BLACK AND WHITE ILLUSTRATIONS BY

James MacDonald

HARCOURT, BRACE AND COMPANY
NEW YORK

COPYRIGHT, 1936, BY
HARCOURT, BRACE AND COMPANY, INC.

*All rights reserved, including
the right to reproduce this book
or portions thereof in any form.*

PRINTED AND BOUND IN THE UNITED STATES OF AMERICA
BY THE HADDON CRAFTSMEN, INC., CAMDEN, NEW JERSEY

AUDUBON PRINTS
BY THE POLYGRAPHIC COMPANY OF AMERICA, NEW YORK

For Hélène Allain
of Wakefield, Feliciana
with grateful remembrance

CONTENTS

AUDUBON PRINTS

AUDUBON

1 *A Mystery—But No Matter*

A BOY named Fougère peered through the shutters of a house in the city of Nantes. A procession was passing, gay but a little wild. Men in long red caps swaggered in crowded clusters. Bareheaded women shouted and laughed. The boy watched eagerly, and since he was already a young republican he cried, "*Vive la république!*" But his voice was doubtful. Already the crowds were growing angry, then savage. Presently men and women in silks and velvets were dragged along at the cart's tail, jeered at by the rough throng. "A bas! A bas!" was the loud cry. "Down with them, down with them! The guillotine!"

Stout and amiable Madame Audubon, sitting in the dusky

room, tried to tell him that these were rich nobles who had harmed the people, but she was weeping. She had friends in both camps. A little girl, Muguet, was at her side.

The noise in the street turned into a roar. "No harm can come to us," quavered Madame Audubon, "for the good captain is a republican. This is the Revolution."

One thing is certain. Fougère stayed at the window. He lacked fear, and he had a lively wish to know what was going on in the world.

These days were full of strange events. While the streets still smelled of gunpowder and were darkened by smoke, Captain Audubon and his wife registered papers of adoption for these two children. The Captain stated that he was the father of both of them.

Except for a hot temper and a strong constitution, the Captain and the boy Fougère bore little resemblance to each other; they might have come from different worlds. Erect, tall for his years, slenderly, firmly built, Fougère had wide, candid eyes, a high color, and well-molded features. His motions were swift; expression played fluently over his small countenance. He had unmistakably what is called the look of race.

Captain Audubon was stocky, red-headed, blue-eyed; his mouth and nose were blunt, his head was set at a devil-may-care angle; it is easy to imagine that he had a rolling gait. On occasion he would cover his head with a curled wig, but this hardly altered his rough and ready appearance. He was the son of a poor fisherman, one of twenty children, who had been set adrift in the world at the age of twelve and had made his way up by lusty strength.

Mystery attaches to Fougère's birth. The full name of the mother of little Muguet was given in the papers of adoption but that of the boy's mother was omitted. She was described only as having lived "in America." Either Captain Audubon did not know or did not wish to give her name. He declared that she was dead. Both children were said to have been born "in America."

Mystery appears in the several names given the boy during his youth. For a number of years after the adoption the Audubons called him Fougère. This, since it means "fern," may have been a pet name to match that of little Rosa who was called Muguet or "lily of the valley." Or Fougère may have represented a family connection. But this name was soon dropped and he was called La Forêt. In his later years Lucy Bakewell, who became his wife, always called him La Forêt. During his youth in France this name was also set aside and he was called Jean, then Jean Jacques. Sometimes he wrote his name Jean Jacques La Forêt Audubon, or used the corresponding initials. When he was past twenty he was described as Jean Rabin in certain legal documents signed by Captain Audubon and his wife. Only one of these papers gave him the name of Audubon.

Some twenty years before the beginning of the French Revolution the Captain had come into the command of a merchant ship which carried silks, velvets, wines, and other expensive articles to the rich planters of Santo Domingo. He brought back cargoes of sugar to France. His voyages were full of adventure since ships flying the black flag were speeding over the South Seas seeking just such prizes. Captain Audubon had sent cannon balls across their bows; he had fought them squarely, or sailed past them. His ship was never captured by pirates.

When the American Revolution broke out he had had to guard against British privateers. For a time he eluded them, but a small fleet of six bore down upon him at last. He fought them stubbornly, was overwhelmed, lost his ship, and was taken to New York a prisoner. Released before the Revolution was over, he managed to join the French fleet under de Grasse and soon was commanding a smart little *corvette*. He saw the surrender of Cornwallis at Yorktown, and knew both Lafayette and Washington. Stubborn, loyal, a hard fighter, as commander of one or another ship he carried out useful missions for the American forces and remained with them until peace was declared.

Captain Audubon then returned to that distant island in the Caribbean which rose like a steep mountain from the sea, around whose base ran a thick border of sugar cane. This time he was sent by a company of merchants in Nantes to look after their trade there. Vertically the sun beat down, changing the young green of the cane to gold. Naked black figures bent in the brakes. Fortunes were to be had trading in sugar and in slaves. Captain Audubon bought a plantation of his own and dealt largely in both. He soon amassed a considerable fortune. In 1789 he left

Santo Domingo, perhaps because he had heard the first low rumble of revolution there, which was to become a hideous warfare between the whites and the blacks.

When he returned to France did he bring two children with him? This is not known. His movements after he left Santo Domingo have not been traced, but he is thought to have traveled by way of New Orleans. Apparently he had been in Louisiana more than once. If he was accompanied by a little boy on this last journey there is no certainty that this was the same boy whom he adopted as Fougère Audubon some three years later.

Evidence has come to light showing that during his stay in Santo Domingo a boy was born to a Mademoiselle Rabin, for whom Captain Audubon evidently felt a responsibility. The date of that child's birth appears among some old papers of no other importance which the Captain had brought with him from the island, and a date close to this was given in the papers of adoption as the date of Fougère's birth–April 22, 1785. On this evidence, and because of the Audubons' later use of the name Jean Rabin to indicate Fougère, it has been concluded that he was the boy born obscurely in Santo Domingo. Perhaps he was, but the obvious concealment of facts raises questions.

A long period exists between the date given for Fougère's birth and the date of his adoption, nearly nine years–a gap which has not been filled in. Where was this boy during that time? Children of quite ordinary gifts can often recall scenes which they witnessed at the age of three or four; and this boy was not ordinary; he had a peculiar genius for observation. He could see tiny objects at great distances; he could note with equal exactness the almost invisible traceries in a leaf or a flower. Yet apparently nothing out of his early childhood, no flash of color, no remembrance of faces, no recollection of journeys or voyages remained with him. Perhaps the changing events of these years were too confused or too difficult for a child to understand and they slipped away from him. Perhaps he never told what he remembered, or told this only in secrecy to those nearest him. He may have been instructed not to tell.

During these eight or nine years before Fougère was adopted, Captain Audubon had been occupied with many affairs, in Santo Domingo, in New Orleans, in France. He was a man of varied connections, as was shown by the ease with which he had joined Rochambeau's fleet. When he reached France on his final journey, the Bastille had been stormed and the mob had forced Louis XVI and Marie Antoinette to drive with the royal children to Paris. The Captain had promptly joined the National Guard, but he had come from a province where royalist allegiances were deep, and he had royalist friends.

The fate of many families in France was now undergoing upheaval. Many were emigrating from France, particularly from Captain Audubon's own province, La Vendée, where the conflict of the Revolution was particularly harsh. Men and women were seeking whatever port they could find for themselves and for their children. Titles were being discarded for new names, and the unscrupulous were taking advantage of the deluge to conceal circumstances that might work against them in matters of money or preferment. Then and later whispers were heard as to the fate of many children, particularly that of the little Dauphin, who happened to be almost precisely the same age as that given for young Audubon—or Jean Rabin. The small son of Louis XVI and Marie Antoinette was generally believed to have been spirited out of prison, and was said to be living obscurely in France, in England, or even America.

It is well within the range of possibility that after his return to France, during the Revolution, a boy was entrusted to the care of Captain Audubon whose identity he was induced to hide. He may have used the approximate birthday and later the name of the little boy born in Santo Domingo to cover the history of another child. Some of those closest to Audubon the naturalist during his lifetime believed implicitly that he was of noble birth. "My own name I have never been permitted to speak," he once said. "Accord me that of Audubon, which I revere, as I have cause to do." On another occasion, late in life, he mentioned the name of an old boat on the Ohio which nearly went down in a storm. "Her name, like mine," he declared, "is only a shadow." But he had then made the name of Audubon famous on two continents. His allusion seems to have been to another name, sunk in obscurity, which belonged to him.

Certainly in his boyhood he must have heard tales of children who had experienced strange events because of the Revolution.

He must have known then that his birth and parentage were not altogether clear. The date of his adoption, March 7, 1794, remains as the first positive date in his history.

The mystery was to occupy him later. Its existence throws light on Audubon's character. He might have turned in protest or anger against Captain Audubon, but all his life he was to speak of the lively old sea captain with grateful devotion. If his name was a shadow there was nothing shadowy or confused about his ways. From first to last he was open-hearted, light-hearted. Whatever the world into which he was born, he found a world of his own without hesitation. As soon as the dark days in Nantes were over he walked out into sunny country lanes and made discoveries—the fat bustling scurry of a woodchuck, the flight of swallows over the silver waters of the Loire, the high pure cascading notes of a meadowlark far above his head.

No one led him to hidden paths in the woods or fields or along the river. On the contrary the Audubons had different ideas. Old Madame Audubon, positive that he was the handsomest boy in France, was anxious to have him learn the ways of a young gentleman. She insisted upon his taking lessons in music and dancing. He was born with a gift for music and quickly learned to play the violin, the flute, the little flageolet. This last he liked because he could tuck it in his pocket and try to imitate bird notes with it out of doors. The graceful steps of the French dances of the time he learned willingly enough, the *gavotte*, the *pavane*, the *minuet*. But they did not occupy him, and neither Madame Audubon's steady coaxing nor the sweets she carried in her great pocket could persuade him to give them much attention. Fencing he enjoyed. His practice in this art used his quick observation and gave suppleness to his hands.

Captain Audubon wanted him to become a naval officer or an engineer and arranged his first studies accordingly. But when the Captain was away at sea, young Fougère was more likely to be in the woods than studying mathematics or mechanical drawing. His room became a clutter of birds' nests, feathers, eggs, shells, lichens, flowers, pebbles, mosses. When the Audubons went to La Gerbetière, their pleasant place in the country not far from Nantes, he had a still wider range. The Captain placed him in a naval school at Rochefort, but he gave his masters the slip, was caught, brought back, and punished by imprisonment. At last the Captain must have been convinced that the boy would continue to resist these efforts to shape his career, for he was soon back at Nantes and in the fields again. A result was that he never received any systematic education.

His absorption in the life of the woods and orchards and fields became a passion; he thought of little else, nor was it enough to watch and follow birds and imitate their notes, or to snare a woodchuck or rifle a nest of field mice. He hunted, and he must draw these small creatures–the quadrupeds, but most of all the birds. He was soon spending many hours over small pencil sketches, of a coot, a magpie, a green woodpecker.

"These were all bad," he said later. "Very, very *bad!* My pencil gave birth to a family of cripples. Yet I felt pleased with them. I thought I had drawn a bird because I had put on paper some sort of head and tail with two sticks for legs. And, oh! what bills and claws, to say nothing of a perfectly straight line for a back, with a tail stuck in anyhow. Those tails! You know how rudders sometimes get loose from a boat and will fall this way and that? Unshipped rudders, they say. Well, those tails were like unshipped rudders. In real life they would fall off the bird!"

Captain Audubon was sympathetic. "Nought that's alive is easy to copy," he said. Even though he did not regard these occupations as important, he helped the boy procure stuffed birds from which to make drawings, and at last sent him to Paris for lessons with the great artist and teacher of the day, Jacques Louis David.

Now Fougère had an undeveloped gift for drawing delicate small things. David insisted upon his drawing large objects in bold outline. More than anything else the boy wanted to capture the look of life and motion, but great plaster casts were set before him, lifeless and white, depicting a remote life of antiquity of which he knew nothing. In the streets he watched the thick clustering sparrows, but he could not put on paper what he saw. Perhaps his searching eyes still did not see enough. He missed his walks in the country, and he was soon back at La Gerbetière.

Here he began his chosen work. David had confined him to black chalk on white paper. He made up his mind to use colors—water colors. Again and again he blotted them and had to begin once more. His tones were too deep or not deep enough; the shadings never pleased him except when he was working on them —not always then. Sometimes he resorted to colored crayons. Stiff profiles of birds in partial color and in not altogether natural attitudes were the most he could accomplish, but this was more of an achievement than he knew. Birds from strange lands had been painted by travelers, sometimes fancifully, but the portrayal of common native birds as they were, in color and precise detail, had not been attempted.

Perhaps he could not have told why he often painted birds on a spray of leaves with berries or fruit. He might have said, "Because that's where they always are—on branches. I paint them as they are."

He might have given a different reason. "I paint them on a branch because they please me more that way." He might have added, "I like the way the stem tips down, and the leaves turn, and the breast of the bird curves upward. Look, they make a little pattern."

He was unconsciously setting himself a difficult task. These two purposes might join or they might not. If he painted birds as they were, they might not always make patterns which he liked. How could he do both? In these early paintings he accomplished neither. Design was there but it was crude. He labored to tell the truth but fell far short. The sedge sparrow, the crow—how he worked over their likenesses! Tails still gave him trouble; they all looked as though they had been joined to the bird as an afterthought and lay flat upon the paper. But in his paintings the slender little claws seemed really to clutch their perch; he often achieved smooth outlines of breast or head or wing; the small heads were sometimes caught in a natural pose.

Often he drew only birds, but he still wanted the whole picture and he would try again to paint them with sprays of leaves. In this, though he did not know it, he was achieving still another innovation. Many years later ornithologists persisted in drawing birds as though they perched forever upon slender wooden cylinders, all tipped at the same angle, about two inches long. Following the instinct he felt as a boy, Audubon became the first to paint them fully against their native background, on waving grasses, among flower stalks, in thickets of leaves, on watery shores.

He toiled on, destroying many drawings, saving a few, numbering these in an orderly fashion. At last he had nearly a hundred. Madame Audubon thought them the wonder of the age. Captain Audubon was puzzled. What would become of a boy like this? He was now seventeen, nearly eighteen—and only birds, more birds, with an occasional groundhog by way of variety.

During his many voyages the Captain had acquired property in America. He made a sudden decision. The boy should go there; he could learn to manage the Captain's American interests. And in America—all things could happen in America! The impractical were transformed; they had only to breathe the air of the great western continent and suddenly they became industrious or they found pots of gold or they had great adventures. What kind of adventures? All kinds! Everyone said so. He himself had known of startling events. He had other reasons for sending Fougère to America which he did not disclose. Later he wrote to an agent, Dacosta, "The reasons which made me send him out there still remain." From the letter it seems clear that these had nothing to do with the boy's faults, which he spoke of as trivial. They could not have had to do with money; for a time Fougère was well supplied with money, and Captain Audubon still expected to recover the fortune he had lost through the warfare in Santo Domingo. Nothing was said about birds. Whatever his reasons were, they persisted, and may have had to do with the boy's parentage. When Fougère went to America Captain Audubon wanted him to stay, though he spoke of him with unmistakable affection.

Fougère was elated. His notions of America were hazy but the haze was bright.

2 *Spring on the Perkiomen*

BREAKING over limestone, rushing in pale eddies, the Perkiomen flooded the roots of great elms and poured at high water into the Schuylkill below the farm. Thin clouds of tiny leaves rose along its banks, pink, pale purple, yellow. The cherry trees bordering the lanes were in bud, and below the dark dense grove of hemlocks the red soil had been deeply plowed.

Well-placed on a ridge stood a broad two-storied farmhouse of red rubble stone. There in the early spring of 1803 young Audubon received a friendly welcome from the Thomases, a pair of excellent Quakers whom Captain Audubon had placed in charge of his estate at Mill Grove. The place took its name from a grist mill, already old, whose wheels were turning beside the Perkiomen.

Men moved in and out of the stone barns, cattle were being driven out to pasture. The whole place was astir, but to Audubon this new country seemed like wild land after the trim order of the French landscape. He had hardly arrived when the Thomases saw him striding off toward high ground. Forests rose in waves of green westward toward the blue Reading Hills. Following narrow footpaths on high ledges he could see great feathery reaches of pine and hemlock to the north and south which might still have been savage.

White men had long since left their print there. This country was already full of memories. Mill Grove had once belonged to William Penn. Not far away Lafayette had crossed the Schuylkill to save his army by strategy. A little to the south lay Valley Forge. Boone, whom Audubon came to know in the West, was born near Reading, and Squire Boone had made a decision as to these rivers which still stood, forbidding fishermen to place their nets from shore to shore since these impeded flatboats by which farmers carried their produce to Philadelphia. Thrifty farms were folded away within these forests though Audubon could not see them. The Quakers had long since come, and the Germans and Swiss had built their substantial houses and great, gayly-colored barns.

Near Mill Grove were many young people who promptly welcomed this strong handsome boy with his broken, plunging English, who said "thee" and "thou" like the Quaker Thomases, and wore the finest frilled shirts and black satin breeches. For a time he could hardly dress with sufficient elegance. He had plenty of money and plenty of time. The Thomases managed the place well; there was little else to occupy him. "A popinjay—I was making a popinjay of myself," he said. "I had a little fancy for fine clothes. I was absurdly fond of dress." Once when he had missed a chance to ride to Philadelphia he went the thirty miles on foot to purchase some new shirts; and he danced with all the girls. In the exhilaration of his first arrival he was playing a part, that of the gay young Frenchman, precisely as it was expected of him, with frills, dancing, gallantry. All his life he was fond of masquerades; he was to play more than one brief part out of mischief. No masquerade ever occupied him for long, and this one was soon over.

As he was walking alone near the old mill one evening he heard a noise like a saw being whetted against a grindstone. The door of the mill was closed for the night; he peered through the windows but the noise had stopped. He went to the miller's house to inquire, but no saw was being sharpened. The rough sound then came from an old hemlock and he looked up in time to see a small owl in the dusk, the Acadian owl, sometimes called a "saw-whet." He tried to follow it but the small dark ghost with its harsh noise was suddenly gone.

With a fish hawk sailing above the Perkiomen he had no better luck, though the bird swept down to the water close to him, rose with a flapping silver fish in its beak and disappeared above the trees.

"Spring—a sure sign of spring, is fish hawks," said a tall stooped man who was casting when Audubon came back from the woods. "When the fish comes upstream to spawn, fish hawks'll foller. You'll see 'em dip quick as thought."

The river, the milldam, the birds skimming over the dark water —he couldn't stay away from them. Along the high wooded banks of the Perkiomen were caves deeply scooped out of limestone, perhaps by prehistoric dwellers in this region, perhaps by the force of the stream. One of them was large enough for him to enter; he had found there an unfamiliar clean empty nest when he first arrived. The next afternoon a pair of dusky olive, yellow, gray-white birds flew past him. Weary, dull, they glided into the large cave. But their subdued colors seemed almost bright the following day as they chased insects, and when he moved toward the cave the male flew impetuously toward it, snapping his bill, sounding an abrupt, trembling, rolling note.

With La Fontaine's "Fables" in his hand, Audubon found a place near the cave and began to read; the phoebes soon regarded him as a fixture. Little by little he moved nearer; at last he was able to slip inside and watch them as they worked, delicately adding grass and moss and lichens to the nest, fabricating a silky lining from feathers and down until something like an exquisite mossy plant hung from the moist rock. Six eggs, white with a few reddish spots near the end, were laid and hatched; the birds now knew him so well that they were unflurried even when he slid his fingers into the nest and picked up the young fledglings.

He put them deftly back and watched other pairs of phoebes in a dark shed near the river or in the rafters of the old mill. The vivacious, not quite sweet note of the phoebes was always to bring back to him memories of Mill Grove.

These days were filled by fresh sights and sounds. The red-wings came, and the grackles. Among the spread flowers of dog-wood he saw the black and deep rose of a grosbeak, his throat clear white against the curled green-white petals. A great eagle glistened in the sky. Muskrats haunted a small narrow wooded island near the shore above the milldam; sleek otters were there, and mink—"minxes": he never learned to call them anything else. Quiet in the grass, he watched their inquisitive ways, saw them stalking mice or small squirrels, and their sudden arched spring as they seized their prey. New flowers enchanted and distracted him—the last of the wood anemones, Dutchman's breeches in gray clefts of rock, the pale flowers of the May apple.

Then though the woods were still fragrant, he lost himself indoors over his drawing board, exhilarated by the multitude of his discoveries and expecting to produce masterpieces. But his drawings seemed no better than those he had made in France. They must be better! He shot a hawk and set it on a rough branch, holding the bird in place by a cord fastened from above. "Bah!" he shouted after many hours of work with water colors and pastels.

At this time poulterers made known their wares by hanging out signs on which a chicken or duck or turkey was crudely painted. "Good enough for such a sign," he said in disgust.

"Alive and moving—I must draw only that way," he told himself.

With pencils and drawing board he went to the river and began sketching phoebes on the wing, darting into caves, poised for a moment on a branch. He sketched other flycatchers and saw that all of them were lax and quiet when they perched, their wings drooping even when they sat upright; all made the same nervous skimming sallies. He had seen herons in the willows on the Perkiomen—little green herons—"fly-up-the-creeks"—and the great blue waders: in momentary poses he thought he saw likenesses between them beyond that of the long legs—a lift of wing, a dip in flight—different as these two herons were. What made these identities he couldn't say. He could only catch them in penciled outline, trying to mirror a character.

He made hundreds of sketches and finished none of them, for the clear reason that birds are never still. But he must finish! And stuffed birds would never do for his final work since these lacked the fresh contours of life. He always hated to see birds in cages, and he had rejoiced when on a neighboring farm he saw a goldfinch escape the trickery of birdlime by tipping instantly backward and dropping down until the lime was a thread and could be broken. Yet he must have birds!

In this country as in Europe songbirds were shot for food and sold on the markets—robins, bluebirds, ricebirds, snowbirds. The wild pigeon was considered a game bird, as was the great, spirited ivory-billed woodpecker of the deep forests. With clear vision, swift, sure hands, and the gift of patience, Audubon was to become an expert marksman. He was naturally a hunter, and he belonged to his time. He was no prophet; he could not have foreseen the outcome of a lavish plundering of the wilderness. Though he did not know it, he had something of the attitude of the Indian toward birds and animals. The Indian hunter killed them for food though not needlessly, and they became his emblems. He wove them as figures into rugs or baskets; he adopted their names as his own; they gave significance to his paintings. For the Indian they were people—the Bird People, the Beaver People. He told stories about them and studied their ways as closely as he would those of the members of his own tribe, but he entertained no sentimental notions about them; his scrutinies were close, his attitudes impersonal. He remained the hunter.

But hunting proved no solution for Audubon. "Alas! they are *dead!*" he cried as he attempted vainly to place in natural attitudes the birds he had shot. When he saw living birds on the wing the blood rushed to his temples; he was humiliated and dismayed, and for a time he gave up both hunting and drawing altogether.

Already on the way toward becoming a prodigious reader, he buried himself in books, turning again to the fables of La Fontaine, which he was always to love for their wise talkative animals and shrewd, gay little birds. He read whatever he could find. But reading was not enough; he was soon collecting nests, eggs, mosses, branches of pine and hemlock, flowers, grasses. His supple fingers learned to prepare birdskins with delicate skill so that at leisure he could study plumages. He worked at the art of mounting birds and small animals. After all, perhaps he might stuff them so that they seemed alive! Squirrels, raccoons, opossums, woodchucks, and even passive snakes and lizards, now quietly peered down from over the doorways and windows of his room and from chests of drawers or the backs of easy chairs. They began to invade the rest of the house to the distraction of neat Mrs. Thomas.

It was the fashion of the day to plait tiny strands of hair into complicated patterns and set them under glass in gold frames, to be worn by ladies as brooches. These had no beauty, but skill was required to fashion them, and Audubon could not resist the effort. He modeled wax into leaves and flowers. He wove softened willow withes into baskets.

His long hands were never still. Toying with small objects he discovered that he could slide or slip them with a barely percepti-ble motion up his sleeve or under a table or into the tail of his long coat.

By sleight of hand he coaxed Mrs. Thomas into a smile when she had seen one snakeskin too many coiled naturally around a candlestick in her trim parlor. Coming in at this moment, he palmed a silver coin for her.

"Thou art a gay young blade," she said mildly.

The Thomases regarded this tall graceful young Frenchman as a little crack-brained.

Suddenly he remembered something he had seen in David's studio, and attacked the problem of drawing birds once more. Instead of a living model David had used manikins of wood and plaster. Audubon carved soft wood to resemble parts of a bird and fastened the whole together with wires.

"It looks like a dodo!" he cried in disgust. "A jumping jack!" When a neighbor strolled in and declared that his little image looked like an old gander, he broke it into splinters.

Soon after this, long before dawn, he jumped out of bed, dressed, got a horse and galloped to Norristown, five miles distant. The streets were quiet when he arrived, the shops still shuttered and barred. He went to the river, stripped, and swam for a while, and at last returned to the village where he succeeded in buying wires of different sizes. Back at Mill Grove Mrs. Thomas offered him breakfast but without a word he took down his gun and ran to the Perkiomen where he shot the first kingfisher he saw. In his room, with fingers that were careful not to ruffle any least feather, he passed wires gently through the body of the bird. By the same means he was able to hold the big spiky head in place, then the firm claws, finally the short barred tail. He lightly fastened the bird against a softwood board which he propped on a table. A turn here, another there, and his fingers had fairly coaxed the kingfisher into life.

"There is the real kingfisher!" he said as he began to draw.

With infinite care he filled in the blue and gray, the rough white, the dark shadings, the firm belt across the breast. With all his observation he had not yet learned to balance his tones. He weighted the bird's large head with shadow. Leaning forward, it looked as though it were about to drive its heavy bill into the ground. But Audubon was exultant in the conquest of a difficulty. This means of creating the effect of life, adapted more and more skillfully, he was henceforward to use for all his paintings, even though he continued to sketch out of doors. He worked steadily all morning and was famished when he laid on the last touch of color. He had had no breakfast.

The cherry trees in the lanes turned lacy white, then were laden with bright fruit. Summer came full of broad color, rich leafage, ripening corn, the rush of white water on the rivers. Audubon was now always up before dawn. Before it was fairly light he would hear the beginnings of songs, many of them unfamiliar, and would trace the curves of single melodies for a moment before these were lost in the medley. In the woods and along the banks of the river he would lie motionless for hours to watch young birds that he couldn't recognize. He hunted constantly. Then, inside again, he set squared paper behind his birds and drew on squared paper to obtain an entire accuracy. Occasionally he placed them on his favorite leaf-sprays or flower-branches, and turned these, altered, experimented, uncertain of the effects. But for the most part now he gave up the effort to create a beautiful design, keeping to the purpose of mere truthful portrayal.

The days were never long enough. He spent six, eight, even ten hours at his drawing board, knowing that the iridescence of a bird's feathers is soon lost, that the most brilliant plumage quickly becomes dull.

At the end of the summer he attempted a painting which might have daunted any artist, that of the great blue heron. He knew little about herons but chose the handsomest specimen he could find, a tall male with slaty-blue plumage and rich black wing tips, curved and silky. He worked tirelessly to place the bird in a posture which his eye told him was a true one. Drawing on a great sheet of squared paper, so large that he had to rig a new drawing board for it, copying freely on another sheet of the same size which would take colors, he tried to achieve the soft curves and clear modeling, the shadings and that special "elegance," as he called it, which belonged to this handsome wader. When his painting was finished he stood away at a little distance to look at it, and knew it for a failure, but he kept it, imperfect though it was.

These faithful tasks were not always compelling. The maples soon rose in broad flames against the black-green of hemlocks, and in a myriad broken forms sunlight fell through sifted leaves. Higher and higher he would climb, leaving the road, following slight trails through tawny brakes, through thickets of laurel. He watched a chipmunk quiet for perceptible moments on a ledge of red stone several hundred feet away. Still farther off he could see a downy woodpecker move round the trunk of a yellowing ash. Across a wide valley on distant hills he could find the coloring and forms of single trees, oak, elm, beech, hickory, walnut, where most eyes would have seen only patches of russet-brown or red or yellow.

He had come into a land where far vision seemed almost a native gift; in this the frontiersman often equaled the Indian, and though Pennsylvania was no longer a frontier many men lived there whose eyes were trained in the frontier fashion. Audubon found that he could match any of them, as later he matched the true frontiersman farther west. His close vision was equally sure. He was learning the most minute patterns in the wings of the last butterflies, the faint, web-like traceries on the petals of late flowers. His eyes were being taught by the clear markings of plumages, of crown and wing, breast and tail feathers. Patterns appeared again in the varying forms of nests, the shape and color of eggs, in a myriad small special habits. Patterns were to be seen in the flight of birds against thickets of leaves or over water or against the sky, wheeling, darting, sailing, tipped up against the wind, plunging into it, varying yet keeping for each bird sequences which could be known and remembered.

As he scuffed through colored leaves and smelled their dry perfumes he had no sense of interruption with the loss of summer. Everything marched. Shadows on the grass had deepened, then grown pale. Birds that for days had been busily feeding wheeled into the air as if practicing for long flight. He heard the brush of many wings, the soft notes of late calls. Flocks were forming. With the heavy frosts the woods seemed suddenly empty, yet he soon found new birds from the north, juncos and cedar waxwings. Ruffed grouse drummed, and he heard the call of bob whites. The cycle which he had watched from the first days of spring had not ended but had moved into a new phase. Here again were patterns, some of them clear; others, as to migrations, he must learn. He had banded one of the young phoebes with a silver thread to learn whether the bird would come back another spring to the caves beside the Perkiomen. He liked certainties and sequences, order, swift changes and sure returns.

3 *Portrait of Lucy*

"SHOOT it if you can, skating by at full speed," shouted young Bakewell as Audubon skimmed down the glassy river. High into the air went a solid beaver hat as he sailed back, and down it came riddled with buckshot at thirty yards. He picked it up without stopping. Backward and forward he went, leaping wide airholes and cutting elaborate figures. A boy who was visiting in the neighborhood wrote that night in his diary, "Today I saw the swiftest skater I ever beheld. I was told he was a young Frenchman, and this evening I met him at a ball, where I found his dancing exceeded his skating; all the ladies wished him as a partner; moreover, a handsomer man I never saw. His eyes alone command attention. His name, Audubon, is strange to me."

One morning after an early breakfast a party of these young men skated many miles up the Perkiomen to hunt ducks. Twilight came before they knew it, and there were many sharp bends and airholes to be avoided on the way back. They started off, laden with game, themselves like a flock of ducks, with Audubon in the lead carrying a handkerchief tied to a stick which he held aloft to guide them. As he curved around airholes the flock also curved around airholes. Darkness came on; they skated faster. Audubon happened on a great hole before he knew it and went into the icy stream; the others were able to stop themselves.

Pulled by the stream beneath the ice for thirty or forty yards, he popped up through another hole, but the shelving snow broke beneath his fingers; the stream still sucked him down. He managed to push against it and to find thick ice at last, crawled to the surface and shouted to his friends. Dry clothes were shared with him, and the party got under way, this time moving more calmly. No harm was done, and these boys went off on many such expeditions.

The Bakewells were an English family who had come to occupy Fatland Ford, a mansion with great white columns, a walled garden, and fine stables, which faced Mill Grove from a neighboring ridge. The older William Bakewell had sought Audubon out but had not found him; they had met at last in the woods, where good hunting dogs brought them together.

When Audubon called for the first time at Fatland Ford a tall and graceful young girl of sixteen rose from a seat by the fire with sewing in her hand. Her eyes were dark under level brows, her hair was a rich brown, her color was delicate. Suddenly shy, Audubon stammered his name and said half in French, half in English that he had come to see Mr. Bakewell. Lucy told him that her father was not at home and asked him to stay. Calmly she resumed her work, and her visitor at last gained enough composure to talk a little, perhaps to ask a few questions. Did she like America? Always inclined to be cautious except in the larger adventures of her life, Lucy answered that she wasn't sure as yet whether she liked America. From time to time she glanced up at this eager boy in hunting clothes whose fine head was so well placed on his shoulders. His eyes were noticeably wide and clear and though they watched her, they seemed to see everything in the room. She smiled a little; her smile was reserved but pretty. Mr. Bakewell came in and Audubon's first meeting with Lucy was over.

Other meetings followed. When the Bakewells came to Mill Grove Audubon was induced to show his paintings. He met Lucy on the frozen river with a party, and the young men pulled the girls up and down on sledges. Lucy's cheeks were rosy in the cold air; he found her more delicately charming than ever, and when they stopped for a while by the phoebes' cave he decided that she did not dislike him.

"Thou art my friend," he said. He was always to call Lucy his friend; though he had other words of endearment for her this through the years seemed to be the one he liked best.

She began teaching him English, which even with her help he never learned to speak well; he always spoke it with a strong French flavor, though he was a fluent talker with an odd dashing brilliance, unless beset by shyness. He gave Lucy drawing lessons in return, and they signaled back and forth between Mill Grove and Fatland Ford by means of chalked signs which Audubon designed with as much care as he had given to the great blue heron. They rode, skated, and danced together.

Not all the winter was given to these meetings or even to the drawing of birds. Audubon had discovered lead at Mill Grove and as result Captain Audubon had sent an agent, Dacosta, to superintend the construction of a mine there and to act as guardian and tutor to young Audubon. Dacosta had purchased a half interest in the place. The two got on badly, though Dacosta at first had seemed interested in Audubon's painting. He ridiculed his attachment for Lucy and spoke slightingly of the Bakewells. In the midst of a quarrel Dacosta cut off Audubon's allowance. When the boy said that he would lay all these matters before Captain Audubon and insisted upon a sum sufficient to take him to France, Dacosta pondered for a moment and finally said that he would write to a banker in New York who would give him money on demand.

After a brief parting with Lucy he was off—walking to New York in order to save the few shillings he had. It was January;

deep snow covered the ground and walking on the rutted post-roads was hard, but the air was sharp and clear, he was seeing new sights on the way, and he was used to walking; at the end of the third day he reached his destination comfortably enough.

The next morning he called on the banker. After a few firm questions on both sides Audubon learned that Dacosta had warned this man to give him nothing, and had in fact explained in the letter that he was now completing arrangements with a roving sea-captain to take the boy to China.

Audubon's hot temper flared up. He was ready to walk back to Mill Grove and wreak violence upon Dacosta. A tactful woman stopped him, a friend of the Bakewells with whom he was staying. She saw part of the story in his angry face and persuaded him to tell the rest of it. Instead of going back to Mill Grove he presented a note which William Bakewell had given him to his brother Benjamin, a man of affairs who promptly offered him any sum he might require for his voyage.

Passage was engaged on a ship bound for Nantes, and after a few weeks he appeared before the elderly Captain and his wife at La Gerbetière. No doubt they were glad to see him, and young Audubon wrote and spoke of them both with increasing affection. If the Captain still had "reasons" for not wishing him in France, these did not prevent his remaining there for nearly a year, living quietly, obscurely in the country. Weeks were required to write letters to Dacosta and obtain answers. The situation was complicated because this agent owned an interest in Mill Grove, and further because the fortune of the Audubons was noticeably on the decline.

In later years Audubon spoke with gratitude of a young doctor living near La Gerbetière, who was something of a student of ornithology. From this Doctor d'Orbigny he received the first genuine encouragement he had had, and the first stimulus toward scientific knowledge. He now read Buffon's great work, probably for the first time. Henceforth he wrote the names of birds according to Buffon on his drawings. In less than a year he had drawn over two hundred French birds.

If he wrote to Lucy we cannot know what he said, but he discussed the question of marriage with Captain Audubon, who gave his consent after a cautious exchange of letters with William Bakewell. And arrangements were completed for a partnership between young Audubon and another youth of about his age, Ferdinand Rozier, the son of a friend of the Captain's, who had just returned from a brief visit to America.

Probably the Captain thought that the tie would act as the force of gravity upon this boy who still seemed gay and improvident. Rozier was dark, slender, cautious, with a narrow frugal face. He had shown sound sense about money, and his father purchased for him a share in Mill Grove. The two young men expected to oust Dacosta.

Their plans were hastened because Napoleon's star had risen. The Captain feared that this strange son of his would be conscripted, and he was spirited aboard the ship *Polly* with a forged passport. Once more the question of his birth came forward. John Audubon was the name given in his passport, which declared that he was born in New Orleans. For a time young Audubon accepted this statement as true, and henceforward he was to be known by the English translation of Jean Jacques—as John James Audubon. He never saw the Audubons again, and he was returning to the country which was henceforward to be his home. Rozier sailed with him under a Dutch name.

The voyage had a smack of adventure. An English privateer, the *Rattlesnake,* chased their ship and English officers boarded her seeking gold. The young men hid their money under a heavy cable in the bow, and prowled around it, on tenterhooks for fear it would be discovered. It was not, and except for a hard storm which sent the *Polly* against a sandbank on Long Island the remainder of the voyage was uneventful. She floated neatly off with the rising tide and they landed in New York.

The two partners were unsuccessful in ousting Dacosta, who had anchored himself well at Mill Grove by legal technicalities. They decided that to sell to him their shares in the estate would be the wisest move.

Audubon was then, as he thought, ready to marry Lucy, but William Bakewell was doubtful. Hunting was all very well for sport; and drawing might be a gentleman's pastime, but this young man had never learned a trade or a profession.

"I am young and useless—I can see that," said Audubon in dejection.

William Bakewell was open-hearted; no doubt Lucy put in an anxious word. A plan was worked out by which the two partners were to separate for a time. Rozier went to a French establishment in Philadelphia, Audubon to Benjamin Bakewell's mercantile house in New York. Later, having acquired experience, they were to unite, when they expected to amass a fortune.

Audubon left with a friendly little screech owl in his pocket that fed from his hand and seemed contented with this nest. Settling in a lodging house he kept the owl in his room. At Benjamin Bakewell's he mounted a high stool and toiled over figures with honest perseverance, and he fled when the day's work was done.

It was nothing for a fast walker to pass from one end to the other of the small town. Within half an hour he could easily enter deep woods or walk along the wild shore of the Hudson. High above its dusky blue waters he saw the rare golden eagle on an autumn afternoon, a speck above the broken veil of clouds, spiraling downward into the brilliance of a stormy sunset.

He collected many small birds, and searched the markets on the Battery for waterfowl, and drew them. Rising before daybreak as at Mill Grove, he could have several hours for these occupations before he needed to present himself at the counting-house.

The little screech owl remained a companion, and gave the same tremulous doleful cries as when free in the orchard or garden; but the other lodgers failed to share Audubon's pleasure in these penetrating unearthly sounds, particularly as they were

NIGHT HAWK. *PLATE NO. CXLVII*

likely to shatter the air at night. The lodgers woke, they said, in a cold sweat, and they complained of the smell of drying skins and preservatives which floated from the same room. Audubon was forced to move, and in fact New York proved for him only a brief halting place.

When his young clerk's book-keeping was erratic, Benjamin Bakewell was patient, but when in a fit of absorption he posted several thousand dollars in a letter without sealing the envelope, this gentleman began to think of polite ways by which he might be led to consider other employment.

At about the same time Rozier had conceived a scheme for making a fortune by sending a large consignment of hams to the West Indies. Perhaps he had heard of the Yankee who had once sold large numbers of warming pans on one of the tropical islands. But the Yankee had accompanied the warming pans, while Rozier trusted only to the flavor and fragrance of the hams, and the West Indians were loyal fish-eaters. He lost money, and was cast into gloom. The two young men met and compared notes.

"The distant fields—I hear they are always greener," said Audubon cheerfully.

Commerce was rapidly spreading; he had learned that at Benjamin Bakewell's. A French colony had gathered at Louisville. The very place for them! They purchased goods and by the autumn of 1807 had made the journey to the Falls of the Ohio. Audubon liked the little town there with its back against the wilderness, and they sold their goods with some success, making trips along neighboring trails as peddlers and scouring the country as far south as the village of Nashville to consider a location for a future store. Louisville seemed to offer sure promises, and in the spring Audubon went east to marry Lucy.

Spring was late and cold that year at Fatland Ford. Snow was spread thinly over the red soil when the apple trees were in bloom. Among the wet pink blossoms he saw a small flock of chestnut-sided warblers, shivering though the sky was blue again. These birds were new to him, and their small yellow crowns, their stripes of black and gray green, their pale breasts—here was a tantalizing study. With Lucy at his side he painted a pair of them, and as he worked, a pair of house wrens began building a nest in the chimney wall outside the window; they often lighted on the sill. The air was full of their lively song. Lucy opened the window a little—then wider. Audubon found insects for them. Within a day or so the venturesome male had hopped inside the room and sang there. He was easily caught in a cupped hand, and Audubon finished a portrait of him. After that the wren never ventured beyond the outside sill but he continued to sing, tipping his head, looking at them shrewdly.

From his drawing of birds Audubon turned to make small pencil sketches of Lucy. He had a gift for seizing a likeness, as he had discovered when he had run across odd characters in the West. But Lucy—could he ever please himself? With her dark eyes, her clear features, her delicate coloring, she made an entrancing subject, he thought, and black and white wouldn't do!

He decided to attempt a portrait in water colors. He worked rapidly, with exultation. The little painting seemed really like her. Then as he gave what he intended as the last touch to her cheek a tiny drop of water fell upon it, blurring the color. His brush had been too full.

Impatiently he walked the floor. How stupid he had been! When at last he dared look at the painting again the color had dried. He picked up a pastel pencil and began to work over the tiny splotch. Triumph! He was able to cover it. But the rest of the portrait was now different in tone. Lightly he worked over all of it and discovered with pleasure that he had softened the whole effect.

"Not good enough!" he said. He could never make a portrait which would show Lucy as she really was, he decided, but it was a true likeness, and this was the softest, gentlest coloring he had ever achieved. He was in a whirl of charmed excitement. He would make other portraits of Lucy which should be still better, and he would use this same overlay of pastels on water colors for his bird paintings. By accident he had discovered for himself a not unusual technique, one which he was to use for all his subsequent paintings of birds—drawings, he called them.

With Lucy he visited the caves along the Perkiomen and saw the phoebe he had banded with a silver thread two years before. They had many walks together in the woods while preparations for their wedding went forward. They were married on June 12, 1808. She was now twenty, he was twenty-three.

William Bakewell must have had many questions about this marriage. His daughter had been reared in a comfort bordering upon luxury, and from any hard-headed view Audubon's prospects were not bright. He had been unable to collect from Dacosta all the money owing him, and with Rozier he had made an unfortunate speculation in indigo, sending this to France just as the Embargo Act came into force. This Act was rapidly shuttling prices up and down; there was no telling how adventures in trade would end at this time. But William Bakewell liked this impetuous young man who could be both shy and gay, who so clearly had his own tastes, and he helped him with money at the time of his marriage.

As for Lucy's questions we cannot know them. Perhaps these were unspoken. She was leaving security, but that was something many women had done in this new country. A rough journey lay ahead. For the broad future this pair had no plans. Audubon did not guess, could not have guessed, where his drawings of birds would lead him. We may surmise that Lucy was entranced by these because he created them, not because she saw in them a future. She had faced and overridden opposition to her marriage, not from her father but from a new stepmother, who was always hostile to Audubon. Lucy had resolution, and she would survive hardships. Her slender figure showed strength.

The morning after their marriage they left in a public coach for that uncertainty which was the West. Long since, they had both heard great wheels rumbling westward over the Reading

Road. Gay Conestogas were always passing with bright red sideboards, blue running gear, and arched covers of white over the graceful, boat-shaped wagon bed. Whole families were moving in these to the Ohio country, as it was called, taking a month for the journey. The hames carrying bells were high, the horses bred for hard travel. At Lancaster Audubon and Lucy stopped for a bit of refreshment at the sign of "The Conestoga Wagon." A fip or a fivepenny bit there bought them a big steaming bowl of punch.

On they went to the Big Chickey where an Indian bridge was swung from one high bank to the other—a tall tree felled so that its top would rest on the other side. Audubon ran lightly across it, but this mode of travel seemed uncertain to a girl in billowing skirts; Lucy went in the coach over the ford.

The pike ascended and smoothed out to follow the Susquehanna. They passed more than one tiny cluster of houses, and a glowing forge by the wayside. The hills seemed near, then swept away into blue distance, and like a great Indian bow the river suddenly bent before them. At last after many tedious hours they saw the white cupola of the courthouse at Harrisburg.

Here they crossed the river on a flatboat, then wheeled slowly along to Carlisle. Dipping to a grove some miles farther along they found a clean inviting tavern with a martins' house above the sign, neatly joined and brightly painted. "The better the martins' house, the better the tavern," Audubon told Lucy out of his large experience in western travel. "You notice, most inns have a martins' house!"

He was right as to the character of the inn. They found a clean table spaciously spread, with many hot dishes, many kinds of "sweets and sours," honey from the comb, and big apples brought up from a deep cool cellar. The place was kept by a pair of rosy Germans and had a wide stable yard. In an open field a group of wagoners was rubbing down their horses for the night, and a camp-fire burned in the dusk.

As the coach climbed a steady incline the next morning the passengers talked gloomily of robbers, who were not uncommon in the mountains since most travelers going by coach into the West carried money with them. But the coach covered the lonely heights in safety and dipped down to ford the Juniata—"Clear Juniata" Audubon always called it as though this were the full name—following its deep, slaty-blue waters for miles, climbing to see these far below steep cliffs where the river seemed to wind beneath the road.

Suddenly a hunting horn sounded above them. Far off came the mellow call of another, then another, until these wild notes girdled the mountains with sound. Two red foxes fled across the road and disappeared among rocks and dark juniper. Down a steep path came men in butternut brown with guns and dogs, shouting "Foxes—any wild critter!" They said they were clearing the mountains of bears and wolves that often attacked stage-coaches and prowled around their cabins in the valley. Foxes must go too, since they robbed the henroosts, and deer because they nibbled young corn. They seemed to be out only for a wild hunt, glad to leave their farms and the roads as well, enjoying a war on the wilderness.

Slow miles followed as the road turned sharply downward, through hackberry and sugarberry and hickory with ravens circling overhead, then rose and rose once more. They reached the top of a great ridge. "Highest peak in the whole land!" shouted the driver with conviction.

At last they faced the West—a rolling ocean of trees, green valleys, pale distances. White rivulets threaded the mountainside, flowing westward. Silver streams in the valleys broadened toward the West.

Two more slow days of travel brought them within view of the winding Monongahela. They circled the hills beside the Allegheny and finally rattled into the thriving town of Pittsburgh, set on bottom land where the two rivers met to form the broad Ohio. Furnaces and forges were glowing. Slender plumes of smoke rose from glassworks and breweries. The streets were full of rushing people—drivers, foundrymen, red-shirted boatmen. On the rivers a few sails gleamed white. Tied to wharves were moored dozens of arks or broadhorns—"Kentucky boats" they were sometimes called—with their great sweeps dipping.

Decisions had to be made. How should they travel to Louisville? They could purchase horses and ride, or they could go by coach. But they had had enough of coaches. A keelboat with fast oarsmen was too great a luxury. A boatman's song floated up to the tavern where they spent the night.

Hi-o
Away we go,
Floating down the river
On the O-hi-o.

A flatboat—they might go in a flatboat. In a few days they had joined a party traveling by flatboat to Louisville.

4 *A Crowd of Frontiersmen*

WHITE mist was lifting from the three broad rivers, and tall men who boasted they were "half-horse, half-alligator" were clambering over the arks or flatboats that lay like a float of tenements on the waters of the Monongahela. Either a rude canopy or a long room was set squarely across the middle of these "Kentucky boats" and they were enclosed by railings. Horses or cows, flocks of chickens, and whole families could travel in them.

> Some row up but we row down
> All the way to Shawneetown—
> Pull away! Pull away!
> Pull away to Shawneetown!

With a boatman at the long sweep and two at the oars set in the blunt bow they moved slowly, for a collision with other clumsy craft in the midst of strong currents meant catastrophe. Fairly down on the Ohio, they hugged the leafy shore to avoid deeply set snags, voyaging three or four miles in an hour.

> Hard upon the beech oar!
> She moves too slow,
> All the way to Shawneetown
> A long time ago.

This jeering song floated over the water to them from the faster keelboats.

Lucy, if we know her, was as prim and exquisite among the flour barrels, kegs of gunpowder and malt, the crates of cotton goods and cutlery as she had been at Fatland Ford. She would not have been the girl who could cast her lot with that of young Audubon if she had failed to see the dream-like beauty of the Ohio River in early summer.

Its waters were silver, blue, with the bending yellow-green of willow fronds along the shores. Honey locusts and tall lindens were in bloom, and the mingling scent of their blossoms floated with the hum of bees on warm winds over the river. Wide green bottom lands rose gently to shaded hills. Islands would break the long view; when these were passed the river would broadly turn, winding among steep knolls whose shadows lay dark on the pale water. They passed thickets of wild grape, hornbeam, sycamore, and saw glittering there the scarlet of a grosbeak, his yellow-green mate showing beneath the gray surfaces of the sunlit leaves, and heard his song, with its marked bold cadences suddenly falling away, which seemed to Audubon like the clearest notes of the flageolet, and listened to the flowing, ringing melody of the water thrush, silver over the silver stream.

Other boats met or passed them at a distance, and from around the bends came the soft slow notes of the boatman's horn. During the day's long voyaging they cared little enough for other craft except to hail and pass, but as late afternoon drew on their boatmen were on the watch either for a neat cabin on shore or another ark or broadhorn like their own near which they might spend the night. River pirates still haunted these waters though they were less frequent than legend has made them. It was well to take no chances of having their boat scuttled while they slept or their cargo seized by a murderous band. More than once the Audubons fell in with a considerable company of flatboat travelers and joined at night in a large camp, sleeping on buffalo robes in rude tents on shore.

At daybreak Audubon would be off to shoot wood ducks or wild turkey or to fish from the flatboat. In the early morning catfish leapt and white perch were biting, and golden, green, and silver sunfish were to be had by casting a line fixed to a slender branch of hickory or hazel.

The days moved lazily, slowly. Many of them lay ahead, for six hundred miles of a winding waterway are not to be traveled quickly in a heavy boat with three oars. They passed the mouth of many small rivers pouring their floods down narrow valleys into the greater valley of the Ohio, the Muskingum, the Hockhocking, the Kenawha. They circled away from small waterside villages, Marietta, Gallipolis, Cincinnati. A moon came up and they could float all night with only the sweep for a rudder. Audubon played his flute and the boatmen jigged on the wooden roof.

"A beautiful lark," said Audubon. Lucy, wishing to be a good ornithologist, asked "Where?" Stiff little puns let him juggle language; he had already picked up a smattering of the western lingo like "poor shoat," or "cut stick." "But I think the ax was not at hand," he told the boatmen who had promised to "cut stick"—be off and on their way—early one morning.

At the end of a mild afternoon they saw the wide mirror of the Ohio at Louisville and heard the slight rumbling of water over shoals warning them of the Falls. The Silver Hills rose blue against a pale coppery sky. The flatboat was steered into the wide mouth of Beargrass Creek, which made a harbor for many boats whose cargoes were to be portaged three or four miles beyond the Falls to Shippingport, there to be loaded on other boats for the farther journey down the river.

The Audubons went at once to the "Indian Queen," a crowded tavern with an open courtyard, where guests were obliged to gather at the pump for meager ablutions. The mattresses were of husk, the sheets of calico; the rooms were usually occupied by four, six, or even eight persons. Rough men were continually coming there from the back country, from down the river—boatmen, traders, hunters in buckskin, men bent on errands of which they did not speak, making their way to unsettled land in the Ohio country or to the Mississippi and beyond. A few Indians wandered through the streets. Not many years earlier the glass windows at Mulberry Hill, the home of George Rogers Clark, had been considered a source of wonder.

Louisville in 1808 was rightly called a frontier village, but behind the word "frontier" many meanings may be found. A life of cultivation had already begun there. The French group in Louisville and at Shippingport was composed of men and women who were said to have fled from France during the Revolution to escape the guillotine—the Berthouds and Tarascons, the Cerfs and Sardous and Fouchés. Some of them were said to have taken new names for fear of reprisals. Even with the wilderness close at hand they achieved something of a formal elegance, in a ritual of calls and dancing, light music and costume. And wide plantations lay scattered over gradual meadows beyond the town, whose owners had come from Virginia to draw liberal fortunes from fields of tobacco. These planters were continually coming and going; their horses, their hospitality, and even the abounding "Kentucky breakfast" which they offered to casual visitors, were already famous. And for those who came to stay in Louisville the "Indian Queen" could offer a more genial comfort than appeared on the surface.

Young Audubon with his reserved and pretty Lucy was immediately made welcome by all these people. He rode and hunted with the planters. The Berthouds became friends of a lifetime, and indeed were soon bound to the Audubons by the tie of relationship since Nicholas Berthoud married one of Lucy's younger sisters within a year. Young Berthoud, an ambitious merchant of sound integrity, found time to puzzle over the new birds and the curious ways of quadrupeds. "He shares my interests," Audubon told Lucy with excitement.

He received a large measure of encouragement for his pursuits in this small river town, encouragement which touched and fired all phases of his work. He had hardly arrived when he painted a cardinal grosbeak for a new friend, Dr. Galt. The brilliant carmine was quickly washed in, the purply dark shadings were in pastels. This little painting was something more than a faithful bird portrait; it was a gay little design with the cardinal set with a spray of green-blue leaves. Dr. Galt was a botanist, as was another physician, Dr. Ferguson; both were always ready to discuss new plants with Audubon as well as unfamiliar birds. Another acquaintance, Mr. Gilly, "drew beautifully." And across the river George Rogers Clark, the old hero of Vincennes, still lived at Clark's Point on the great tract of land to which he had retired when his country disappointed him too greatly. In its forests Audubon was welcome to wander and when Clark moved to Locust Grove outside Louisville to live with the Croghans, both Lucy and her husband were frequent guests there. Clark had always been a student of natural history; during his many marches in the wilderness he had somehow contrived to observe birds closely; he had a great store of information which he enjoyed sharing.

Lucy said charmingly, "If I were jealous I should have a bitter time of it, for every bird is my rival!" When Audubon was away selling goods in the back country or traveling east to renew the stock of the small firm she stayed at Locust Grove, or with the family of General Jonathan Clark at Trough Spring. And whether or not William Clark came to Louisville in these years Audubon would surely have heard from his brothers and from the Croghans of the fruits of the Lewis and Clark expedition, which had returned to St. Louis two years earlier, rich in scientific observation. William Clark, whom Audubon certainly knew either in Louisville or later in St. Louis, had been the map maker on the long journey to the Northwest, drawing birds, animals, and fish for the scientific record.

"Most remarkable thing you ever saw!" Major Croghan said to Audubon, describing something nearer at hand, an immense cloud of chimney swifts descending at evening upon a tall sycamore outside the town, entering the tree through knotholes. Audubon spent many early morning hours and others at the end of the day watching the tree, climbed it and wound himself around one of its limbs like a contortionist in order to see inside, failed, and by an elaborate plan managed to enter from below at night without startling the birds. Thrusting a lantern above his head he saw them so close together in dusky rows that a finger could not have been laid between any two, lining the tall hollow trunk—some eight or nine thousand of them, he decided by a rough estimate.

Posting himself outside with his head against the tree, he listened; all was silence until nearly daybreak; then from within came a sound as if the tree were splitting; for about half an hour a large millwheel might have been revolving within by the force of a powerful stream, and the swifts began to emerge, making their way in a dark stream to the chimneys of Louisville. They proved to be males for the most part, but at the end of the second nesting season more females were to be found among them. Suddenly by the middle of August they had all gone in a great cloud southward.

For such expeditions Audubon's early habits and his capacity to work for long hours stood him in good stead. He could have a fair stretch of time to use as he liked before he was obliged to stand with Rozier behind the counter and sell shot pouches, cutlery, malt, and raisins. Before daybreak one dark winter night he posted himself behind a pile of drift logs near the shore of the Ohio to wait for wild geese, and heard for a time only the faint wash and rumble of the Falls. He missed the geese but saw the rare snowy owl of the North, which sometimes comes to a more moderate climate in the coldest months. Deep cavities or potholes lay among the shoals where fish found the shelter of calm water. Near these the owl was watching. Lying flat on a rock in midstream like a stealthy cat watching for a mouse, his body lengthwise, his head down but turned toward the water, he looked like a soft patch of snow and seemed asleep, but if a fish rose to the surface from the pothole, out went his barbed claw; he carried it away, devoured it, and came back. When one pothole failed to yield fish he slid over to another. He was joined without a rustle of sound by his mate in the pale early darkness. With the first streak of light they were lost like small white clouds in General Clark's woods.

If a trip by one of the partners into the back country was required for the business of the young firm Audubon was always willing to undertake it. His easy way of making friends was no disadvantage in trade, even though he often traveled over more wild country than the work of the day demanded. These trips were much to his liking and were often prolonged.

The broad, softly sloping valley which was Kentucky opened before him. When Daniel Boone first came there forty years earlier elk and buffalo had ranged these hills, but they were gone now. Elk horns might sometimes be seen in the rafters of a log cabin, and spoons were carved from the buffalo horns which might still be found near the salt licks—great horn spoons like those which the Indians sometimes had, so hard to carve that "break it or make a spoon" became a saying of the backwoods, or an oath was heard, "By the great horn spoon!" And the hills were still traced by buffalo paths which had become Indian trails and might be taken by a good rider. These were now safe enough;

the Indians had gone with the elk and buffalo, and pirates of the road were not seeking victims on the smaller traces.

No swamps were here, no dark forests of evergreens. So high and airy and well spaced were the trees in many regions that early settlers had been able to drive their wagons under spreading branches to reach favored sites for their cabins. If Audubon chose to follow the flocks of gay little green and red parroquets abounding here he could ride for miles over firm ground, through woods, hardly bending his head, with only a faint Indian trail or the sun for his guide. The pale yellow, green, and white of the sycamores seemed to catch and filter a soft light, and the many water courses took it up. Never were there so many winding rivers, clear like the Kentucky, moss-agate like the Green, some of them lost at their sources in great caverns—the Mammoth, the Onyx, the Crystal Caves, as yet hardly known to white men except by legend. The soil was sweet and rich, renewed by the limestone upon which it rested. Slight sink-holes—"dimples" they were called—sheltered lichens and mosses and even the nests of the pewees. Berries, seeds, lush leaves, soft wild fruits—the mulberry, huckleberry, sumach, persimmon—on which many birds fed, were abundant through the long summer.

Audubon could not know then that the mild climate, the many waterways, the rich growth, made Kentucky a favored dwelling place for birds, or that this land lay within the broad path of migration from Louisiana and beyond the Gulf. He could only surmise the changes in bird life from section to section over the breadth of the land, but he was continually seeing birds which were strange to him; he was dazzled by the myriads in the great flocks of spring and autumn and by the rich variety he found everywhere, unknown warblers in the deeper forests, snowy egrets, whooping cranes, whole heronries—of blue herons, the great blue and the smaller blue, the black crowned night heron—and the brilliant, gay wood ducks whose flight was sudden, strong, and high. He listened to the hollow *yank, yank, yank* of the ivory-billed woodpecker in the deep woods and saw this magnificent bird again and again, showy, with white curving lines down his back, a fine spread of wings, a red and black crest. He heard the American bittern with its odd voice like the workings of an old-fashioned wooden pump, without knowing what it was—a lusty fighter, "the booming bittern." He learned to call wild turkeys with a piece of bone through which he could make the clucking, answering notes of that wild shy bird.

His hearing seemed to match his sight; he could catch the soft tread of turkeys over twigs and branches at a distance, or hear the rustle of their wings. He was learning many bird calls and melodies for the first time, learning to gauge distances of sound, tracing the curve of a strange bird's flight—listening, watching, listening, making notes in the woods, bringing birds back at nightfall to Louisville to toil over fresh sketches and paintings.

There were hot summer days when the cardinals dusted themselves in dusty trails, when the smell of tobacco rose from the planters' fields under burning sun, when the catbirds fed on ripening blackberries or industriously sought out small insects. Young birds were feeding, scattering. A thousand new circumstances were to be watched, learned, too many for the drawing pencil. Audubon formed a habit which was to become permanent, of writing down the day's observations and even small happenings in his journal, perhaps writing in French at first, more and more often using English.

In all this bright new abundance he was concerned only with discovery; he hardly considered at all his wish to place birds on the page with flowers or branches to make a design which pleased him. First of all he must *know*.

Rozier became gloomy as this passion mounted: Audubon grew still more carelessly light-hearted. When as a small boy he at last could wander outside Nantes after the dark imprisoned days of the Revolution, the life of birds had spelled freedom, the freedom which birds have always meant to the earthbound; now he found this on an immensely wide scale, spreading over the meadows and valleys of Kentucky and again eastward over the Alleghenies and back, as he traveled to buy stock for the little store.

Once when he was riding toward Pittsburgh with several horses laden with goods and also with his supply of money, he left them all suddenly on the road and slipped deeper and deeper into the woods to watch the motions of a warbler. The horses were quietly eating grass by the roadside when he returned; his goods were untouched, and he continued along his way with only a sober second thought or two. He was sure to tell Lucy of such adventures, and perhaps she was troubled, but Audubon's gayety was likely to be irresistible; they were both young, and though the new firm could hardly be called highly prosperous, for a time at least it did not fare too badly.

On a March day in 1810 a visitor came to the little store who was destined to become a force in Audubon's life though they had only one direct encounter. This was Alexander Wilson, who had been first a poor Scotch weaver and in a quiet way a poet, and who after many hardships had made his way to America, hoping to study and portray birds. Most of his difficulties had come from poverty though a few perhaps sprang from his temperament; but he had succeeded in identifying and painting a large number of American birds, and he had found in Philadelphia a publisher of his work, the "American Ornithology." This was to appear slowly, a volume at a time, and was sold by subscription. Wilson had come into the West with the hope of obtaining subscribers and at the same time of increasing the number of his discoveries and his paintings.

Perhaps Audubon and Wilson could never have become friends; their differences in temperament were too great. Anxious, reserved, dour, and disappointed, Wilson was not an easy man to meet. Audubon, much younger, was in the full tide of high spirits, and still without plans as to the future. As each looked at the other's work it was inevitable that something of the spirit of rivalry should arise. Wilson had advanced to the stage of publication; there could be no doubt that he was first in the field, and so he remains—the first American ornithologist. As he considered the paintings of this unknown young trader he may have recognized powers greater than his own, just as he almost surely saw birds in Audubon's collection which were still unfamiliar to him. Audubon had artistic gifts far exceeding those of the reticent Wilson, and other gifts as well. He had above all the power of stirring the imagination, not only by the brilliance and beauty of his paintings but by his character. Everywhere he went Audubon was to create some sort of excitement. Many were to dislike, misunderstand, and even despise him—the followers of Wilson among them—but he had an equal genius for making devoted friends among men of all kinds, and this gift was to be of great service to the science and the art which he had chosen.

Wilson sparely noted in his diary that Audubon's paintings of birds were "very good," and added, "Saw two new birds he had." The two went hunting together. Audubon did not subscribe for Wilson's work; probably he could not afford to do so, and Wilson said that he left Louisville without having "received one act of courtesy from those to whom I was recommended, one subscriber, or one new bird. Science or literature has not one friend in this place." He complained that everyone there was intent only upon making money. But he had certainly encountered one man for whom this was not a main pursuit. His notes were not consistent, and Audubon's experience had proved it to be far from true that science had no friends in Louisville.

Wilson went his lonely way southward, one of a long procession of naturalists who were to come by the Ohio and enter the American wilderness in the hope of unlocking strange secrets there. Much later, in his published writings, Audubon spoke of Wilson as "my predecessor" and gave him warm praise more than once, insisting that much of his work had not been sufficiently understood and recognized. At the time, this visit undoubtedly sharpened Audubon's conviction that his own observations and his paintings belonged to the world of science.

He still hardly thought of himself as an artist, and perhaps this was as well, for possibly no one whom he met would have known how to foster his genius. He was better left to follow his bent with perhaps such turns of suggestion as could have come from woodcuts, Bewick's or those of others, which he may easily have seen in the libraries of his friends. Their unstressed decorative values in the portrayal of birds and animals may have given direction to the clear impersonal art which was to be his own.

At about the time of Wilson's visit he had another encounter of significance–his meeting with Daniel Boone.

Long before, Boone had learned that the Kentucky land which he believed was his had not been properly recorded in his name. He had moved to West Virginia and then to the banks of the Femme Osage in what is now Missouri, where once more he lost a land grant through a false title. In 1810 he petitioned Congress for a true grant in the Louisiana Territory because, as he said, of his services in opening the West, and he eventually received this; but the matter hung fire, and he may have come to Kentucky to obtain what assistance he could in this direction from men of influence. Then or later he came back on foot, for another reason which did him great credit. He came to pay a debt at Frankfort. The story has it that only fifty cents remained to him when the debt was paid, and that he was in high spirits.

Boone was now an old man, erect, strong, with steely eyes, wearing a homespun hunting shirt, bare-legged, moccasined like an Indian. Audubon either happened to be in Frankfort when he was there or went when he learned of Boone's arrival. In the autumn woods they hunted together, and Boone showed Audubon how to bark squirrels by concussion—shooting not the squirrel but the bark of the limb on which it sat. That night before a blazing fire Boone was induced to talk of some of his adventures in Kentucky, and Audubon set them down in the journal which he now regularly kept.

"Tell us how you flusterated the Injuns, Dan'l," said a hunter.

Prompt and matter of fact, Boone began one of his stories. They were all well known, but hunters could not hear them too often. "Once I was hunting alone on the banks of the Green, when the Injuns still belonged here. We was waging what might be called a war of intrusion in Kentucky, and I followed after Injuns as I would follow after bears or deer or catamounts. But Injuns are smart and they outsmarted me that night. I had covered over my fire and had just laid me down to rest when it seemed like a thousand hands laid hold of me and pinioned me tight. You understand Injuns will be quiet themselves when they get caught, and I was bound I'd show 'em I was no more afraid of death than they were. I let myself be led to their camp without a word. Great rejoicings when we appeared at their camp! They tied me to a tree with leathern thongs, and the squaws fell a-searching in my hunting shirt for anything they might think valuable. Happened I had a flask filled with *monongahela.* They began to beat their bellies and sing and passed my bottle from mouth to mouth. I wished it was ten times the size and filled to the top! But the squaws drank more than the warriors, and I began to think after all my bottle of strong water wasn't going to help me, when a gun went off in the woods. The warriors all jumped to their feet and after a few words with the squaws they went off into the woods to find out about the gun. I expected the squaws would be left to guard me.

"Well, it was just so. The squaws sat down and the remains of my whiskey began to gurgle down their throats. They tumbled down and rolled about, and they began to snore, and little by little I unlaced the thongs that bound me to the tree. There was still other thongs binding me tight, so I rolled over and over towards the fire, and after a short time burned them asunder. I stretched my sinews and picked up my gun. But I had determined to mark the spot, so I found a thrifty ash sapling and cut out of it three large chips with my knife. Then I ran off, taking care to walk like an Injun and leave an Injun's tracks and other signs, and I threw myself deep into a canebrake. I got through to the other side and finally made out to reach the settlement.

"Later a Virginian rode out to Kentucky and laid claim to a large tract of land, taking for one of his corners the very ash tree on which I had made my mark. So it read in the deed, 'at an ash marked by three tomahawk marks of a white man.' He must have knowed the difference 'twixt Injun marks and white man's marks. There's a plain difference.

"But the tree growed and the bark covered over the marks, and this Virginian had some trouble about his boundaries. He heard I had marked the tree so he wrote for me to come back to Kentucky and see about it. When I got there we went out to the Green River Bottoms and I considered for a while and began to think that after all I could find the very spot, and the tree too, if it was yet standing. Great changes had taken place in those woods, and it was evening when we got there. We waited for the moon to rise and I made for the course in which I thought the ash tree grew.

"As we came toward it I felt as if the Injuns was there still and as if I was still a prisoner among them. We had to await the return of day to find the course so we camped, and at sunrise I was on foot, and after a good deal of musing I decided an ash tree then in sight must be the very one.

"The Virginian went to get some witnesses, and when they come up they looked upon me as if I had been George Washington himself. I walked to the ash tree, which I now called mine, and took an ax and cut a few chips off the bark. Still no signs of my marks. So I cut again, careful, and scraped and worked away

GOLDEN-WINGED WOODPECKER. *PLATE NO. XXXVII*

with my knife until I *did* come to where my tomahawk had cut into the wood. I scraped with care until three hacks came to light as plain as any three notches ever were. So the Virginian got his land."

That night Audubon shared a room with Boone and talked with him into the late hours. Perhaps he had already pleased Boone by his marksmanship; there was little to show that Audubon was different from the hunters they had left before the fire. Gone were the days when he wore frilled white shirts and black satin breeches; he was wedded to the rough garb of the hunter, which was Indian in part, with a deerskin shirt and leggings and a belt that held a sheath knife and a tomahawk. Boone talked with him of his fur-trapping days up the Missouri, and perhaps Audubon heard from him how to travel for days in the forest with only parched corn for food, though he may have learned this from George Rogers Clark, who had often sustained himself on dried corn on long marches in his fighting days. When they prepared for sleep Boone refused a bed, took off his hunting shirt, arranged a few folds of blanket on the floor and lay down upon them.

What Audubon gained was a vast liking for this stoical old scout; and Boone, whom he was apparently to see more than once in the next ten years, may have given direction to purposes which had unconsciously been forming as he had ranged through the woods of Kentucky. If he did not know that he was an artist it was equally true that science would never fully claim him, or even the mysterious wheeling life of birds or the ways of four-footed creatures who kept close to the ground or the simple pursuits of the hunter—none of these alone.

He loved them all; perhaps even more he loved the ways of life belonging to the wilderness. These might never be so primitive, so sharp as when Kentucky was unknown ground, but deep woods and strange watercourses could still be sought; the look and smell of wild land could still be his; and he possessed an aptitude for turning small events into adventures when others would have passed them by. He was careless of practical issues much as Boone was, not disregarding them altogether, in fact possessing a greater talent for business than has generally been supposed, but never regarding this as of first importance. What he wanted was unspoiled country, its curious sights, its wealth of small mysteries, the pleasures for the five senses which it offered.

"Young heads are on young shoulders," he said a little later to Rozier, who was insisting that the firm had made many mistakes. It was true that they were not prospering. Other stores had been set up in Louisville by older and shrewder men, and trade everywhere was proving difficult because of rapidly changing prices. Audubon agreed readily enough that they might do better elsewhere—westward of course! They hit upon the idea of going to the small village of Henderson, a hundred and twenty-five miles farther down the Ohio.

The year before, a son had been born to the Audubons at the "Indian Queen," a handsome child whom they called Victor. As soon as she was able to travel Lucy had gone back to Fatland Ford with the baby for a visit, but she returned to Louisville when the move to Henderson was decided upon. Rozier had gone ahead.

The little party of three made the two days' journey by skiff with two Negroes for oarsmen. It was a warm October. Sunlight, rich and hazy, lay over the hills. The maples, oaks, and ironwood were lighted with color. Wild vines, purple-red, trailed to the water's edge. Long curving sprays of black mulberry were purple-gold. The canebrakes were pale and dry, the fragrance of sassafras was in the air. The Ohio lay still as a pool, riffled only by the stroke of the oars. Except for an occasional skiff or flatboat they were alone; there were hours when they might have been explorers of two centuries before. Deer stood poised delicately on a high ridge, and Audubon shot wild turkeys, a grouse, some blue-winged teal. A fire was made on shore in the midst of the blazing color of the trees, and they had a savory supper, but they did not pause for the night.

The moon came up touching the river and the dark-tawny bottom lands. As they turned past a bend, a slight fence and a newly planted orchard lay before them clear in the silver light. They skimmed silently past deep thickets. As day broke Audubon saw a great horned owl among island willows like a patch of soft bars, yellow, black, red-yellow, among the yellow leaves. He fired, the bird fell, and he was overboard in an instant, swimming to the little island. But the owl might have laid a trap for him. On a bar thinly covered with water he was above his knees in quicksand before he knew it, sinking rapidly, and would have been lost if the Negroes hadn't shouted to him not to move since every motion would send him deeper. Lucy, with Victor in her arms, looked on in distress, but they made a bridge of their oars and some driftwood over which they could walk, and slowly pulled him from the sinking treacherous sand. He had to leave his owl.

They reached the mouth of the Green, and after a few more miles the skiff was shoved against the red banks at Henderson. Red Banks the village had been called because of this bright heavy clay. Some fifteen years before only a stockade was there to protect a wandering band of German settlers. Then members of the Transylvania Company had come in canoes down the Green and had planned a spacious town with a commons and streets a hundred feet wide, which they named for Richard Henderson. A few log cabins were now loosely scattered along these broad streets, and plantations had been cut into the surrounding country, but this land was still wild enough. Dense canebrakes grew along the river above and below the settlement; a few miles away were saltlicks which had once been so greatly frequented by elk and buffalo that whole hillsides were undermined by greedy tongues. This region had been favored by an Algonquin people or by others even older, "river people" whose great mounds could still be seen, one of them in the village itself, others placed at intervals beyond it. Huge heaps of mussel shells told, in imperfect language, something further of an ancient civilization. Stone tools and beautifully polished banner-stones could be found there, some of them apparently showing the outlines of the magic "thunder bird." All through this region were buried emblems in stone which brought remembrance of the natural world, pipes which may have been totem pipes, with the image of birds, or a frog, a snake's head, a deer's foot, a fox, or an owl.

The Red Banks trail ran south from Henderson to Nashville where it joined the great Natchez Trace; it cut northward to Vincennes. Another branch followed the Kentucky side of the Ohio to a point opposite Shawneetown. Here the bloodthirsty Harpes had roamed. The robber Mason had known these trails, and islands below the settlement had been the stronghold of river pirates. Most of these marauders had been brought to justice within recent years but the land was sparsely settled, and wolves still howled around the plantation houses at night.

For a few weeks, during the warm promise of the Indian summer, Audubon and Rozier sold some of their stock, but most of the planters of this region were accustomed to travel, and on their trips to Pittsburgh or Philadelphia or even to New Orleans they were likely to purchase for themselves the plain goods and few luxuries they demanded. On the whole the firm did a meager business. Before mid-winter the partners decided to try to dispose of their goods at some one of the French colonies along the Mississippi.

On a plantation, Meadowbrook, near the mouth of the Green

lived Dr. Rankin with his large family, a man of learning and geniality. He was interested in natural science, and from the first he had liked both the Audubons. Lucy and little Victor were invited to stay at his house while the young partners plunged still deeper into the West.

5 *At the Great Bend*

SNOW whirled over the river as they started. Audubon and Rozier were traveling with a party of hunters and trappers in a keelboat manned by French *voyageurs*, members of that hardy mixed race, part Indian, part French, which had known the rivers of the continent for two hundred years. Swarthy, boisterous men, they were gay in their blue shirts, red caps, bright sashes. The long keelboat, in contrast to the clumsy arks, had trim, firm lines.

At the bends of the river they rowed cautiously through the white gusts, but they soon picked up speed, and the patroon, with a long steering oar shaped like the fin of a dolphin, kept a true course. The first night on board was dreary, even though the boat was well anchored and they had a small cabin in which to sleep. The river slapped and pounded. They had passed the wild little settlement of Shawneetown in the driving snow where lawless American and French wanderers often converged to mingle with a remnant of Indians. They had skirted Cave-in-the-Rock, which had long been a stronghold of robbers, set high in a great bank, above which towered pines.

Inland the cold was bitter. At daybreak clouds of waterfowl were moving toward the river, where flowing water and the sheltering banks provided a measure of warmth.

Flurries of snow kept ahead of the keelboat, but this was new, staunch, and well trimmed, and the *voyageurs* knew the Ohio in all weathers. On the third night they entered Cache Creek, a half-concealed little river which ran almost alongside the Mississippi in Illinois, with a broad mouth that made a good harbor. This had once been the refuge of that infamous river pirate Colonel Plug, who lurked there to prey upon boats on both rivers and who had devised many ingenious ways of seizing cargoes and of murdering all hands. Now the Cache seemed known only to mallards, teal, mergansers and wild geese. Its waters and the snowy shores were covered with floating waterfowl, their sleek heads and backs gently bobbing with the current. Little incautious flocks of green parroquets hovered closely together in the lower limbs of leafless sycamores.

At sunrise the party awoke to find Shawnees standing silently near the boat. In a sheltered wood nearby some fifty families were encamped, brought there by a rich harvest of nuts and acorns, which in turn was bringing game almost to their tepees—raccoons, opossums, and black bears.

Up the river came another keelboat manned by French traders who paused at the Cache only long enough to give warning that the Mississippi was rapidly filling with ice. The patroon decided to remain until the weather broke. Rozier was stirred by apprehension. Their boxes of drygoods, kegs of powder, barrels of whiskey—perhaps they would lose the market for these if they waited. Audubon could only regard the delay as his own particular good luck, for he discovered that the Shawnees were about to cross the river and go inland on a hunting expedition. The time had long since passed when the Shawnees followed the warpath; they were friendly enough and could speak a smattering of English or French. He had no difficulty in arranging to go with them.

With half a dozen squaws paddling the long canoe and as many Shawnee hunters in the party, they struck across the heavy current and soon landed on the Kentucky side. For several hours the men squeezed their way through thickets, waded through lagoons and low bottom lands and at last reached a wild little lake where hundreds of swans floated—whistling swans or trumpeters—brilliantly white in the shadowed water. Indian fashion, the hunting party had divided. As the first group fired, the swans rose and flew toward the other. The Indians wanted the beautiful snowy skins, which would pass through many hands before they were worn by ladies in Europe. They soon had brought down more than fifty swans, within their reach, which they carried back to the Ohio by the same hard route through brush and water.

One of the hunters blew loudly on a conch shell, and the squaws, who had been gathering nuts, quickly came to build a great fire and make soup of nuts and bear fat. Audubon then stretched out with his feet to the fire, as did the hunters, while the squaws prepared the skins. The next morning as he walked about the camp in the crisp winter wind he saw a squaw at work tanning deerskins. She had cut vines and fastened them between two trees, from which swung a bark cradle holding her new-born twins. Occasionally she pushed the cradle as she worked.

In the morning a Shawnee told Audubon that he had discovered the hiding place of a large bear and invited him to come with two others on the hunt. This Indian bear-hunt was far different from that of white men, who used dogs, started up the bear, and followed him through woods and canebrake with a clamorous fight of men and dogs at the end. The Indian was cool and methodical. He followed a scarcely visible trace through the woods, occasionally pointing to a faint track which he said meant "bear." When they reached a great dead log lying on the ground he waved his hand toward a strong sapling; Audubon, whom the Indian evidently wanted out of the way, was to climb it. Bears cannot climb a slender tree but they will mount in an instant of rage a tree large enough for them to clasp, seeking an enemy.

What followed was sportsmanship of a peculiar kind. The

Indian lay down on the ground before the log, drew out his knife, and without a sound worked himself inside. He disappeared. All was silence for a few moments. Then his feet showed again, finally his whole body. He had known where to strike, but if the bear had been aroused as he entered or had been making his way to the open air, a close and difficult combat would have followed.

"The white hunter would have talked about such a feat forever," said Audubon afterward. "The Indian only hauled out his bear with a twist of grapevine, skinned him, hung the four quarters on trees, and we went on with the hunt. Squaws came and took back the meat and the skin."

By dark the whole party had returned to Cache Creek. Next day the Indians broke camp and went down the river in their canoes, bound for the Arkansas.

The weather had grown somewhat milder, and Rozier thought that if the Shawnees could travel, white men could do so. Audubon volunteered to walk the five miles to the Mississippi to see what the prospects were for ascending it; he found only a little floating ice there, and the patroon decided to try the journey.

"But we must be prepared," he said, "to haul the *cordelle*." The rest of the day was spent in shaving the oars to put them in the best condition and in making new tugs of hides, or *cordelles*, by which they might be forced to haul the keelboat upstream, walking along the shore.

The few miles to the mouth of the Ohio were quickly passed;

at the Mississippi they faced a different prospect. Boats usually crossed the river to follow the farther side, avoiding the heavy current along the Illinois shore where the Mississippi pounded to meet the Ohio. Now with floating ice and a winter wind crossing was impossible, nor could the oarsmen match the force of the current, though they accomplished the difficult turn upstream. From then on there was nothing for it: they must haul the *cordelle*.

The patroon remained on board with his steering oar. His was a heavy enough task; he had to fight the Mississippi and at the same time warp the keelboat away from the shore toward which it was constantly tending because of the tugging force of the men who were hauling it. Their labors were no less heavy, for they too fought the Mississippi and dragged the heavily laden boat.

They all hauled, with the leather tugs thrown around their shoulders in a noose. Audubon's great physical strength made him a welcome companion for the *voyageurs*, and he enjoyed this slow hard journey. He was having his first sight of the Mississippi, yellow and gray under the wintry sky, lazily sweeping in small foamy waves. "And while I was tugging at the *cordelle*," he told Lucy, "I would keep my eyes on the forest or the ground, looking for birds and curious shells."

Down the broad track of the Mississippi from the far north had come waterfowl which were new to him. Peering into the thick woods along the shore he could see small flocks of snow-birds, plunging into heaps of snow, trimly in flight again. Chickadees would alight so close to the slow procession of men that it almost seemed possible to touch them. But there could be no stopping except for a short meal. If he saw curious shells he could only try to print their patterns upon his memory. The many shells of the Ohio Valley, so far from the sea, had always seemed mysterious to the white settlers, and Audubon, who was always charmed by odd or beautiful natural forms, had begun to collect them.

They made seven miles the first day and camped at night. With breakfast at sunrise they began again. The weather was steadily growing colder. Floating ice on the river began to form in sheets, then in solid cakes. The second day they traveled more slowly. They hoped to reach a point on the Mississippi opposite Cape Girardeau, where they might await a favorable time to cross the river. Then they could make their way to Ste. Geneviève either with oars or the *cordelle*. But the river was now almost solidly frozen, the skies dark. They reached the point where the Mississippi swept downward, then back into the Illinois country in a broad bend, opposite Tywappitty Bottom, and the patroon decided that they must camp until a change came. Islands broke the wind here and gave them some shelter.

Fearing the onset of a blizzard they all worked furiously, felling trees which they slid into the water alongside the keelboat; these they fastened so as to protect the hull on both sides from the grinding ice. More trees were felled and piled high for firewood. Around a partially cleared space with a few tall oaks for shelter they built a circling wall of snow. Their goods were brought ashore and covered with sailcloth, and a great fire was built. Next day they cut holes in the ice and fished. Along the higher banks they found opossum holes and set snares. Before a week had passed venison, wild turkeys, raccoons, and opossums hung from branches overhead.

Rozier fell into a black mood. He was certain that nothing but disaster lay ahead. Finally he decided to lose himself in sleep among the buffalo robes. "The sorrows of my partner were too great to be described," Audubon told Lucy later. "He wrapped himself up in his blanket like a squirrel in winter quarters, with his tail around his nose. Rozier was seldom seen except at meals—or when something went wrong!"

Audubon on the other hand had seldom been gayer. "I never regretted one day there!" Everything pleased him in this wild spot. "Nobody can have any idea of what a good fire is who has never seen a camp-fire in the woods of America! Imagine four or five ash trees, three feet in diameter and sixty feet long, cut and piled up with all their limbs and branches, and then a fire kindled on top with brush and dry leaves!" Wolves howled around the camp but were kept at a distance by the steady towering fire, which lighted the branches of the oaks overhead.

The wolves remained for days just out of range. One day they appeared on the river as a flock of trumpeter swans alighted on the ice. With their bodies low they crept toward the swans, but the great birds were wary. They permitted the wolves to approach within a hundred yards, then sounding their clanging calls as at a signal, they flew up the river far more swiftly than any wolf could travel, circling part way back again and suddenly dropping to batter the ice with their wings, making a rumbling, cracking noise as of thunder. Gracefully, triumphantly they rose into the air again and sailed down the river high over the wolves, whose noses were tiptilted eagerly into the air as if they could smell the fat and juicy birds. The swans lighted far below them and once more battered the ice with their wings.

A party of Osages, camping not far away, soon discovered the white men's camp, and came, making friendly gestures. They spoke almost no English or French, but communication was achieved, and Audubon, who admired their fine bearing, visited their camp in turn. When he made a drawing of one of them in red chalk they shouted and laughed as though this achievement were a great joke. He followed them in pursuit of game for what he could learn of the woods and canebrakes and lakes of this region, of the ways of the forest and of Indian ways. Often a young man named Pope, who had joined the party at Henderson, was with him, one of the many young men who were to follow him through wild country. They watched the squaws weaving and making baskets, learned something of their use of vegetable colors, saw them gathering roots and berries from beneath dry leaves for food or medicine. The Osages, delighted by Audubon's searching vision, gestured and pointed to teach him the ways of birds which they saw him watching.

At night they frequently came to the camp, bringing their squaws who worked on baskets of wild cane while the hunters smoked serenely, and persistently laughed at Audubon's drawings. He was making sketches in profusion, of the patroon, the *voyageurs*, perhaps a comical one of the squirrel-like Rozier, wrapped to his chin in furs. He made many drawings of raccoons, opossums, rabbits, squirrels, of the thwarted wolves, of the swans, and with the whole crew of boatmen and hunters and Indians around him he wrote of each day's happenings in his journal, continuing the habit which was to become as fixed with him as that of rising before daybreak.

As the firelight threw a rosy-yellow light on the walls of snow young Pope would play his violin; when his writing was finished Audubon would bring out his flute. The *voyageurs* would sing—delicate little songs which had come long ago from France, about a girl or a swallow or a rose or a clear fountain—

A la claire fontaine
M'en allant promener
J'ai trouvé l'eau si belle
Que je m'y suis baigné.

Lui ya longtemps que je t'aime,
Jamais je ne t'oublierai.
Sur la plus haute branche
Le rossignol chantait.
Chante, rossignol, chante,
Toi qui as le cœur gai.

Audubon must have learned some of these songs in his youth in France, and the little airs which he played on the flute were known in turn to these French-Indian boatmen. Sometimes they danced as he played with Pope, and then the Osages were convulsed. They thought both the music and these gyrations extremely funny.

As several weeks passed with no change in the severe weather the party grew restless, then uncomfortable. The supply of bread gave out. For a time the dry white meat of the wild turkey took the place of bread with bear's fat for butter. This finally became distasteful, as did both bear and possum meat. Audubon decided to walk north to the point on the Illinois side facing Cape Girardeau where perhaps he might succeed in crossing the river and bring back bread or meal.

With young Pope as a companion he wound his way through woods and around canebrakes, walking until dusk when they happened on a trail which they supposed led to the river. Following it for some distance, they found themselves back in camp. Rozier roused himself from his unhappy slumbers long enough to speak. "What, no loaves of bread?" he cried scornfully. "No bags of meal! Boobies!" He curled up in his robe again. The Osages present rolled over with amusement, and Audubon laughed as much as anyone. He decided to try the journey again at sunrise the next day.

This time they went directly across the deep half circle of land around which the river made the great bend. At sunset they had

Cape Girardeau in full view. It was too dark to hail a canoe from the other side; they were obliged to camp for the night in an abandoned log hut. A light snow fell during the night; when they arose, icicles hung from the trees glittering in sunshine so brilliant that wild turkeys in branches overhead seemed dazzled and did not stir when Pope and Audubon walked beneath them.

With bright scarves and a firing of guns they signaled to Cape Girardeau and presently saw a canoe threading its way through broken ice, sometimes almost upended by the pushing current but finally reaching the Illinois shore. The French trader who had made the journey learned what they wished to buy and in the mid-afternoon returned with a barrel of flour, some bags of meal, and loaves of bread. The flour was rolled into the cabin; some of the bags of meal were hoisted into the crotch of a tree. Others they carried on their shoulders, and they thrust their gun barrels through the loaves of bread. Thus their hands were free in case they were obliged to use their guns. By steady trotting they reached the camp not long after midnight. The next morning others in the party contrived a rude sledge and went for the flour and the rest of the meal.

Two more weeks passed, in which the ice cracked and broke, piled up and froze again, making great ramparts that hid the islands. Slowly the river began to fall, and as it fell the ice ground against the logs protecting the keelboat and splintered them. With the help of the Indians they cut more logs and lashed these to the boat with thick cane, and thought it was protected. They had failed to count on the Mississippi in winter. Suddenly at midnight the patroon aroused them. "The ice breaks! Get up! Get up! Down to the boat! Bring axes! Hurry or we may lose her! Here, a torch so we may see!" Ice was slipping with loud reports as of heavy guns; the river was overflowing the banks.

Floods had risen with mild weather on streams far to the east which poured into the Ohio, and had turned that river into a flood which now was rushing into the Mississippi with hurtling violence, pushing the ice there into huge ice fountains that rose and fell far upstream, and began to break as the weather turned wet. When dawn came the whole river was a piled, heaving cover of ice which had been ground so fine as not to offer a solid inch of foothold. Masses of this were pounding against the keelboat, splintering the logs lashed there as buffers, working through to the cane. More bundles of cane were lashed to its sides. Before this task was finished the boat was riding easily. The river had risen, and the ice had begun to cascade downstream.

Breathless, exhausted, they watched the Mississippi rise higher, higher. A crash like volleys of cannon was heard far below them.

"The Mississippi he have pushed his way against the Ohio River," said a *voyageur*.

Within four hours the Mississippi was partly open and the patroon decided to attempt the trip upstream before the weather changed again. The boat was loaded and the camp was given to the Osages. "We bade them many farewells," said Audubon, "as when brothers part."

Danger in plenty lay ahead of them. They were obliged to pole their way along the shore against the strong current, shoving against the bottom when it could be touched, but often swept into the wider stream, perilously close to the ice. Often this was higher than their heads. But it was still moving, and here and there they struck open water where oars could be used. At last they were able to head across to Cape Girardeau. Ice still threatened them as they pushed slowly upstream. "Once more we were in motion between ice," Audubon wrote in his journal. If a sudden thaw had come they would have been in still greater peril.

By slow stages, camping at night, they reached the Grand Tower, that tall rock near the western shore which had long been a landmark for travelers on the Mississippi. Here they must take to the middle of the stream if they were to avoid bars, small islands, and well-known snags and sawyers. Heavy clouds had blown over the river. The patroon decided to begin again the heavy tedious work of hauling the *cordelle.*

The party rested for a whole day opposite the great rock. Far above it and below, the shores were dark, the gray ice and the brown waters were heaving. Suddenly the patroon cried out, "The sea eagle! Look! It's the only one I've seen since I left the Great Lakes." The great blackish-brown, coppery bird was slowly descending from the upper air in magnificent flight and hung for a moment against the cloudy sky, dipped strongly and swiftly for a fish and bore this aloft in his talons, lighting for a moment on a ledge of the Grand Tower so that the proud contour of beak and shoulder was clear, and vanished on the farther side.

Audubon had never seen this eagle, and excitement left him breathless. He was certain that it was unknown to science, and he determined to name it the "Washington Eagle." It seems not to have been a new species, as he thought, but a partly grown bald eagle. None the less, the savage strength, the wild flight over the dark river to the ancient rock, had been glorious, and though he would have liked to stay at the Grand Tower for much longer observation, he harnessed himself for the trudging journey with a *cordelle* willingly enough. In the West he had seen an eagle!

A long pull followed. With the *voyageurs* he waded through small streams that poured into the Mississippi or broke through the ice that blocked them. Open water showed from time to time where oars could be used; then the whole party would return again to the shore, stopping in the late afternoon to let Audubon and one or two of the hunters bring in game, making a camp-fire, taking a long hard sleep with one of the men told off each night to stand guard.

Fighting the river inch by inch, they passed lonely gray islands, combed with thick brush, banked with the wreckage of flatboats. All the men were plastered with mud. By no means out of spirits, they reached Ste. Geneviève at last.

Set well back from the river because of floods, Ste. Geneviève was the oldest white settlement west of the Mississippi. After seventy-five years it was still a French village, French in the look of its shuttered houses and shops, even in the shape of its muddy streets. At this time St. Louis, farther up the river, was hardly larger. Both settlements were a rendezvous for *voyageurs*, fur-traders going north, travelers from New Orleans, trappers going into the far west, Indians, missionaries.

At Ste. Geneviève Audubon and Rozier found a ready market for their goods at high prices. The ice on the river had created scarcity, and they were among the few who had broken through to this frontier post. Rozier was no longer depressed. Audubon was not half so pleased as he had been at the Great Bend or for that brief moment when he saw the eagle at the Grand Tower. He found at Ste. Geneviève a Frenchman who had accompanied William Clark and Meriwether Lewis on their great expedition, and listened entranced to this new account of a journey of which he had already heard much in Louisville. The Rocky Mountains—nothing would have suited him better than to start westward at once. And Boone was no great distance away on the Femme Osage Creek.

There was no chance to consider such tempting possibilities now. He had a decision of another kind to make. Rozier wanted to remain in Ste. Geneviève, the more so since he had found there a girl whom he admired and was already courting. The partnership papers, drawn up in France, had stipulated that Audubon and Rozier were to remain partners for nine years, and only four had passed. Though he enjoyed the stories of the West which he heard there, Audubon did not like the rough post and thought it an unsuitable place for Lucy. He decided to sell his interest in the remaining stock to his partner and return to Henderson. Rozier made a partial payment in cash and offered notes for the remainder. "He made out to grow rich," said Audubon afterward, "and what more could *he* wish for?"

The journey to Ste. Geneviève had taken more than two months, and in the leisurely fashion of the time the transactions there had been slow. Perhaps Audubon found an excuse to visit Boone at this time. In any event it was late spring, or early summer of the southern country, when he started back to Henderson on foot, with only a dog for a companion, crossing the river at Cape Girardeau and following little-known trails toward Shawneetown.

Audubon had a sensitive touch with all animals, all living creatures; this made him able to put his hand in the phoebes' nest at Mill Grove. His dogs always seemed to have an instant sense of what he wanted. When he was watching birds they would lie by his side for more hours than it was reasonable for dogs to remain quiet, and he trained them to bring back not only game birds—that was simple enough—but the tiniest warbler without injury.

With Zephyr at his side the trip went happily enough. The weather was bright, the prairies were full of brilliant color, green from the tall grasses with swaying tops of wild sweet william. The titlarks and snowbirds had long since vanished. The chickadees no longer had a friendly eye for travelers but were shy and busy among the thickly flowered redbuds. He flushed meadowlarks as he walked, and in the freshness of early morning heard songs from the air, from thick grasses, from the edge of tiny streams—changing arcs of song from the four quarters of the sky and from a fresh and opulent earth.

Prairie warblers hid themselves in briary tangles that still were yellow green with new leaves. Audubon lingered to watch them and was captivated by the look of one on a low spray of wild phlox, poised there for a moment, a waving bit of green upon blue-green, rusty red upon pink. He made a rapid sketch with a note of colors which he was to use for a full painting.

One night he spent at the camp of some friendly Osages and saw calabashes swung outside their tents where purple martins were nesting. Occasionally he found a neat cabin where he was made welcome, with a pone made from freshly ground corn, and perhaps some fresh milk, or a bit of game. More than once he made his own fire and camped alone.

One day he walked later than he realized over the prairie. Twilight came on suddenly and the nighthawks were wheeling in the air and skimming over the deep grass. There seemed to be no shelter at hand. He was about to make some sort of camp when he saw a faint glow of firelight ahead of him; before long he came toward a small log cabin whose door was open. A tall figure was passing and repassing before it, an unkempt woman. When Audubon asked if he might spend the night in the cabin she answered gruffly "Yes," but offered him nothing.

As he entered the doorway he saw a finely built young Indian lad before the fire, resting his head between his hands with his elbows on his knees, without motion, apparently without breath. A few coonskins lay at his feet; his long bow rested against the wall. Audubon spoke to him in French, and he raised his head, pointing to one of his eyes, and explained brokenly that this had been blinded only a little while before by the rebound of an arrow which had split.

When Audubon drew out his watch to see the time the woman's attitude changed completely; she hastily explained that she had plenty of cooked venison and jerked buffalo meat and that he would find a cake on the hearth in the ashes. With ungainly motions she danced about, eager to see the watch at close hand. Audubon took it off and handed it to her with the gold chain. She asked its value, put the chain around her coarse neck, and said she wished she had such a watch. Audubon, paying little attention to her, ate some of the venison, sharing a portion with Zephyr.

While he was eating, the Indian lad rose from his seat as if his sufferings were unendurable; he passed Audubon several times, and once, when the woman was not looking, pinched his arm so sharply that Audubon nearly exclaimed out loud. The Indian, with his one good eye then gave him a look so dark and forbidding that Audubon was uncannily chilled. The Indian sat down again, drew out a long knife from his belt, felt the edge, put his hand behind him and brought out his tomahawk, which was also a hatchet pipe. This he filled with tobacco. At intervals, with his one strange dark eye, he sent a look in Audubon's direction.

At last Audubon asked the woman for his watch and wound it. Saying that he wanted to see what weather was promised for the next day, he took his gun and walked out of the cabin. Outside he slipped a ball into each barrel and scraped the flint. It would have been folly to leave over a strange trail in the dark with perhaps more than one enemy at his back. He returned to the cabin.

There were no beds, only a pile of bearskins; one of these he took, and lay down with Zephyr at his side and his hand on his gun, pretending to be asleep. In a few minutes two tall strong young men, as coarse in appearance as the woman, came in with guns over their shoulders, bearing a dead stag slung on poles. They asked for whiskey which they drank in great gulps.

"Who the devil is that!" they exclaimed as they noticed Audubon. "And what is that rascal doing here?" they asked, pointing to the Indian. "Hush!" said the woman. She took them aside. Audubon heard the whispered word "watch" and was not slow to guess the rest. He lightly touched his dog, and saw that Zephyr seemed to know what was happening, for he turned his eyes alternately at the group and at his master.

The boys called for more whiskey and were soon reeling around the cabin. The woman also drank heavily, and presently Audubon saw her take a large carving knife from a shelf, which she carried outside; he could see her gaunt figure in the dim light and hear the grinding whirr against the stone's edge. In she came, handing the knife to one of her sons, and hissed, "There! settle him!" She motioned toward the Indian. She herself advanced toward Audubon.

His gun was cocked and he was waiting for the attack when through the door came two stout travelers with their guns leveled at the pair of young men. Audubon covered the woman with his gun and Zephyr was growling around her feet at the same time. With the help of the Indian the three were tied fast with leathern thongs and unceremoniously bundled against the walls. The Indian, in spite of his eye, seemed about to perform a dance, he was so overjoyed. He explained that he had tried his best to communicate with Audubon, but there had never been a moment when either of them could escape. He had stumbled into the house almost by accident when his eye was injured.

"You may suppose we slept much less than we talked," Audubon told Lucy afterward. The strangers had once had a similar experience in a lonely cabin. Single travelers were almost defenseless under such circumstances, and the offense was serious. It was harshly punished the next morning by the two travelers, who burned the cabin, gave the skins and implements to the Indian, and drove the trio into the woods, administering a lawless justice in a land where as yet there was no law.

Audubon went on to Shawneetown alone. If he saw a pair of orioles among the pointed silver spires of a young ash this would have been enough to make him forget the ugly events of the night. His eyes were filled with fresh colors; the low green landscape, sloping gently now toward the river, was astir with small motions, bold flights, the ripple and turn of song, the rustle of wings.

Walking steadily, he soon reached Henderson and Lucy.

6 *On a Gay Horse*

BARRO was a newly caught wild horse of the breed which long ago was brought from Arabia to Spain and from Spain to Mexico, and thence northward to the western prairies. When the early Spanish explorers came to grief there, the horses survived and bred with wild horses of the plains.

The beauty of the Arabian horses had not descended to Barro. "He's as homely as a worm-fence and as clever as a possum on the hunt for turkey's eggs," said his owner, who had ridden him to Kentucky from the headwaters of the Arkansas.

Barro's forehead was bulging, his mane was long, thick, unkempt, and constantly swung forward. His tail, which seemed designed in the original plan to be a splendid tail, drooped thinly to the ground. But his chest was broad, his legs were clean and sinewy; his nostrils indicated spirit. He was a bay with legs deepening to black. He had never worn a shoe, and his black hoofs were sound. "Try him and welcome," said his owner. "His gaits are easy and he'll stand fire as well as any horse I ever saw."

Audubon mounted Barro, who carried him with great smoothness to the woods. As they approached a huge log, six or seven feet thick, Audubon pressed his legs to the horse's belly without using the spur. Barro bounded off and cleared the log as lightly as an elk. Audubon made him leap the same log several times, which he did like a trick pony going through his paces. He rode Barro into a swamp. "I knew it was muddy and tough," he said. The horse entered the swamp with nice caution, placing his nose near the surface of the water as if to judge its depth. They rode through the swamp, and though Barro had to push through heavy, soggy soil in many places he was good-natured and hesitated only to make sure of his way.

After this they went off at a gallop, and Audubon shot a wild turkey cock from the saddle. Barro, undisturbed by the report of the gun, went up to the turkey like a pointer.

"Can he swim well?" thought Audubon. "For there are many excellent horses that cannot swim at all, but will lie on their sides and float with the current, and the rider must either swim or drag them to the shore, or let them go their own way."

When he rode into the Ohio, Barro made off at an angle against the strong current, his head well above the surface, his nostrils expanded. He breathed freely, with none of the grunts which many horses make in the water. Audubon turned him downstream, and then up again, directly against the current, where he swam as easily as before.

Barro had his own tastes. He liked hen's eggs, but it is not reported that he ever robbed a nest, and it is not known whether he sucked them like a weasel or ate them whole, crunching the shells. He also had a fondness for pumpkins. Lucy rode him and he carried her gently over rough trails.

Audubon and Lucy and little Victor were now living at the Rankins', in their comfortable two-storied log house with a wide covered passageway dividing its two parts. The arrangement seems to have been merely a friendly one; Audubon was not pressed at this time for money. He had brought back fair returns from his trip to Ste. Geneviève and had soon set up his store again. The sales were still small but the profits on what he sold were high, and though he was nothing of a farmer or a planter he seemed to know good land when he saw it, perhaps by a rich look that seemed to escape other less observant eyes. He had begun at this time to invest his surplus money in land, which he invariably sold at increased prices. In the store he was fortunate in having young Pope, who had returned from Ste. Geneviève before him, as a clerk. Pope was faithful and honest; besides, in off hours he could talk about birds and even join Audubon in expeditions into the woods.

These years, which had begun with so little promise in the new spare little town, had abundance. Audubon often rode with Lucy. Once they made the long journey to Fatland Ford and back with Lucy on Barro. They had many pleasures together. Lucy was a strong, graceful swimmer; on summer days they would swim in the Ohio. Little Victor grew well, and within two years another son, John Woodhouse, was born. With Lucy, Audubon danced all night at plantation weddings, and he trod the pea vine to a lively tune on bare ground outside a squatter's cabin when a trip on horseback brought him to a halt there.

It was understood that he was to supply the Rankins' table with fish and game, a sufficient undertaking, for the family was large; he was often away on Barro hunting. When he returned it was for good exchanges of talk, not only with Lucy but with Dr. Rankin, who was always interested in news of the woods and rivers. His friends and neighbors could count upon his abundant harvest of tales, some of them hunters' stories, gravely told and very tall. He could offer all sorts of small diversions, mimicking the horned owl's note, simulating an Indian yell and giving the hair of his audience an authentic lift. His music on one of two or three instruments and his French songs were always welcome, and he fenced with those who knew the art. He took snuff after the sociable habit of the day.

He was usually willing to admit his own mishaps. Once when he went up a tree to look at some young woodpeckers in their hole, he slipped his hand inside and drew out not a young woodpecker but a lively blacksnake. He slid down the tree in a hurry with the blacksnake coiling around a limb above him. "Weren't you scared?" asked one of the men to whom he was telling the story. "Me scared!" exclaimed Audubon drily. "But no! It was one damn scared blacksnake."

Like most hunters of the time and place he let his hair grow long; this has suggested a vaguely poetical look, but not to those who know frontiers. Audubon has been pictured as a mild dreamer, idling his hours away in the forest, seeing the beauties of nature in a rosy mist. He was nothing like that. He was sharply aware of the darker phases of wild life. It is significant that he admired hawks as much as bluebirds—"whose least note I love." When his curiosity was aroused he could be as swift and sure and relentless as a hawk in seeking out birds. He was not a dreamer in any true sense at all, admirable though dreamers may be. Not a line in all his many writings of later years or in his journals suggests this. He was always outside himself, even among men, watching their ways, reading their faces. "Their eyes often tell me what the mouth denies," he said.

Nor was he ever a solitary, though he could be happy enough in solitude. He was always picking up companions along the road, and he thoroughly liked the more sociable birds—sociable among themselves. "Nothing can be more gratifying than the society of woodpeckers," he once wrote. He liked the "mirth and gayety" of the golden-winged flickers. He was often in the thick woods along the Green with the Rankin boys or others at his heels. He might have been a piper leading the children of the town or from nearby plantations with him on his errands, but he had no need of a pipe or even of his flageolet. His bird calls were enough, or his talk about birds, or his way of pointing out nests or feeding places or the ways of fledglings.

The boys in turn taught him much that he had not known; all his life he was to speak of the close and faithful observation of young people, and of how much he had learned from them. They showed him a nest of the golden-crowned wagtail or ovenbird, well hidden under pink beech leaves far from the river in a dry place, so softly arched as hardly to be noticeable among the wind-blown drifts. Not far away was the pair, resorting to a few simple tricks to lead the invaders away, so shy that they seemed ready to disappear beneath a tangle of vine. Audubon had returned to Henderson in time for the rare ecstatic song of these wagtails, only to be heard by those who are persistent in their wanderings and willing to wait for hours, motionless, perhaps without reward.

"Treason!" he would hiss if one of his young followers made a movement or a sound during such long pauses. They wanted to laugh; he had many small jokes with them. The whole tribe looked like a pack of young Indians with their deerskin shirts and leggings and Indian hatchets. They looked for the hiding places of the peregrine falcon in cliffs along the Green, and watched its sudden rocket-like flight into the air above the faint white swirl in deep cold-green water. Once Audubon brought down a teal within thirty paces of where he was standing. A falcon swooped down at the report of his gun, stole it and was off. The boys told him that this bird had a breastbone shaped like an arrow which it drove into a teal or mallard, striking on the wing, killing its prey on the instant.

They often told him such queer stories of the woods, which sometimes had a touch of primitive magic. They said that the hearts of the green parroquets distilled a deadly poison. They said that in winter most birds went far into the deep forests where they crept into hollow trees and lay as if dead until spring. They said that jaybirds went to hell on Friday. They said that bears sucked their paws in their winter sleep, and they had many stories of bears that had hugged men to death. They said that raccoons sat beside streams with their tails hanging into the water, waiting for crabs to nip them, when they would whisk the crabs neatly in front of them for a meal.

Stories like these were told by Negroes, sometimes by wandering Indians, often by white hunters. They were often highly fanciful, but at least the creatures of earth and air and water were talked about by those striving to make a place for themselves in the wilderness. Often hunters were brutal; white men were careless of life in all ways on the frontier. When great flocks of wild pigeons darkened the sky they were shot for the excitement of shooting, and a flock of small strange birds might suffer the same fate only because they were strange. Fear sometimes seemed to lie beneath these moods of destruction, or sheer excitement, but in a not altogether haphazard fashion these people lived in their new world. Audubon was not alone in his searching curiosity or his enjoyments.

When parties went out for deer he was with them, and in the frosty woods he joined in routing out the thieving possums. Like the hunters he knew every trick of that wily creature, tricks to obtain whole clutches of eggs, the best young chickens, even the fattened fowls, or the finest fruits. "Let the crows and the ravens flourish," he told his neighbors. "They'll beat off the possums!" But on the whole these planters preferred to hunt with hounds and with a rousing supper at the end.

One night when Audubon was staying at a neighboring plantation he was aroused to join in a bear hunt some miles away where bears were robbing a cornfield. The overseer's horn rang out. A Negro swiftly cast bullets; others saddled horses, called the dogs, and in a few minutes Audubon was off on the amiable Barro with his friend and four stout slaves. The night was hot, misty. They overtook others on the way, but the large party contrived to let down the bars of the cornfield without a sound, entered, divided, and posted themselves at intervals. At a signal all the horns were blown, and with shouts the men and dogs charged toward the center of the field to drive the bears into trees there. The drive succeeded. Fires were built and quickly blazed high; in their light two small bears were seen in crotches. It was nothing for any hunter to bring them down. A big she-bear was seen in another tree, high and fairly well concealed.

BLUE-WINGED TEAL. *PLATE NO. CCCXIII*

The Negroes, who had brought axes, began cutting at the trunk with great strokes. At last as the tree fell the dogs rushed in, but the bear laid about her, killing one of them at a blow, inflicting heavy damage upon the others, and in a sudden dash shaking off the rest of the pack to charge upon a Negro who was mounted on a piebald. The bear slashed at the pony and plunged her teeth into his breast. Scipio, who had only a sheepskin bound by a tight girth for a saddle, was an excellent horseman and kept his seat with a short rein on the plunging piebald. He shouted to his master not to fire at the bear; he and his pony were thrown to the ground by a stroke of the powerful paws. In an instant, with a well-directed blow of the ax the Negro had killed the bear. In another instant he was down on his knees beside the pony, tending him so skillfully that the piebald was destined to survive. The dangerous slaughter was not yet ended. Other bears were discovered in a tall tree, which were routed and killed by the combined forces of smoke, gunshot, knives.

"Those dogs, horses, fires, and trampling men destroyed more corn in a few hours than did the bears in all their visits," said Audubon, yet he had liked the gusty color.

In the spring when the woods were still wet and cold he joined in sugar-making on the banks of the Green or the Trademaker, and he enjoyed country barbecues in summer when a whole scattered countryside would gather in some favored spot to forget that they had no close neighbors. Corn pones and sweet potatoes were baked, great haunches of venison roasted. While the blue smoke curled upward there would be singing, lively dancing, the rough game of gander pulling, and rivalry in marksmanship as men trimmed the wick of a candle without extinguishing the flame. Nails were lightly pointed into a board for targets, and the hunters, with Audubon among them, would drive them through the board to the head with bullets as surely as by a hammer swung in the hand.

Mounted on Barro, he went east for new goods in the early autumn of 1811, taking a roundabout route through the south with the hope of finding new openings in trade, or perhaps only to explore the country. He followed the Red Banks trail to Nashville, and may have lingered there. He then took a cross trace to Knoxville, a small, thriving village set down by the Tennessee. Trails met at Knoxville, coming down from high-peaked narrow blue mountains.

Barro seemed completely himself on a long journey. If a wild turkey appeared in a dusting-place, brushing the barred iridescence of his wings, burying his sheathed head, Barro would be after him at a lope. He would almost succeed in flushing coveys of quail and he robbed more than one field of a golden pumpkin. Grouse were drumming, and Audubon shot enough game to keep himself in provender along the way, making his fires at night while Barro munched the last of the season's grass. Off at a touch in the morning he would loiter if Audubon wished to loiter, and pause at the edge of a clear spring until told to drink. When Audubon wanted to explore a thicket beyond a watery hollow he would nose his way as smoothly as an alligator, "and stand, when I want him to stand—he will stand as still as any great heron, though not quite in the same position." Now Audubon watched more than one heronry and saw the snowy egret winging over dark hemlocks. One after another flocks moved in long diagonals to the South—purple martins, swallows, red-winged blackbirds, goldfinches. On moonlit nights he kept himself awake to watch and listen with Barro browsing at his side. He knew that many birds migrated at night; he was now sure enough that this was the habit of the catbird and of certain warblers, but he foresaw that he would have to follow through many such nights in other years to reach the end of these secrets.

The pair meandered higher and higher through the mountains facing crisp autumn winds, camping or spending a night at some cabin perched above a laurel-covered cliff. They traveled through Cumberland Gap—

> Cumberland Gap is a noted place,
> Three kinds of water to wash your face.
>
> Cumberland Gap with its cliff and rocks,
> Home of the panther, bear, and fox.
>
> The first white man in Cumberland Gap
> Was Doctor Walker, an English chap.
>
> Daniel Boone on Pinnacle Rock,
> He killed Indians with an old flintlock.

Audubon would have liked the song for the celebration of his friend, and he was stirred by the wild spread of scene. Moving on powerful wings, he saw again the great golden eagle as the mountains turned black-green and coppery.

Riding out of the old town of Abingdon in Virginia, he overtook a traveler who knew the country well. Their road lay through high, shelving country with rivers to ford. Suddenly the stranger pulled up his horse and said, "Wager you can't guess how far we are from the Natural Bridge."

Audubon thought for a moment. He listened; he had heard a faint familiar note in the woods. "Take you."

The stranger scoffed. "Lay you a dollar."

"Done," said Audubon. "The Natural Bridge is about a hundred feet away."

"How do you know that?" exclaimed the stranger. "After all you must have been in these parts before."

"No," Audubon insisted, and the man was convinced that this was true. After a bit of banter the wager was paid, and as they rode over the bridge Audubon explained how he had determined the distance, pointing to a small dusky-olive bird making swift sallies into the sunny air for insects. "She told me how far we were from the bridge—or her mate." It was a phoebe, whose haunts in cavernous rocks he had known well on the Perkiomen, always circling near her nesting place, one of the earliest of birds to come north, one of the last to leave. The note which he had heard was less assured than in spring, more casual, hardly more than a plaintive echo, a dubious breath, but he knew the few notes of the phoebe too well to be doubtful, and he could now determine the distance of sounds in the woods as accurately as any Indian.

He was soon off main-traveled roads again, and crossed the Roanoke. Where he went in Virginia or on what errands can only be guessed. Captain Audubon had had a business connection with merchants in Richmond who were said to owe him money; it is possible that Audubon went there on an errand connected with this debt. Or he may only have made the errand fit his wish to explore. He finally rode through Maryland to Lancaster and on to Fatland Ford.

Here by a sudden decision he joined Lucy's brother Thomas in a partnership by which the firm of "Audubon & Bakewell, Merchants," was to be set up by young Bakewell in New Orleans. In this enterprise he invested a fair sum of money, and in Philadelphia he purchased new goods for the Henderson store.

For a time he lingered at Fatland Ford, working over sketches of birds. Something about the place seemed propitious for these undertakings. A number of the studies which he finally included in his great work were signed and dated as belonging to these visits, among them his Blackburnian warbler with a spray of wild phlox, and his song sparrows. However far he circled, however widely he observed, completion on paper was never far from his mind.

Somehow the year had wandered into late November when he

started west. Somewhere, in Richmond or Philadelphia or elsewhere along his road, his appearance had changed. As he cantered along over hard roads Barro was the same Barro, picking his way neatly over frozen ruts or layers of ice. But Audubon was not the same Audubon.

By the time he reached the Juniata he was no longer wearing his hunter's garb but that of a common French sailor, blue dungarees and a short jacket with a red madras handkerchief wound around his head and large gold earrings in his ears. His beard and mustachios were his own, but they flowed and curled so abundantly that they looked as though he had fastened them on with glue for a masquerade. He looked gayer, wilder, than any common sailor, and no doubt took more snuff than usual. Whatever his reasons for acting the part, he never troubled to mention them; perhaps he had none; perhaps he was bent only on some prank among the French colony in Pittsburgh. Whatever his reasons, he enjoyed this to the full. As he was sitting at the table in a tavern close by the falls of the Juniata a stranger entered and asked whether he minded a companion for breakfast.

Audubon answered, "No, *sare,*" with the strongest of French accents.

The stranger asked a further question which Audubon thought silly. "Are you a Frenchman?"

"Oh, *no, sare.* Hi em an Eenglishman!"

"An Englishman! Why, how can that be?"

"I am an Eenglishman," said Audubon slowly, "because I 'ave

han Eenglish wife." Questioned still further, he declared firmly, "I belong to every country."

When the stranger, whose name was Nolte, relaxed his questions this nonsense stopped. Nolte saw that this was no common sailor, and the two struck up something of a friendship. They decided to travel on into Kentucky together. Vincent Nolte was a merchant and speculator, born in Leghorn, whose affairs had taken him on long journeys over the world and many times through America. Audubon knew how to talk with such a man, and some years later Nolte was to remember and to assist him.

Nolte was accompanied by a servant on horseback and his own horse was handsome. "I wish you had as good a one," he said, casting a glance at Barro, who as they started pricked up his ears and lengthened his pace. Nolte caracoled his horse to give him speed and then put him to a quick trot, but in vain. Barro remained a length ahead, then two, then a smart distance. He was in the stable at the next inn eating oats and eggs as Nolte came up. Audubon, who had ordered an excellent supper, was standing in the doorway of the tavern, still looking the bold French sailor lost in the wilds of America.

At Pittsburgh Nolte bought two flatboats by which to carry a cargo he had purchased and invited Audubon to make the journey with him down the river. The weather was cold, the river full of ice, but the trip went pleasantly enough. Audubon amused his host by drawing everyone on board the boats, and showed him some of the sketches of birds which he had managed to make on his long journey. At Limestone they decided to make a detour into Kentucky on horseback. They parted in a friendly fashion at Frankfort.

The year of wonders had begun. On the homeward journey Audubon was jogging along comfortably through the open barrens when he saw a strange sudden darkness in the west. Accustomed to storms, he thought little of this though he speeded Barro a little, hoping to reach a friend's house no great distance away. Suddenly he heard a distant rumbling as of a violent tornado; again he pressed his knees against Barro's sides. But Barro almost stopped and moved only by placing one foot after another with as much care as though he were moving over smooth ice. Audubon thought he had foundered and was on the point of dismounting to lead him, when Barro began to groan pitifully, hung his homely head nearly to the ground and spread his four legs. He now stood entirely still but continued to groan, and all the low trees and shrubs began to move and wave along the ground. The earth itself shuddered and heaved and sank in waves for a few moments. The sky grew quickly light again, and Barro frisked along the road.

Audubon hurried him, fearing that the earthquake had brought disaster to Henderson. He burst into the Rankins' house to find everything safe, and perhaps astonished the quiet Lucy who had never seen her husband as a sailor.

Toward dawn a few nights later another violent rumbling was felt and the whole household rushed outside for fear of falling timbers. The earth waved like a field of grain in a strong wind; birds wildly circled overhead. Suddenly the doctor remembered his jars and phials and instruments, neatly arranged in a corner cupboard on shelves, and dashed back into the house, and in the distraction of the moment never thought of closing the cupboard doors which would have held all his treasures within; instead, to keep them from dancing off onto the floor, he kept shoving them back, himself dancing all the while, pushing back the jars, thrusting back the knives, but saving only a few of his mixtures.

This was the great earthquake of 1811 which was to continue at intervals in the West throughout the next year. Islands had been sunk in the Mississippi by the great convulsion. The great river itself had become a raging whirlpool in the region of New Madrid, spinning boats around on their sterns, plunging some of them to destruction. Land in western Tennessee was transformed; lakes were completely sunk beneath the ground and others formed in new places. In Kentucky the shocks were less violent, but they continued; no one felt safe, and to heighten the common terror, a great comet appeared in the sky, trailing a fiery tail and to the minds of many persons portending evils and misfortunes.

With the land shaking beneath men's feet, the sky a trail of fire, the western waters also showed strange apparitions. The first steamboats appeared on the Ohio. Men and women living in squatters' cabins along the Ohio, accustomed only to the placid, silvery water and the occasional movement of a canoe or a broadhorn, saw in the first noisy steamboat another promise of destruction. When the *Orleans* reached Louisville on a still moonlight night shrilly blowing off steam, the inhabitants rose from their beds in terror and ran into the streets, fearing something like a comet and an earthquake combined. When they saw the creature in motion they were terrified by its fearful rapidity as it circled in open water at the rate of five or six miles an hour.

Word reached Henderson beforehand that the *Orleans* was coming, so the townspeople were somewhat less fearful than those who had first beheld the mechanism without warning. They crowded to the wharf. Audubon was in the crowd, and as the *Orleans* steamed near he dived into the river under the boat and came up on the other side. This was a spectacular and daring feat! The crowd was breathless. Who knew what the under parts of a steamboat were like? The whole machine might have exploded on top of him.

When the first steamboat had made its way to New Orleans, a hurricane came sweeping out of the West. Audubon had gone to Shawneetown on a trading errand and was jogging quietly homeward on the Kentucky side. He had reached a little valley lying between two small streams. "For once in my life," he said, "my thoughts were entirely taken up with business."

He noticed a hazy thickness over the country; for a moment he thought of another earthquake, but he stopped at a little stream to quench his thirst. As he bent down he heard an unfamiliar murmuring sound and looked through the trees to see a great yellowish oval spot in the haze—something he had never seen before. The tops of the tallest trees shook violently, small branches and twigs fell in whirling, slanting masses; the forest was suddenly in noisy motion, creaking, bending, writhing. Whole trees of gigantic size crashed down within a few feet from where he was standing.

"The horrible noise sounded like a Niagara," he said. "Branches, twigs, foliage, and dust whirled onwards like a cloud of feathers, and left a wide space filled with fallen trees, naked stumps, and heaps of shapeless ruins about a quarter of a mile wide, which to my imagination looked like the dried-up bed of the Mississippi, with thousands of planters and sawyers strewed into the sand and set at queer angles."

Even when the hurricane had swept on, millions of twigs and small branches were sucked in its wake as by some huge magnet. For hours afterward these floated high in the air with a thick, moving dust cloud beneath them. The sky was green; a smell like sulphur was in the air. The mass of fallen trees and tangled branches was almost insurmountable. Audubon was obliged to lead Barro, who had taken the hurricane calmly, in a scramble over great trunks, through the dense thickets, through an overhanging cloud of dust, pelted by the falling leaves and twigs.

Slowly he pushed and broke his way through. When at last he reached Henderson with his buckskin clothes almost in ribbons, it was to find the village undisturbed. Almost no wind had been felt there. The hurricane had cut a narrow swath to one side of it. Elsewhere log houses had been overturned and their inmates killed. Far to the northeast the broken tops of trees showed its force. For many years the little valley between two streams which Audubon had crossed was to remain a dark, almost impenetrable wilderness. Briars quickly filled small spaces. The valley became a favored haunt of wolves, bears, panthers. The shyer birds began to nest there.

7 *Many Trails and a Snug Cabin*

A WELL-BUILT log house of spacious proportions stood on one of the wide streets of Henderson, with a barn, smoke-houses, and an ample yard. It was neatly shuttered and comfortable within. A piano stood in the parlor with a rack of other instruments—a violin, a flute, a guitar, a flageolet—and a generous pile of music nearby. The rooms were furnished with pretty tables of cherry or walnut, with carved or flagged wooden chairs, good carpets and rugs, handsome andirons, large mirrors and silver candlesticks, a silver tea service and plenty of silver for the table, with china in the cupboards, and many books. A few finely mounted birds were placed over the fireplace or over windows and doors, and the log walls of the rooms were lined with bird drawings. On a big table were a pair of silver compasses, paints, pencils, crayons, rules, microscopes, presses, squares. Guns hung from antlers in the open hallway, and knives and pistols and an Indian tomahawk pipe lay on a shelf.

The whole place was prosperous, the barnyard well stocked. Sunflowers waved in the garden, and turtle doves, jays, mockingbirds, picked up grain along with the poultry. In spring green goslings were afloat on the pond beyond the barn. Audubon not only raised tame geese but wild ones; he had found a clutch of wild goose eggs which a tame goose had hatched, and during a harsh winter had coaxed some wild geese to join the flock by a careful scattering of corn, and a few came back the following autumn. He had a tame trumpeter swan that had been wounded, and he found a small sparrow hawk in the woods nearby, dropped from the nest and still covered with soft white down, that he brought home for his "Kentucky boys," as he called Victor and John, naming it Nero because of the murderous look in his bold eye.

Soon Nero was out on the wing, seeking grasshoppers and occasionally given a small dead bird which he would seize as it was tossed into the air. For a time his parents and the other young of the brood seemed outraged by this domestication, and chased him. He would then swiftly retire to his home behind a shutter. Gradually his family let him alone. He was fastidious about his food; he refused woodpeckers, and became something of a joker, sailing down from a hidden perch, falling upon the back of a tame duck, which would waddle off, fluttering, squawking, outraged but helpless, with Nero sticking close until an insect or small bird drew him away.

"To the last he was kind to us," said Audubon, who thought the sparrow hawk, so graceful and swift on the wing, so erect on the branch, one of the most beautiful of this family. "Kind is not the word, you say, for a hawk? Well, but this Nero was like a friend. Frolicsome, then–he was frolicsome."

A frolic led Nero to his fate. He swooped down once too often upon one of the inhabitants of the barnyard, this time upon a hen with a brood, whose small head evidently contained ideas about hawks. The fight was royal. Nero met his match and was destroyed.

Audubon still remained lucky in buying and selling land. Never a shrewd bargainer, he made money in these transactions because more and more men were coming into the West seeking homes, and the price of land was going up. For much the same reason his store remained fairly profitable, and also because he easily made firm friends and kept them.

In these years he hunted tirelessly, fished, traded, worked in his store, devoured books, traveled on foot and on horseback, mounted birds, and constantly set himself the task of drawing. His work seldom pleased him. "I think nothing of it except when in the very act of drawing," he said, and there was no one to tell him that this was a usual experience for an artist. He was still by no means sure that he was an artist, and he was teased by problems of scientific classification. His notations were still mainly in French, according to Buffon, but he was constantly discovering problems which Buffon could not help him solve. When Wilson died in 1814 Audubon could hardly have failed to learn of the tragic poverty of this ornithologist's last years or that publication of his work was not yet complete. These circumstances might have halted him. He went on with his early plan, which was more ambitious than Wilson's, to portray American birds among their natural surroundings.

Often he made single studies. He had hardly returned from Ste. Geneviève when he painted the brooding hunched form of a turkey buzzard, life-size, painted this so truly and substantially that the bird's whole character loomed clear against the white paper. He was steadily occupied by the complex patterning of the plumage of owls, and painted barn owls on a branch with the Ohio and its low-lying hills dusky green in the background. He tried to solve one of the most difficult of problems, to paint a bird so that it would seem in free motion through the air, not merely set within the foreground of a scene. In a small water color he accomplished this, showing a bay-breasted warbler, jewel-like in grayish green and shadowed black and tawny red, in flight—flying northward perhaps to a nesting place in Labrador—with the pale blue hills of the Ohio beyond.

The painting of birds' eyes steadily engrossed him and he triumphed early over the problem; he was miraculously sure as to colors and shapes and somehow by the placing of tiny sharp highlights achieved an effect of wildness which was never timidity or distraction but the unchanging watchful look that sets birds apart from humans.

His concern with small effects of light and color was becoming intense. He had already discovered latent tones in old wood. It happened that the use of old wood had long been a romantic convention in nature painting, introduced to create an atmosphere of melancholy decay. Audubon was to use it in many forms and textures again and again, but never according to this stale formula. He found lucent blues there, deep yellows, touches of red; he studied the bold lines of the grain in split or shattered branches and began to use these in compositions. These were not always successful, as in his early painting of the pewee flycatcher, but the decorative intention is plain, and curiously enough his use of old wood or even of lichens seldom suggested age or decay, but light and brilliance.

In these years he was clearly concerned with the conquest of design, though this grew more difficult as he used more and more exquisite natural forms. He still liked the bold outlines of birds in flight without backgrounds, with the mere placement of outlines and the patterns of spread tails and wings, and the relation of two or three birds making the decoration, as in some of his paintings of hawks. His quiet study of snowbirds in early winter on gray-black gum branches with hanging oval berries foreshadowed some of his more subtle later work. He was coming into consciousness of many forms which were always to enchant him—the pink mallow in flower, blown into changing patterns by the wind, the wild grape in fruit, and the narrow leaves of the cane.

He fronted many problems in color and pattern which he was to solve slowly, only by most patient labor and experiment. He tried to portray purple grackles stripping stalks of Indian corn, and succeeded in showing the clutching, ruthless strength of the feeding birds with a bold contrast between the yellow corn and the dark rich glow of eyes and feathers. Other paintings were taking shape—his orioles in the flowering tulip tree, his studies of the great wild turkey, the cock and the hen, and the peregrine falcons—he tried these over and again but could not please himself. He still invariably destroyed drawings or paintings when others were finished of the same subject which seemed truer. Yet with all his failures and dissatisfactions his portfolios steadily grew heavier, and overflowed with sketches of birds, leaves, flowers, fruits, insects, and—because he couldn't let them alone—squirrels and mink, otter, raccoons, opossums.

Obstacles he met in sufficient number as his plans multiplied. When he shot a rare bird this might fall into a deep tangle where by the most determined efforts he could not reach it, or he might make a stirring discovery at so great a distance from home that when he reached his drawing table the lustrous feathers were dimmed. One cold spring he found a number of cliff swallows far down the Ohio, but the lad with whom he was hunting lost those they had shot somewhere in the woods, and it was four years before he saw cliff swallows again. He had already formed a plan to portray both the male and the female of the chosen species and even the immature birds in a single painting, and he often had the experience of finding one without the others, and was obliged to wait for months or even until another season to complete his group.

But there were days of extraordinary sights, as when he saw some goshawks trailing a great crowd of swiftly flying pigeons over the Ohio. Suddenly one of them turned aside to a flock of blackbirds, and the blackbirds swiftly closed together and were like a dusky ball passing through the air. The goshawk claimed four or five of them with ease, squeezed them, dropped them into the river. As the blackbirds reached dense woods they plunged, and the goshawk wheeled and dipped and picked up his prey from the surface of the water.

On one errand or another Audubon went to Ste. Geneviève more than once, and almost surely saw Boone, from whom he could have heard further beguiling stories of regions to the West still hardly known to white men. On the way back and forth he encountered his friends the Osages, and seems to have stayed with them, and to have learned a smattering of their language. He watched their sugar-making, and saw their clay bowls for the sap swung by grapevines. It was they who gave him a hatchet pipe, and from them he collected an abundance of lore as to the use of herbs and roots, dried leaves, and seeds. Indian remedies were always interesting to Audubon though he did not employ them. He had a special scorn of all medicine, as he had for any meat but game. But this lore seemed part of the wilderness, part of the life which had flourished there whose passing he came more and more to regret. He wrote down the Indian uses of Indian turnip and wild muscadine, of grasses and cresses and black mulberry; and these notes began to weave themselves into narratives running through his head about birds, trees, fruits, and life on the frontier. They began to form in sequences as a kind of panorama.

On foot in the spring with a dog he crossed the Mississippi from the Missouri side to find the Illinois bottom lands partly under water. He slid along for miles over the drowned prairies, swam more than one river, waded through small streams, and at evening saw a great herd of deer with a low fringe of green behind them, their slender bodies mirrored in the shallow silver, their white tails tipping and moving. Nothing else was memorable from this journey except a friendly welcome at a settler's cabin, which was bright and clean with a swept hearth. After a good supper there he slept well and woke at dawn, refreshed.

"I walked off gayly, my dog full of life, but met no one till four o'clock when I passed the first salt well, and thirty minutes more brought me to Shawneetown. As I entered the inn I was welcomed by several whom I knew, who had come to purchase salt."

Nothing extraordinary had happened; he had made no new

discoveries; yet because of such trips up and down the western country and over the Alleghenies and back down the Ohio, his vision grew keener, his delight in the natural world steadily increased. He constantly lived the life of the eyes, seizing exact color tones, minute outlines, patterns of movement in grass and water and trees. He made more than one journey up the Wabash to Vincennes, where his friend Nicholas Berthoud had connections among the French settlers. But it was the many small worlds along the full and flooding river which drew him most, the life of water birds, muskrats, box-turtles, lizards with their markings, bright-winged insects, and water moccasins.

Audubon had three or four of these ample years, enough to root him in his chosen way of living so deeply that he could never be changed. He was then struck by forces beyond his control—fluctuations in the money market, bank failures, the new tariff, the rise and fall of land speculation. So far he had only been lucky. His aptitude for business had never been encouraged in his youth or later; and by the time he needed it he was immersed in his own pursuits.

The new firm of "Audubon & Bakewell, Merchants," in New Orleans failed. Thomas Bakewell had established it only to face the complications in trade caused by the War of 1812. The investment was a complete loss. Bakewell came to Henderson, and the two decided to build a grist and lumber mill. But the country round about yielded little grain and no great amount of lumber. The mill was like many another enterprise upon which frontiersmen had embarked. Memory was powerful even in the laying out of towns on the frontier. Most often towns were laid out with narrow thoroughfares and closely neighboring houses because these had been part of city life in Europe. The wide streets of Henderson were an exception. Mills were a usual part of commerce everywhere. Surely a mill would be a good venture in Henderson—almost anywhere!

The mill, very large, very high, was built into the side of the red clay bank on the Ohio. Audubon watched the bank swallows boring fresh holes day after day as the workmen shoveled into the steep slope and demolished their nesting places. These small lively swallows would bathe and drink on the wing and return to their labors, friendly, unable to understand that this group of human beings would continue to destroy their habitations.

The mill was finished at last, the expensive machinery installed. There was only a little business. Audubon had invested nearly all the money he had in it.

"Now we know the country is unfit for such a thing!" he exclaimed to Dr. Rankin. "We might as well have settled in the moon!"

"The times are bad." The doctor tried to console him.

"The fault was ours," said Audubon roundly. "We should have studied this over. We should have known better."

The machinery gave them endless trouble, and they lost business while it was being repaired.

"How I labored at that infernal mill," said Audubon afterward. He was there day after day.

But presently its walls began to be lined with bird drawings. He was absorbed in painting nighthawks, whose rapid motions had always pleased him. He had watched them "strutting through the air in courtship," flying low in windy weather. He had seen them with spread wings against a thicket of white oaks, where their velvet blacks and grays and browns with the arcs of white markings had a singular grave beauty.

Thomas Bakewell came in during one of the frequent lulls in business to find him painting an otter. On an autumn evening Dr. Rankin stopped there for a bit of talk with Audubon. They came out together, and suddenly Audubon noted a flock of small birds winging their way southeast over the river. "What are they?" he cried. Without waiting for an answer he unhitched his horse from a tree, mounted, and was off. How long he was gone or where he went nobody knows. The story is that he pursued the flock through Kentucky, through Tennessee and over the mountains into North Carolina, returning at last with two small birds for a trophy.

There were many such stories. He was said to have followed an unknown species of woodpecker on foot for many miles to the south, scrambling through thickets, swimming rivers, penetrating far down into the Cumberlands. Perhaps he made such a journey, but he was too good a shot not to have brought down at least one of these birds at almost any time. It seems more likely that one bird led to another, and that once away he could not resist the promise of further trophies in deeper wilds.

At least he was thoroughly tired of the mill. There was a jumble of partnerships. Thomas Bakewell withdrew, and though a fair arrangement was doubtless intended Audubon was left with a mounting burden of debt. Other partners came in, and at about this time Lucy obtained from her father the share of money in his estate which she could expect at his death. A large part of this was also invested in the mill. Still the returns remained small, and Audubon decided to invest a fair sum, either of Lucy's money or his own, in the building of a steamboat. When it was finished he sold it, at a profit, but the buyer had paid him in worthless paper and was well down the Mississippi in the boat when this was discovered. Audubon procured a skiff and with two Negroes for oarsmen started in pursuit, making the long journey to New Orleans, only to discover that this dubious individual had other creditors who had followed him more swiftly. They had seized the steamboat.

He returned to Henderson and was told that the unprincipled purchaser of his boat had come before him, furiously angry because of his efforts in New Orleans. He was warned that the man would attempt to kill him. His right hand had recently been injured in the mill, and Lucy insisted that he carry a dagger. There was a bad encounter in which the man struck him with a bludgeon. Audubon turned on his enemy with a thrust of the dagger, and his enemy had to be carried away on a plank.

This made a great stir in the village, for the man had friends. Partisans on both sides carried arms for several days, and at last Audubon was hailed into court. Justice was rude, the judge was solemn. "Mr. Audubon," he said, after hearing all the testimony, "Mr. Audubon, you have committed a serious offense—a very serious offense, sir. You failed to kill the rascal!"

All this meant lost time, lost money, when he could afford to lose neither. He tried to climb out of debt by purchasing a tract of government land to the west of Henderson, from which he hoped to gain something through the cutting of timber, to be sawed at the mill. He employed a party of men to fell the trees who seemed honest enough but who were unknown to him. One day they failed to appear with their usual load, and he learned, much too late, that they had loaded a flatboat with his draft oxen and his logs and had gone down the river. This time he could not follow.

Generous with his friends, most of all when he found them in distress, he had freely endorsed notes for several of them. But widespread bank failures occurred in Kentucky at this time and when the notes were called the signers could not pay. Accordingly the banks levied against Audubon.

Before this he had been obliged to sell Barro. He walked to Ste. Geneviève with empty pockets, hoping either for assistance from Rozier or seeking a new opening in trade. He found neither, and paid his board bill by drawing a portrait in black chalk of the Frenchman in whose house he had stayed. It is not an altogether skillful portrait, and it was not flattering, but it has the air of a true likeness. This man, to judge by the drawing, was not easy to get along with. Sulky, sensitive, with a large head, rumpled hair, fine and even noble eyes, a soft mouth, he looks out stubbornly, rather angrily. His heavy body is solidly set within his dark coat. Rough and unfinished as the drawing is, it is enough to prove that Audubon could have been a notable portrait painter if he had wished, or if circumstances had permitted him to develop his gift. He had a basic sense of character, a close perception of revealing lines. And it is clear that he gave an absorbed attention to his task.

Hastening back to Henderson, he walked the long distance in a few days, and faced a bleak outlook. There seemed to be no way out of his difficulties.

One afternoon in the worst of the anxious period which followed, he saw a small bent man landing from a flatboat who wore a long, badly stained coat of yellow nankeen, a waistcoat of the same material buttoned up to his chin, with enormous pockets, and a tight pair of pantaloons buttoned down to his ankles. His black hair was lank, his beard was long, he carried a little bundle of dried clover on his back. He walked rapidly to the mill and inquired for the house of Mr. Audubon.

This was Samuel Constantine Rafinesque, a naturalist who had come into the West as Wilson and many others had done, in the interests of science. He bore a letter of introduction in which the writer said, "I send you an odd fish." Not too innocently,

Audubon asked to see the odd fish. The stranger smiled with good humor and answered, "I suppose *I* am that odd fish, Mr. Audubon." Audubon politely invited him to stay at his home. "I was heartily glad to have the naturalist under my roof," he declared afterward.

His opinion may have been somewhat altered during the night. He heard a great banging in Rafinesque's room and hurried there to find his guest running about the room innocently naked with Audubon's favorite violin in his hand battering it against the walls to kill bats that had entered in pursuit of insects drawn by the candle flame. Rafinesque continued to skip and jump and bang, but his aim was poor, and he begged Audubon to procure a few specimens for him. "A new species," he cried, out of breath. Audubon tapped a few bats with the bow of the violin, and, as he said, ended "the war." He noticed that dried plants were strewn around the room in great confusion. "Never mind, never mind, Mr. Audubon," said Rafinesque, "*I have the bats!*"

A game started when a little later Audubon showed Rafinesque some of his paintings and Rafinesque declared that no such plant existed in nature as appeared in one of them. Audubon replied that the plant was abundant. When they hastened to the shore of the Ohio and found it, Rafinesque leapt into the air, danced, picked many specimens, and was more convinced than ever that the plant was unknown to science. Rarities—he adored them! When they returned to the house the candles were lighted. Audubon caught a scarabaeus and assured his visitor that it would crawl on the table with a candlestick on its back. Rafinesque was enchanted, but the experiment may not have been a complete success.

It became clear that the wonders of nature would never be quite sufficient for Rafinesque. He could always think of creatures and events more marvelous than daily life or ancient history could provide. He later wrote a book about Kentucky in which whimsical fancy and scientific truth were strangely mingled.

Perhaps Audubon grew tired of his strange visitor's perpetual questions; he may have been in a reckless mood because of the hard tangle of his business affairs. It was not for nothing that he had consorted with western hunters who could pull the long bow and spin the tall tale. He liked a rousing big story for its own sake. He began to try out his visitor in a mild way, as western hunters and trappers invariably tried out the stranger or greenhorn, to see how much they would believe. He showed Rafinesque a few drawings of birds, whispering that no one had ever seen the like before—as was true. He mentioned a rare swallow which he had seen only once—a swallow whose head was a brilliant scarlet. A great *rarity!* Rafinesque was vastly interested in fish; well, he should see a fish that *was* a fish! Audubon said that this fish, the Devil Jack Diamond Fish, could only be observed from a distance. It was enormous, and its scales would strike fire with flint. They were bullet proof. Perhaps the basic fish in Audubon's mind was the mud cat, of which many tales were told, or the gar pike, or the alligator gar. He was offering the gaudy science of the backwoodsman, half truth, half tall tale.

Rafinesque made notes on all these wonders and even copied some of the drawings. He insisted that to visit a canebrake would be a crowning pleasure.

"I determined," said Audubon, "that my companion must view a canebrake in all its perfection!"

They crossed the river and entered the woods and after several miles of hard walking came upon "as fine a sample of a canebrake as could be found in that part of the country." The cane was dense, growing in places to a height of twenty feet among tall forest trees. "Bears and panthers—they are common here," he told Rafinesque casually as they entered the cane. Soon they were obliged to walk backwards, wedging their way through stalks, slipping and sliding over wet ground, their faces stung by nettles and the long leaves of the cane. Rafinesque became jammed between close-growing stalks and would gladly have turned back. "But a canebrake—you must see a canebrake!" cried Audubon. "You must be able to describe it. From experience! And botany—we shall study here the great science of botany!"

They heard a crash, and a black bear thrust his way through the brake not fifty yards away. He snuffed the air, and Rafinesque, terrified, struck into a deeper thicket where he became hopelessly entangled. The bear disappeared, and Audubon pulled his friend out of the cane to the sound of thunder overhead. A great storm was coming up. They were now crawling on hands and knees. Rafinesque panted. Leaves and bark stuck to their clothes and they were scratched by briars. Rain poured down in torrents, lightning struck close by. "Courage!" cried Audubon. "Patience!" He gave Rafinesque a sup of brandy and plunged into another dense thicket. Fire broke out not far away, and the water in the jointed stalks began to explode like shells. The naturalist began to rid himself of ballast, flinging away shells, stones, lichens, mosses which he had picked up during the early part of the expedition. They now proceeded so wildly that Audubon, who knew the canebrake well, almost lost his way, but at last as the storm diminished they circled back to the Ohio and were ferried to Henderson.

Rafinesque remained with the Audubons for three weeks. He expressed no further interest in canebrakes, but he collected a large number of plants, shells, bats, mosses, lichens, fishes. One evening, when tea was ready, he was missing. All his specimens had been removed from his room. Audubon spent the night searching for him, and wondered whether he had perished in a swamp or had been devoured by a bear, or had come to grips with the Devil Jack Diamond Fish.

Let us not waste too much pity on Rafinesque. During his visit in Henderson the world had taken on something of the brilliant color which he desired. His ideas were always immense; he was to attempt nothing less than "the whole history of the earth and mankind in the western hemisphere." Though he discovered that he had been hoaxed, in later years he invariably spoke of Audubon with pleasure.

For Audubon this sport was soon ended. Bitter disappointments were upon him. Every one of his projects failed. Lucy was obliged to take a position as governess in the Rankin household. Panic swept the region. The mill was given up to creditors, and he had to sell everything he possessed—his house, its comfortable furnishings, Lucy's pretty silver and china, his own paints, pencils, crayons, compasses, microscopes—all the special tools with which he worked. All of Lucy's inheritance had been swallowed up. Audubon had now only the clothes he wore, his drawings, and his gun. But even these drastic measures were not enough. A deeper humiliation followed. He was arrested for debt and sent to Louisville, where he was put in jail. He was able to declare himself bankrupt and was finally released. He went to the home of Nicholas Berthoud in Shippingport, and Dr. Rankin sent Lucy with the boys there from Henderson in his carriage.

In the blackest depths of discouragement he told himself, "I *have* talents." Again he said, "I have eyes!"

"With you I am always rich," he told Lucy.

He began at once to draw portraits in black chalk at low prices. His right hand, injured in the mill, had healed slowly but he had learned to use the left with almost equal ease. After a time he would sometimes use both at one time in drawing as a matter of interest for his sitters. With this novelty as an attraction he obtained a considerable number of commissions. He could promise "a strong likeness," and he could fulfill the promise. Again his drawings proved that he possessed a notable gift for portraiture. He drew a little old Frenchman wearing the red liberty cap, full of gay belligerence. His portrait in oils of an old dragoon in worn regimentals revealed the old man's lusty pride in his tawdry costume. A profile sketch of a traveling preacher showed insight of a more subtle kind, for this man was plainly eager, open-hearted, with a finely modeled head.

Shippingport offered a pleasant haven to the Audubons for a short time. Many of the French colony at Louisville had come there to live. The little waterside place was wholly, unmistakably French. With clear bubbling wells, graveled walks, trim gardens, it was fresh and green. The Berthouds and others had imported flowers and shrubs from abroad. Comfortable brick houses in a high-roofed French style had been erected with wrought-iron galleries above and below. There were open commons and pleasure grounds with a maze of box which might have graced the gardens of a château, and an excellent race-course, where Audubon saw a tiny jockey named Jim Porter who pushed his horses to victory for a few years. He then suddenly began to grow swiftly taller and taller and became a giant who could easily step over a five foot fence.

Shippingport was always busy. A great wharf of puncheons had been built, and a treadmill ferry ran across the river. The Tarascons owned a prosperous mill. Flatboats or steamboats were always coming or going, many of them with cargoes to be portaged. The river bank was gay with the colored shirts of the boatmen, their boisterous songs and fandangoes.

In the pleasant houses there was plenty of gayety of a more worldly order, with dancing and music. Audubon played his flute or violin for balls and taught the young people the steps he had learned long ago in France. The place must in all ways have brought him a large measure of homesickness, for he received the news there that Captain Audubon was dead. The Captain's large fortune had dwindled and was left in trust for the use of his wife during her lifetime. After her death it was to be divided between Audubon and his foster-sister Rosa; but the estate became involved, and in the end Audubon asked and received nothing from it.

At the time these events must have raised questions once more in his own mind and perhaps that of others as to his birth and early life, leaving him with a sense of uncertainty that was acute. Who was he? What were his true origins? And how could he emerge from the narrow possibilities that lay before him?

He tried to set up a little drawing class at Louisville, but he was not successful, and his little flurry of popularity as a portrait painter was soon over. The number of persons who desired the luxury of a drawing or painting of themselves was on the whole rather small, by no means enough to occupy his time and give him a living. When a gifted young man in Louisville proposed to establish himself there as a portrait painter at about this time he was urged by his friends not to make the venture since so talented an artist as Audubon had failed.

Rozier's success in Ste. Geneviève no doubt led him to make

another journey there, or perhaps he was finding the tether too short and broke it in order to go off to wild country alone. On this journey, according to tradition, he went on to St. Louis and the Femme Osage to see Boone, who was living alone in a small cabin. He was now eighty. A portrait still exists which Audubon is said to have painted from memory on his return to Shippingport; Boone's son brought it from Kentucky many years later and gave it to members of the family of General William Clark in St. Louis. It is painted in oils, with which Audubon had boldly begun to experiment at this time since he was making a business of portraits. The painting was on paper, pasted on a board. Perhaps he made a pencil drawing from life, then filled it in.

Audubon was never to please himself as an artist in oils, even after years of practice. His natural medium was the lighter, more transparent medium of water colors or pastels. Here he used oils without fluency, as if he cared nothing for paint, as if he were intent only upon reaching through to the character of Boone. He painted sheer character. Here are the steely, pale, impenetrable eyes, the clear brow, the narrow lips, the unyielding pose of the long head. But where did he find the rich color of the neckcloth, of so rich a red that it burns and seems alive yet does not overwhelm the effect of the pale old face? And how did he come to choose the dark wood green, almost black, like a hemlock forest at nightfall, which makes so simple and so right a background? The colors all have an enduring quality. He may have learned to mix them from his friends the Osages; the rumor has persisted that he learned from them much about pigments, but the simple choice of color must have been his own.

The painting has the plainest faults if one chooses to find them, yet it is stirring and may even be counted the best of the few portraits of Boone that have come down to us. Audubon had cut through the technical difficulties which beset him because he was intent upon portraying his old friend as he had known him. It tells of friendship, and equally, a basic passion for truth.

Boone died in September, 1820. A few weeks later Audubon had started out on a long and difficult journey. When portraiture failed to yield a living in Shippingport and Louisville he moved with his family to Cincinnati, where for a brief time he found employment for the humblest of his talents, stuffing and mounting birds and fishes for the new Western Museum. He also made portraits, when he could obtain commissions, and tried again to set up a class in drawing. He seems to have earned a fair sum of money, but later his wandering habits were mentioned by his employers.

Lucy did not call them that. "On more than one occasion his genius for discovery was used against him," she said hotly and loyally.

Lucy helped him make the final decision at a hard moment. A little girl who had been born to them in Henderson had died there, not long before they left. Now a second daughter, Rosa, born in Shippingport, had died. From day to day Lucy was obliged to consider the future of the two boys, eight and ten years old. The adventure upon which Audubon was about to embark was by no means the first. She must have remembered all his earlier experiments. Neither of them could forget the failure at Henderson because it had been too recent and too severe, and because people constantly reminded them of it. Lucy had much the harder part. Audubon would have the pleasure of following a beloved vocation; he could lose himself, could forget his anxieties, in the woods or on the rivers. Lucy lived constantly with the knowledge that the very grandeur of his plan might mean complete failure.

He had decided once and for all to complete his work on American birds and to seek publication. His portfolios were full of paintings and sketches; he now had several hundred, but he intended to find many birds still unknown to him and to others, belonging to the southern forests, swamps, and bayous; he would learn more of the great migrations. His plan was to go down the Ohio and the Mississippi, explore Louisiana, travel eastward through the territory along the Gulf to Florida and down to the Keys, of whose bird life he had heard tantalizing rumors, then back again up the Red River into the broad region watered by the Arkansas. In this darkest period the plan for his great "Birds of America" took final shape.

Lucy and the boys were to stay with the Berthouds in Shippingport. Audubon tried to obtain a position as clerk on a river steamer in order to earn his passage and a little added money, and had the humiliation of being refused by a number of agencies.

Unfriendly word of his failure at Henderson had preceded him.

He was now thirty-five or older. He started with a few companions in a flatboat. He hadn't a penny.

"Without any money my talents are to be my support, and my enthusiasm will be my guide in my difficulties," he wrote in the early pages of a new journal which he addressed to his two boys, thinking that sometime they might care to read this.

8 *Along Water Boundaries*

AUDUBON had secured free passage on one of two flatboats going down the Ohio and the Mississippi, carrying salt and miscellaneous articles to sell at villages along the way. In return for his berth he was to keep the party in game. Altogether a party of ten set out, four boatmen, three owners, and two other passengers whose fortunes were not unlike his own. One was an overgrown boy of thirteen named Joseph Mason, another of the many boys who would follow Audubon anywhere. He had been one of his pupils in Cincinnati, and had a small gift for painting. Audubon valued him as a companion mainly because he was a fine shot. With the multitude of his plans he needed an assistant, and he had made an arrangement with Mason's parents by which he would support the boy on the trip and continue his drawing lessons in return for his services.

Captain Samuel Cumings was making the trip in order to complete a chart of the Ohio and the Mississippi for navigators. He had little money, and the slow flatboat was admirable for his purpose, for he could take soundings. He later published "The Western Pilot," the first reliable guide for travel on the two rivers, in which every village on their banks was described, every island, the mouth of every tributary, with the precise course to be followed along the deepest channels, past rocks and snags and towheads. Silent and precise, a sympathetic figure, Captain Cumings was absorbed in his task.

The crew was mixed. One of the boatmen was a lively Irishman who danced, sang and cracked jokes at every turn. Another was so lazy that he would let his coat be singed rather than move away from a camp-fire at night, and the boat often went askew because he failed to pull on his oar. Mr. Aumack, who owned the flatboat on which Audubon traveled, was a surly man who took pains to remind him that he was paying nothing for his passage. More than once they came to the brink of a quarrel. The other owner was intent only upon the sale of his wares. Except for the companionship of young Mason, Audubon was much alone on this trip. The party separated for meals, each cooking his own food over the small iron stove or a fire on shore.

In spite of these unfriendly touches the journey began well.

Audubon had made his one dashing trip down to New Orleans in pursuit of his steamboat, but he had had then little time for observation. Now he was to have leisure in abundance. From his days on the Perkiomen he had known many rivers, the Schuylkill, the Susquehanna, the Clear Juniata, the Ohio, the Kentucky, the Green, the Trademaker, part of the Mississippi, the Wabash. He had explored the small creeks and streams about Henderson and in the Illinois country for miles. All his life he was to love water courses, water boundaries, the fresh colors which he found there, the hidden bends, the lush growth, the moist air, the sudden lighted distances with water steely or white or green.

They started in bright October weather. "Gayly we were overtaken by a skiff containing a couple of young gentlemen from New Orleans," he wrote. If most of his own companions were dull or unpleasant he had many an agreeable interchange with passers-by on the water. The skiff accompanied the flat-boats for a short distance and he made friends with the plain people on board—some settlers going on to new land. "Drawed all day," he said, "floated eighteen miles, the woman in the skiff mending my good brown breeches."

Gayly too he went ashore with young Mason for the necessary game and to look for birds. They could walk for miles and easily rejoin the boat down the river, cutting across bends, exploring the back country. When the boats paused at waterside villages and set up counters to sell their wares, the two would wander afield.

Audubon took time to sketch dark fissures in great cliffs, views of the river, the village of Henderson when they passed it, and the famous Cave-in-Rock. For what purpose he was making these sketches he did not say but they seemed to be weaving themselves into some large scheme. He watched closely the flight of waterfowl and made fresh notes, not altogether the notes of an ornithologist, finding of blue-winged teal that the "blue of their wings glistens like polished steel when they are flying in flocks, with their wings alternately thrown into shade and exposed to bright light." Constantly he sketched or painted birds, sometimes in the autumn woods, often in a low cramped space on board the flatboat with the distractions of talk about him. He worked for long over his painting of a rusty grackle, trying to reproduce the metallic iridescence, the brown rustiness, and the sinister look of the pale yellow eyes. He decided that he liked what he had done. "Made a handsome drawing of it." Waterfowl he drew again and again, sometimes making rapid pen and ink drawings of them in his journal, sketching them in black chalk, studying the handsome plumages of the mergansers and mallards, pintails—sprigtails he called them—and green-winged teal.

The clumsy boat frequently ran aground on sandbars and was halted by shoals. But "her hide is thick," said the one jolly boatman, "and she won't sink." She didn't, and they floated on to encounter wind and rain and hail, but when they reached

Fort Massac on the lower Ohio Audubon wrote that the view there of the river was "magnificent," and that the afternoon was calm "with one of those *whimsical* sunsets that only belong to America."

As soon as they reached the yellow-brown waters of the Mississippi he found that "the passenger feels a different atmosphere *at once*, a very different prospect—the curling stream and its hue are the first objects—the caving-in of the banks and the thicket growth of young cottonwood is the next." It was now colder, and they landed on towheads. "A towhead," he wrote, "is a small willow island overflown in high water." He still had his own way of writing or speaking English.

Fast on a towhead they had "a dreadful night of wind," and he played his flute during the slow hours. The river was full of swift currents, uncharted snags and sawyers and islands, and they passed the wreckage of many flatboats that had come to grief and now thrust only a blunt bow or a broken sweep into the air. But these pauses suited him exactly; when he couldn't manage to go ashore he could draw. Along the shore the boats made many brief landings, and with Mason he would scramble through tangles of willow and sawgrass, seeking nests, birds, and game of all kinds. The great migrations had begun. For once he was wholly out in the open with nothing between himself and the sky as in great successions of movement flocks of birds followed the broad trough of the Mississippi Valley to the south.

Waterfowl began pointing down the river as the weather grew sharp.

Sometimes the flatboats traveled only fifteen miles in a day, and the days began to lengthen into weeks. In watching or following birds or exploring inland Audubon and Mason often walked or scrambled for twenty or thirty miles between dawn and dusk, through swamps or over brown fields.

The days passed so quietly that the sight of the Chickasaw Bluffs was a great event, with their red, yellow, black, and lead-colored strata of soils and their thousands of holes, empty now that the bank swallows had gone. After a storm he had a great piece of luck, for Mr. Aumack succeeded in winging a white-headed eagle and brought it alive on board so that Audubon could paint it. "The noble fellow looked at his enemies with a contemptible eye."

Working steadily on his painting of the eagle during many days, he was cheered by another one of those whimsical American sunsets, "with light frost, rich clouds of purple and light green—this indicated wind." The wind came, and he was confined to the dusky cabin of the boat without an occupation as they plowed cautiously along the shore. At last they found anchorage. "We are landed at the foot of island No. 35 a few miles above what the navigators call the Devil's Raceground, but the whole of the Mississippi being so much of the same nature, it feels quite the same to follow the devil's tracks anywhere along its muddy course."

At the White River they entered the cut-off to the Arkansas, where they made a cordel of grapevines with all of them pulling the boat upstream, walking through cypress swamps and cane-brakes and shallow ponds and green briars. By the time they landed at the only tavern in the region they had walked a good many miles, "a full dose for any pedestrian per day in such a country."

"At the tavern the supper was soon called for and soon served and to see four wolves tearing into an old carcass would not give you a bad idea of our manners while helping ourselves, the bright staring eyes of the landladies notwithstanding."

Afterwards they went to a large building which, Audubon thought, had seen "the great councils of Spanish dons." Here were "three beds containing five men, yet all was arranged in a few moments, and as the breeches were coming off our legs Mr. Aumack and Anthony slided into one and Joseph and myself into another. To force acquaintance with the strangers of course being necessary, a conversation ensued that lulled me asleep, and nothing but the want of blankets kept me from resting well.

"The morning broke and with it mirth *all about us*. The cardinals, the Iowa buntings, the meadow larks and many species of sparrows cheering the approach of a benevolent, sunshining day." Downstairs he was introduced to a "medley circle" of travelers and heard tantalizing stories about the upper Arkansas which made him want to go there at once. "So *strong* is my enthusiasm to enlarge the ornithological knowledge of my

GREAT CRESTED FLYCATCHER. *PLATE NO. CXXIX*

country that I wished myself *rich again* and thereby able to leave my family for a couple of years." He turned the idea over and over and saw at last that it was out of the question.

Through the cut-off and back on the Mississippi again they slid along and passed the mouth of the Yazoo, "a beautiful stream of transparent water, covered by thousands of geese and ducks and filled with fish, the entrance with low willows and cotton trees." And treasure of treasures! "Mr. Aumack killed a great-footed hawk." Audubon had made studies of this hawk before but these had failed to satisfy him; he would make the attempt again. When the boats tied outside the float of keels and flatboats at Natchez he was hard at work. All about him steamboats whistled, trying to make a landing; the shores were crowded by other flatboats bearing sugar cane, cotton, corn, flax, which was being loaded or unloaded by shouting boatmen. In the midst of the hollow crack of boats slapping against each other, the plap of water, the measures of a song, he was lost, working on his hawk. He hardly looked at this famous river port until evening, when he glanced up and saw it "in miniature," as he said, from a distance.

Flatboats had been drawn ashore and planted alongside low houses in the mud to make the crooked little streets of Natchez-under-the-Hill. Up what he called "a sidling road" sledges toiled bearing water from the river to the upper Town, and horsemen cantered back and forth. The ruins of an old Spanish fort lay in a gulley to one side. Along the top of the flat bluff could be seen the fringes of trees, two church spires, and a few solid, spacious buildings which had remained from the Spanish rule.

The next morning he was out early, passing through the Lower Town. Boatmen reeled and dipped through low doorways of ill-smelling groggeries. Within could be heard the clink of coins or a scuffle. Blousy women poked their heads out of small square windows. Somewhere along the streets land pirates often concealed themselves after raids into the rich back country or on unfrequented roads. Their great pathway was the Natchez Trace, "the Devil's Backbone," so old that De Soto had described it as worn deep in the earth. The Trace cut a long bending line through Nashville and became the Red Banks Trail, which Audubon had known well, for it ran through Henderson.

In contrast, Natchez-on-the-Hill was trim and spacious, with neat shops, and streets bordered by chinaberry trees. Planters were riding in and out. Suddenly Audubon ran into Nicholas Berthoud who had come down the river in his fast keelboat, passing the flatboats somewhere on the way. "Letters from Lucy and the two boys!" he cried. Audubon had had no word from his family for two months; nothing could have been more welcome. Berthoud invited him to continue the journey to New Orleans in the keelboat a few days later.

Audubon set out with young Mason to earn, if possible, a little money. After their tramping through briar and swamp their shoes were in tatters. They prowled through the streets until they found a shoemaker and Audubon made a proposal; he would draw the shoemaker's portrait in exchange for a pair of stout new boots. The shoemaker's wife peered around the corner. "And also your wife!" cried Audubon. "Your pretty wife, she too must have her portrait. Two portraits—two pairs of shoes!" The bargain was struck, the portraits were quickly drawn, and Audubon went off with his young friend, both of them well shod.

He succeeded in earning not only shoes but a little money. "Procured the drawing of two more portraits for five dollars each," he noted in his journal. "This was fine sauce for our empty stomachs."

Hoping for more sitters, he went to the rooms of an artist, "a portrait painter called *Cook*, but I assure you he was hardly fit for a scullion."

Elsewhere he made two more sketches for five dollars each, and since he and Mason were living aboard the flatboat he began to feel something like opulence. He had a further stroke of luck when an acquaintance permitted him to see the latest issue of Wilson's "Ornithology," which he studied closely. He had seen and drawn birds which did not appear there.

In the flurry of leaving Natchez he handed one of his portfolios to a Negro and failed to make sure that it was put on board. This contained a little painting of Lucy which he particularly prized, as well as some of the best drawings he had made on his recent journey and all his silver paper for preserving his paintings. Nothing could be done about it except to drop off a letter at the next landing, for the keelboat was moving rapidly down the river, towed by a steamer, when he missed the portfolio. He was in a dark mood, reproaching himself for his carelessness, knowing that the drawings would have to be made again, halting him on what was already a bitterly slow progress toward his ambition.

He set to work, finishing sketches he had made in the earlier stages of the journey. At the considerable port of Bayou Sara where they paused, he drew a portrait of the captain of the steamboat and received for it five dollars in gold. When this was finished he stayed up half the night finishing the drawing of a pair of warblers, anxious, unsettled, uneasy as to the future.

At Bayou Sara the steamboat left them and Berthoud's keelboat proceeded down the river alone. After they passed Baton Rouge the Mississippi began to widen; its shores were almost bare, since booming floods had repeatedly swept away acres of land here with trees, houses, barns, cattle. People inland spoke of the shores of the Mississippi as "the coast." They talked of going to "the coast," and indeed the shores looked like some widening bleak coast. But dark watery coves showed here and there with the deep green of swamps and bayous, and Audubon could begin to see great numbers of birds which he had known in the North, warblers, buntings, vireos. He watched those thieves, the boat-tailed grackles, violet and coppery-green among the live oaks, a noisy congregation wheeling with a firm steering movement of their tails, creaking their wheezy notes. He shot a pair and painted them, sharply conscious of the likenesses and differences between these and the rusty grackles, achieving the bold, wise, severe look by which the boat-tail masks his sly purposes.

After a week, in early January, a great flock of fish crows brushed overhead, and early the next morning a thicket of spars topped by bright flags came into view around a bend. This was New Orleans.

A broad flight of steps cut the levee and led to a public square, and a market was spread along the river bank. Palmetto leaves were spread on the ground to make stalls; bright boxes were set up to display a cluttered variety of wares. Men and women from all the world seemed to have converged along the gaudy street. Negroes, mulattoes, Spaniards with gold rings in their ears were busy trading, and Yankees in blue or butternut brown showed tinware, clocks, cotton goods. Indians sold game or woven baskets. Soft creole speech rippled quickly. Selling strings of birds, game of all kinds, kegs of bear oil and buffalo meat, were French trappers like the many Audubon had known at Ste. Geneviève and St. Louis, who had come in from the shores and swamps and bayous with their spoils. Purple finches, ivory-billed woodpeckers, bluebirds, red-winged blackbirds, bobolinks, were piled in heaps, fat and sweet, to be sold for food.

The Cathedral of St. Louis looked out over the river, and long, spacious buildings filled the other two sides of the public square. The pale pinks and blues and yellows of stucco houses showed down small streets, set close to the brick walks or *banquettes*. Cabriolets passed, and carts squealed loudly, and six tall Kentuckians strode by. A boy at a corner held a hunting net in which were a live green heron, some mockingbirds, a summer redbird, and a little crowd of white-throated sparrows, all frightened and fluttering. Audubon stopped to ask him his prices, but they proved to be too dear for his purse. He had only ten dollars. A few hours later he discovered that he lacked even that, for his pocket had been picked. The smell of good food was in the air. Steam from luscious gumbos rose from pots over charcoal burners in the streets, but he had to pass these by.

With young Mason he went back to the keelboat, got his gun and tramped off down the levee away from the city where the river bent and overflowed into small creeks and bayous. Odd-looking sloops were anchored there with swarthy sailors stretched along their decks who might be smugglers, who might have traffic with the pirate fleet over which Lafitte still ruled. A mysterious life went on beyond the tall rushes and sawgrass, within the channels, beyond the dark cypresses among the sea-islands. Audubon learned before long why all the cartwheels of the city squealed. They squealed by law—a law which had come down from the days of the Spanish rule, when the governors had learned that smuggled goods were brought quietly into the city by night in carts whose wheels were well greased. "Let the cart-wheels scream!" they proclaimed.

Far down the river these two companions shot a few teal flying over wild rice, roasted them in a fire, and carried back enough game for another day or two to the keelboat, which was to be their home until Audubon could find employment.

"No work yet—rain, warm, frogs all piping," he wrote a little later. It was a discouraging search. He refused to hire himself as a scene painter at one of the theaters, not only because the task would be uncongenial but because he feared employment of this kind would damage his prospects for portraits and as a teacher. He found a man who wanted his portrait drawn but received a pittance for his work, and was "tormented," he said, "by many disagreeable thoughts."

With hardly a penny left he met a French merchant named Pamar who wanted portraits of his three daughters but thought Audubon's prices too high. He had raised them in desperation, thinking that perhaps he had lost patrons by cheapening his work. To prove his talents Pamar asked him to make a quick sketch of a little girl who happened to be playing in the room.

"My pencil was sharped," said Audubon, "and sitting on a crate I was soon at work and soon was finished." The likeness was amazingly good, and Pamar amiably offered to leave the question of payment to Audubon. He asked a hundred dollars for portraits of the trio of girls. Delays followed, but also, as Audubon said, "Here is fond hopes. How I calculated that one hundred dollars! What relief to my dear wife and children! For, said I, if I get this I may send it to her."

The Pamars proved to be hospitable friends. Audubon was often at their table. He soon moved with Mason from the keelboat to rooms near an old convent, where he heard a mockingbird sing from moonrise to midnight and again in the freshness of the morning from a neighboring chimney top and where in the late hours he would hear the watchman's cry, "All's well, all's well." The bird too repeated the same cry, so precisely that he would have supposed that it was the watchman again if the hour had not been wrong and if the "All's well" had not been cried too often.

By the time the Pamar portraits were painted he had come again to his last penny; but all at once, perhaps because of this merchant's influence, he had several sitters for portraits, then a little rush. In a single week he rolled up the sum of two hundred and twenty dollars. Adding fifty of the hundred he had received from Pamar, he sent Lucy an order for two hundred and seventy dollars and, with this for full measure, a crate of fine dishes. The loss of all their pretty furnishings in Henderson still rankled. He was determined to replace them. Perhaps Lucy had specially regretted the loss of her dishes; so he sent dishes. He always pursued a zigzag course between high elation and dark spirits. With this excellent start he was certain that the future was opening out before him with dazzling promises. Dishes, fine furniture—they would have everything. No doubt Lucy was touched by the dishes, but what could she do with them at this time?

He took a holiday and set for himself a difficult but amusing task, to draw a brown pelican, with its oddly posed head, green pouch, long, tipping, drooping back, large well-exposed, flat feet, and sturdy spread of wing. The results did not please him, yet he felt that he had made a beginning in his knowledge of pelicans.

A hunter brought him a great white heron, which was still harder to portray. He worked almost a month at this, in the midst of his portrait painting, and still felt that it was not good.

New birds—more new birds! He must have them! He sought out some of the half-breed trappers on the market, chose one or two who seemed clean shots and hired them to bring him the specimens he particularly wanted—or any strange bird they might see. Their prices were high. "The Harpes were not the only land pirates," he said to himself. But these men who had trapped and hunted in the Louisiana bayous had useful knowledge.

From dawn to daylight he worked at his bird drawings, taking infinite pains with the sheen of feathers, the outlines of eyes, of beaks, of feet and their scaly coverings, and claws. For drawing those of the smaller birds he now used quills of a trumpeter swan, finding them both firm and elastic.

From daylight till dark he worked at portraits or the search for commissions. From dusk until far into the night he worked again with birds. In a few weeks, with pride, he sent Lucy twenty new finished paintings. He was now in high feather, for by good luck his portfolio was returned to him from Natchez with only one bird drawing missing, and Lucy's portrait was with the rest.

Warm winds were soon blowing. Along the river wild rice was turning freshly, brilliantly green with thin feathery plumes.

The black ash was in leaf, the willows were pollarded. Audubon saw a Brazilian eagle spread his wings toward the sun.

Suddenly from the south came a prodigious flock of golden plover, hundred of thousands of birds, numbers such as had rarely been seen in this region, streaming through to alight on the river banks for several days.

On a calm, drizzly day a dense flock of purple martins passed over the city, moving to the northwest—a flock something more than a mile and a half in length and a quarter of a mile wide that had come from across the Gulf.

Portraits or no portraits, he was off to the river banks and the swamps and marshes. The long coast line of Louisiana, the winding Mississippi with its delta, the broken bayous and inlets, the cypress or tupelo swamps and the oak-covered sea islands were the haunt not only of immense numbers of water and shore birds which nested and bred there; they also offered resting places for flocks that made the long journey of half a thousand miles across the Gulf from the tropics, on their way north. The rich soil of all this watery region with its profusion of tender leaves and berries and quickly ripened seeds let them feed and fatten for the further stages of their journey.

Far down along the shores of the river he went, following pirogue trails inland along creeks. Ducks rose in profusion from the marsh grass, redheads, canvasbacks, mallards, with taut wings and spread tails in dancing changing patterns of metal-blue, brown, red, green, white, black. If only he could draw them in strong flight!

Delicate against the sky, in the gray-green and silver of a willow thicket he saw a small colony of slaty-blue and white herons–Louisiana herons, "the Lady of the Waters"–standing steeply among the leaves. A gangling snowy egret stood among the rushes. A pair of little green herons, called by the creoles *cap-caps*, flew up a small creek. In the midst of mud and water he made quick pencil sketches, and then was away to make fresh discoveries.

Toward evening he had come back to a bend in the river when he was beginning to think himself lost, and found an old flatboat pushed up among rushes. A kite was circling high overhead and he dropped into a corner of the boat to watch it. Evening drew on and he heard from the top of the broken cabin the angry little chirr-chirr of a Carolina wren. She objected to his presence. He watched her as she gradually accepted him, poking about for spiders and other insects. She peered into an auger hole, thrust herself into it, peeked out of another, crept under some masses of drifted timber and was out again.

"Weasels and minxes are her foe," he thought. He had known these wrens well in Kentucky. He had made sketches of them before, but he began again. That tail, those soft feathers, that light grayish look over the red brown as if she were covered by a faint mist, distinguishing her from the male–could he ever please himself, ever paint her as she was? Her mate flew to the ledge of the old cabin and decided to sing.

And if he couldn't please himself drawing wrens, how could he hope to capture the look of the many new birds he was continually discovering? Those mallards and pintails—sprigtails he always called them—how could he ever truly paint them! He had worked at them for long, as far back as his stay in New York when he tried to be a clerk, but he had completed none to his own satisfaction. He dropped his sketch of the wren. He hadn't yet mastered his medium, he reflected. When he used color, instead of a bird the beholder was aware of the grain of the drawing paper. He could always see it.

The sun set; the wren sang on for nearly a quarter of an hour, letting fly his brilliant, rippling, changing notes. The pair disappeared. Audubon could not sleep in spite of the fresh tranquillity of the night.

The next morning at dawn he was off again, following a faint trail toward salt marshes, coming out on a little spit from which showed the green of sea islands. Terns rose in great flocks like snowy spray and fell again in white cascades over small silvery waves—not white altogether; the small dark heads or crests, the red bills of royal terns, the orange feet and bill of the sea swallows made tiny broken splashes of color. Gray gulls floated among them. He heard the strange cackle of laughing gulls. He thought he heard the deep baying of hounds, but the sounds came from a flock of black skimmers rounding a point below him. Snipe and sandpipers ran along the shore. The terns rose and rose again and fell in beautiful pointed forms against green water.

"I returned to our lodging with a compound of ideas not easily to be described," he wrote in his journal. Confusion, hope, lovely forms and colors, a thousand questions, were all mingled together.

He set himself the difficult task of portraying the gorgeous beauty of painted finches on a spray of Chickasaw wild plum, setting them so that the brilliant diagonals of blue and gold and bright red formed a design that pleased him. But he could not pause for other such enchanting problems. Again without money, he was obliged to sell his talent for likenesses. A gentleman wanted a portrait of his wife but declared he could not pay for it. He offered a lady's saddle in exchange.

"Not to disappoint him I suffered myself to be saddled," said Audubon somewhat ruefully. He sent the saddle to Lucy, who had perhaps no more use for it than she had had for the dishes. He secured a few more commissions but found it more and more difficult to paint both birds and people at the same time. He wrote in his journal, "I am very much fatigued of New Orleans where I cannot *shoot two birds with one stone*."

One morning as he walked along the levee he saw a tall stout man in a coat of light green, a pair of flowing yellow nankeen trousers, and a pink waistcoat. On his head was a wide flopping straw hat. His shirt was frilled, and tucked into the waistcoat among the frills was a large bunch of flowers, and among the flowers was a baby alligator waving a small pointed head. The gentleman carried in one hand a cage full of painted finches. In the other he bore aloft an umbrella on which was inscribed in large white letters, "Stolen from I." Audubon thought that the stranger looked rather like a painted finch, in paler colors, but there was nothing bird-like about his port. He moved pompously, and as if oblivious of others about him he was singing loudly in broad Scots–

My love, she's but a lassie yet,
My love, she's but a lassie yet!
We'll let her stand a year or twa,
She'll no be half sae saucy yet!

But he was no Scot, and Audubon had not watched men on the rivers for nothing. He was sure that this strange songster hailed from Maine.

"Will you let me examine the birds in that cage?" he asked politely.

"What the devil do you know about birds?" asked the Yankee.

"Little enough!" thought Audubon. Aloud he said grandly, "I am a student of nature, sir, and I admire all her works from the noblest figure of a man"–and he cast an admiring look up and down the ample figure–"down to the crawling reptile in your shirt front!"

"Ah, a-a-a naturalist! Come with me, and you shall gaze upon many curious birds!"

At the stranger's lodging Audubon entered a long room where paintings were placed along the walls and several cages of birds hung at the windows. The birds were by no means rare, but Audubon was surprised to find that the paintings had merit.

"Aye," said the stranger pleasantly, "the world is pleased with my work." He took up his brushes and palette, then suddenly asked if Audubon had ever seen a percussion lock. With such a lock he said a gun could be fired under water, and filling a large basin he immersed a gun. The report was terrific. Water splashed high over the walls, and the birds beat their wings against their cages.

"The devil!" said the Yankee. "Let me show you that I'm rather a marksman too!" He splintered the wooden pin that held his easel and then rang for a lighted candle which he tried to snuff with a bullet. He was not successful. He put the candle out.

"Your alligator seems uneasy," said Audubon.

"True, true! I had quite forgot the reptile."

He placed his pet in the basin of water. Audubon prepared to leave, but the stranger insisted that he sit down beside him while he painted. As he skillfully applied his brushes he told a very long story of no interest.

Perhaps Audubon learned a little about the use of oils, with which he was still experimenting from time to time, but the whole visit—the man himself—made nonsense. He set down an account of the experience in his journal for its oddity. He was always jotting down notes about queer people whom he met.

At this time he began to seek out other artists, hoping that some of them might help him find commissions for portraits. One artist told him that his bird paintings were all very bad—but offered to put in backgrounds for him. Another, Vanderlyn, kept him waiting like a beggar in an anteroom, and on seeing his portraits, remarked that their outlines were much too hard. When the birds were shown him he thawed a little.

The sweat ran down Audubon's face with embarrassment as he laid the drawings one by one on the floor. A military officer who was present came forward and brusquely praised all his drawings, and offered him a commission for a portrait.

An expedition was being formed to survey the boundaries of the territory in the West acquired from Spain. Audubon was eager to join this as a draftsman, thinking that he might earn a modest salary and at the same time study the birds of the far West. He timidly mentioned this possibility to Vanderlyn, who was well known not only in New Orleans but in the East. Vanderlyn wrote a letter in his behalf but the plan came to nothing.

Instead, Audubon drew the portrait of the military officer and hunted for other commissions. His clothes were now old and shabby; he fancied that some of his acquaintances preferred not to talk with him in the streets because of them. By chance he ran across the merchant, Vincent Nolte, whom he had met long ago at the Falls of the Juniata when he was disguised as a French sailor and was riding Barro. No chance for disguises now! His poverty was plain; there was no way to cover it up. But Nolte was friendly and Audubon consented to dine with him on condition that no one else be invited.

Money—if he had only a little! His chances seemed to be dwindling. New Orleans was full of artists, American and European, who had come there hoping for a harvest from the rich Louisiana traders and planters. With so many others seeking similar ends Audubon had done well to keep his head and Mason's above water.

His landlady, always suspicious of this odd painter with his birds, became insistent as his clothes grew shabbier and his expression discouraged. He owed her for washing as well as rent. He was now giving a few lessons but the money was not enough to live on; and more pupils could hardly be expected as the spring and summer advanced, when most of those who could afford such luxuries as drawing lessons were in the habit of going to the plantations or the North. His great plan for exploring the South for birds, eastward to Florida, westward through the Arkansas territory, had come to nothing. He faced the possibility of returning almost empty-handed to Shippingport.

Mason came in one day with feathery grasses and early spring flowers from the marshes. The fresh colors and delicate unfamiliar forms entranced Audubon yet cast him into despair because he had finished so many of his paintings and had sent them to Lucy without having used some of them, and because the future had in all ways gone empty and dark.

The next day he was off on a trip to the bayous and swamps

down the river with Mason, somehow capturing a pirogue. These pirogues, of cypress, were light of draft and could be pushed into the shallowest water. The trappers said they could be paddled over a light fall of dew. The marshes were laced by the slender threads of trappers' water trails through grasses and dense woods. Here in great numbers, as in a great wild, shy colony, were muskrats, beaver, mink, otter–those small animals whose fine pelts were desired all over the world. They paddled silently through gray-green forests with Spanish moss hanging from above like tangled nets, and around the "knees" of the tall cypresses, which Audubon thought were like great sugar-loaves thrust up through dark water. Here were painted finches, in flashes of bright blue, scarlet, lemon, green. Purple finches–the last of them before they went north–gleamed crimson in the sun in high branches against the pale blue sky. Linnets and seaside sparrows, indigo buntings and brilliant orange-yellow prothonotary warblers lighted and dipped overhead. All at once a shower of warblers whirled through the air; when they had passed Audubon could still see the flash of wings, hear the many differing notes, watch the varying motions, creeping, darting, flying upward.

Here and there the pair of watchers suspected that nests were to be found but they could not pause. The strange waterways leading into open pools and deepened streams entranced them as much as the ways of unknown birds. They pushed the pirogue through rustling, floating sheets of pink water hyacinths. Along the marshy banks were irises, some in sheathed bud, some in full flower, tiny wine-red irises, a lake of giant blues where Audubon waded waist-high in bright fresh color, others of rich salmon, of rose madder—there seemed no end to this fresh transparency of bloom. These many flower forms—he couldn't see enough of them, of the white spider lilies hidden deep in the swamps, fringed and delicate, shadowed by pale drifting light, or the violet spikes of the pickerel weed where a marsh wren lighted for a tiny fragment of time.

A salt tang was in the air with all this cool profusion. A thousand images and ideas and plans danced through Audubon's head. The water birds and shore birds, how could he come to know them all with his limited resources, the differences in plumage of many of them at different seasons, their nesting habits and migrations? And all the warblers, those strangely confusing tiny creatures whose young birds it was easy to mistake for new species? In his study of Wilson's volumes he had seen what he believed to be mistakes, and he could fill many of the omissions. But how, and when—when? And these new forms of flower and leaf and stem, the firm outlines of unknown shrubs and leafy branches—all these belonged to him, making a dazzle of patterns and fresh color, but how was he to possess them and create them again with colors of his own?

He carried back to the city a sheaf of flowers and leaves wrapped in wet mosses, and painted in a fury, making rapid studies. His spoils were soon withered and dry but he continued, sometimes combining with these birds which he had already completed, making new paintings. The blue grosbeak had delighted him, the brilliant color of the males, the soft browns of the females. He painted them in a drift of dogwood leaves whose shadowed forms fell in green blues and lucent pale greens. Among the feathery fine lavender flowers of the pride of China he placed the white-eyed flycatcher.

But an infinite amount of work lay ahead, an infinite number of fresh and lovely designs. He had intended to be away only seven or eight months, and that time was nearly gone. He was forced to take stock of his situation. He still had a few pupils but these would soon leave New Orleans. By the greatest amount of luck he might succeed in obtaining enough commissions for portraits to enable him to pay his bills and engage passage for himself and Mason on a steamboat for Louisville. At worst they could walk. Nothing else lay ahead, neither enough work to support himself nor any chance at all to follow his chosen pursuits. He would have to go.

The decision was bitter and humiliating. Failure, which had come to him with great severity at Henderson, was now upon him in a far darker form. His great plan for painting the birds of America—a plan which had slowly taken shape through a long period of years—was coming to nothing. Publication was as remote as the Rockies or the moon. He decided to go, knowing that his departure might mean that he was giving up, perhaps forever, the deepest purposes of a lifetime.

But there are sometimes advantages in floating as completely with the tide as Audubon had lately done. The tide may turn. One of his last pupils was Eliza Pirrie, a girl of sixteen from Oakley, a plantation in Feliciana not far from Bayou Sara. As he gave her some final lessons her mother noted his despondency and questioned him. Mrs. James Pirrie was a woman of tact and decision, with a glint of humor in her brown eyes and at the corners of her firm mouth. Older than Audubon, she soon had the story of his hopes and disappointments. She recognized talent when she saw it; otherwise she would not have placed Eliza under his instruction. She offered him a position to teach her daughter drawing and French during the summer months at Oakley. Mason was also invited to come. The two were to live at the plantation and their afternoons were to be free. Audubon was to receive sixty dollars a month, which meant security. He accepted this plan in a rush of gratitude.

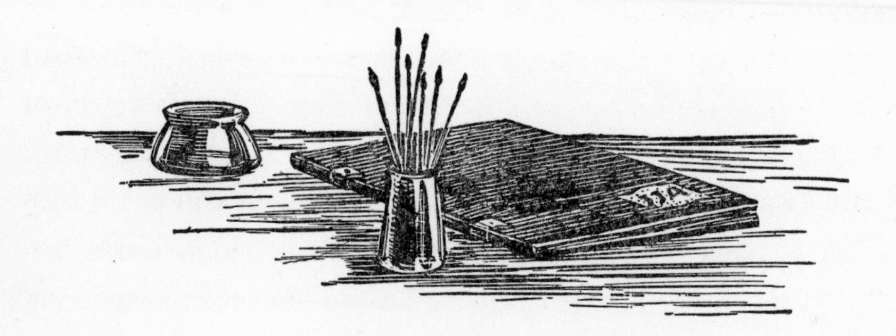

9 *Patterns on the Page and in the Sky*

WHEN Audubon landed at Bayou Sara and went up the steep road to St. Francisville and saw houses that had been built there under the Spanish rule, as he passed spacious plantations on the road to Oakley, he probably would not have called Feliciana a frontier, nor would he have spoken of Mrs. Pirrie as a woman of the frontier. Yet Lucretia Pirrie had known this region as a wilderness and had had adventures of a sort that can occur only in wild country. Her father, Captain John Alston, had come here with his family from the Carolinas some forty years earlier, and had soon set himself against the Spanish rule. A price was put on his head; for months he was in hiding. He placed his three young children in a cabin deep in a cypress swamp on the other side of the Mississippi with an old Negro to guard and care for them. There they survived terror, privation, danger, suffering. Nor was Mrs. Pirrie alone among her plantation neighbors in the remembrance of such experiences. As the Louisiana Territory had passed from the Indians to the French, from the French to the Spanish, as American possession had been inaugurated and the War of 1812 had been fought, this beautiful region had been an outpost and its inhabitants had known more than one rude conflict.

Even now Feliciana, partly surrounded by the bending Mississippi, traversed by dark swamps and deep bayous, was not wholly wrested from the wilderness. A hunter said that its forests were "so thick you'd have trouble running your knife in 'em up to the hilt." The Houma and Tunica, peaceful tribes of the Choctaw, still camped unceremoniously where they pleased, on any plantation, and the Negroes were still close to an ancient primitive life, practicing dark rites in spite of prohibitions and telling stories of birds and animals whose meaning white men could not penetrate. Even their language was strange, with the African mingling with the French to make the soft *patois* known as creole.

Land pirates still cruised along Indian trails. Strangers who failed to come to the plantation house or who cast an appraising eye upon horses were regarded with suspicion. Every house was full of firearms. Every plantation was a small village, ready to face any enemy. Yet the houses with their wide galleries, their long French windows, their bordering formal gardens always seemed open. Fields of jonquils, rare yellow lilies, pink and white rain lilies, might be seen from almost any window in spring. As at Shippingport, plants and shrubs had been brought from old gardens in France. Good libraries, growing libraries, were to be found in these houses, with new periodicals from France and England. Every house had its muster of musical instruments, violins, guitars, flageolets, harpsichords, and new music was constantly coming in, much of it copied by hand, the light tinkling airs of the most recent French and Italian operas, and old dance tunes from England, Ireland, Wales.

Feliciana was still a frontier—but perhaps the word frontier should be given a wider color. Here were strange meetings of the civilized and the wild. Eastward were the Indian tribes of the Mississippi Territory. Westward was the wild land on the Red River and the Sabine and in "the Texas." Feliciana was thrust between, a broad region that kept something of the life of the planters of Virginia and the Carolinas, something of eighteenth century French and Spanish outlines, with simplicity.

Nothing could have pleased Audubon more than this conjunction. In his own character he contained many of the same mixed elements. The new music delighted him, the substantial libraries. How he contrived to read widely when he was cramming his days full of teaching, hunting, drawing, preparing skins and making notes must remain a mystery, but inveterate readers are usually made of stout materials. Most of all he enjoyed "Gil Blas," for its humor and because he saw himself in this Spaniard whose education had consisted of shifting from one adventure to another.

At first he was shy meeting these people. He had lived simply, even roughly on the flatboat and with Mason; he felt uncouth and was certain that his table manners had suffered. Gradually his constraints vanished. The days floated along easily. Neighbors would ride up to bring him rare plants or birds. When he chose he could take an Indian hunter in the employ of Mr. Pirrie as a guide on his expeditions. And to instruct Eliza Pirrie was anything but arduous. A slim spirited girl with cool gray eyes, she was already sought by many suitors, and though she had a talent for drawing this was to be for her only a minor accomplishment.

When the morning's work was over Audubon was off to the woods. The dark magnolias with their great fragrant flowers, the holly, the great beeches, the tall yellow poplars, the wild muscadine, even the red clay had excited him from the beginning. Wrens would float to the ground like stray leaves; he could hear the whistle of cardinals. A blue-winged yellow warbler flashed through a sweet bay and he saw a little cloud of the Carolina parroquets which he had come to love in the Ohio Valley. Deep in a thicket he watched a mockingbird playing near a gray fox that had stolen from his hole and was sunning himself on a stone. The mockingbird jigged about on a nearby gum tree, then hopped to the ground, stopped, skipped from stone to stone, trimly spreading his wings and tail until the white patches showed, fluttering and stretching as if for exercise. Quickly he fluttered back and forth over the fox, skipped away and came back again, again, until the sleepy fox in annoyance pulled himself up on his forelegs and slid away.

Lying under a cucumber tree Audubon watched a pair of mockingbirds for hours. A hawk dropped swiftly toward the male but with a movement even swifter the mocker darted up at the hawk, which turned tail and fled into the upper air. In the garden at Oakley he had seen a mocker chase a dog and even a cat to cover. He soon found that everyone on the plantation protected mockingbirds, so much their song was loved, so greatly were their neat and daring ways enjoyed. Their carelessly constructed, coarsely lined nests were rarely disturbed.

Not far from Oakley lay a deep moss-hung cypress swamp and others could be found by ferrying across the Mississippi to Point Coupée. In a pirogue Audubon passed far up thin dark streams among cypresses with only small patches of blue showing high above the tall feathery tops. He would hear a faint splash. A mink had moved with a sudden arched spring upon a sharp-tailed sparrow. He saw weasels, which the French trappers called *fouines*—sneaks. Echoing over the waters was the *yank, yank, yank* of the ivory-billed woodpecker. Letting his pirogue float in a little pool, he would sit for hours with pencil and notebook in hand, hardly moving perceptibly even when he saw something he wished to note. He watched a raccoon ambling along a log and remembered some of the stories he had heard from Negroes—

stories of coons and possums and rabbits in which these creatures made a world in themselves, with talk and trickery. Some of these tales he had heard from trappers who knew most of the waterways of Louisiana; they had learned animal stories from the Choctaws and passed them along in the soft creole *patois*—stories telling why the buzzard has a bald head, and why the katydid sings all summer.

Among the pale spider lilies were water moccasins, and he found pearly snail's eggs on the lily stems. An alligator lifted half of a long body near him and slid beneath black water. The bright small flare of the prothonotary warbler—a male—lit for a moment one of the dusky-gray cypress "knees." Suddenly the air seemed full of such brilliant flashes.

He walked to Oakley with a red-cockaded woodpecker in his hat which he had winged on leaving the swamp. Tired as he was, he sat down to draw him, first setting him free in the room. He wrote that the woodpecker "immediately reviewed the premises, hoping and hunting for a place to work through and using his chisel bill with great adroitness, throwing chips to right and left." The bird explored downward all the way to the floor, then ran up a brick wall "as easily as if up the bark of his favorite pine, picking between the bricks and swallowing every insect he found." Audubon drew him as he looked under cracks and finally opened a window and let him go.

Whenever he could he made drawings from living birds. Tirelessly he made sketches of leaves, of the patterns made by flower-filled branches, of fruits as they ripened, the papaw, the persimmon, the swaying muscadine. He watched a richly colored spider entangle a horsefly in her net and cover it in a moment with her silk, shooting it out in a stream until she had a white silk oblong ball. He began to fill a notebook with delicate exact paintings of many oddly formed insects, exquisite dragonflies, caterpillars, bees, spiders, butterflies. He painted frogs and little blue-green lizards. He killed a full-grown rattlesnake and worked for sixteen hours at the drawing, having poised the snake as if for attack with open fangs.

He finished this by candlelight. The time had been far too short, he thought, as he rose from his drawing board; but he had succeeded in transcribing the blunt contour of the head, each shade and pattern of the zinc-colored, brownish-gray, and yellow scales. The next day he dissected the head to make sure of the structure of the jawbones and teeth, and he decided that the warfare of snakes and birds must have a place in his gallery.

He chose mockingbirds because they were gallant fighters. He had seen blacksnakes in a merciless attack on birds, but as he thought of a pattern of mockingbirds and orange blossoms, he could see that a blacksnake would make too heavy a bar upon the page. The rattlesnake, so boldly sinuous in outline, so precise in the diamond-shaped forms of the scales against the loose ovals of orange leaf and petal, and so right in shaded color—the luminous green and white—it was settled! It should be a rattlesnake.

The more closely he planned his arrangement the more certain he grew. The neat gray of the mockingbirds, their trim outlines, the light green of the eggs were harmonious in color and form with the snake! He painted the birds in a wild storm of fear and action against the approaching fangs—in such tenseness of body and feathers as only one who had watched these birds—many birds—day after day in flight and in a hundred strange situations could know them.

In his own time and in later years Audubon was said to have painted birds in unnatural attitudes, with an effect of artificial drama, contorting, distorting these small feathery figures. His painting of the mockingbird attacked by a rattlesnake was to thrust him into an angry controversy whose echoes have not yet died away. But naturalists of his time had often seen only the simpler attitudes of birds, and few observers possessed Audubon's sure and rapid vision which could catch variations which others missed altogether.

Walking through deep woods he came one day to a little ravine into which he dipped, and at the bottom found the tracks of raccoons "as close together as those of a flock of sheep in a fold." Before he discovered the careless nest on an old stump he heard sharp and angry notes, like squeaks above his head, and looked up to see two male great-crested flycatchers fighting angrily, with sudden sallies and a whirl of yellow green and dusky feathers, one of them, the conqueror, darting toward the other's tail, which he was plucking, then retreating for another attack. Thus Audubon painted them, without backgrounds, as he had seen them, one above the other against the sky, with erected crests and stiffened quills, this time not filling the page, using only the two figures yet by his light placement of the birds with their outstretched wings and repetitive colors, creating a bold design.

He was now steadily absorbed in the problems of pattern, experimenting with shadows and forms of live oak and white oak leaves. In his painting of prothonotary warblers he used a slanting downward drift of dry cane vine with berries in dim yellows and grays and blacks, yet the eye is lifted by twists of tendrils and by the poses of the bright-colored birds.

In the smoldering heat he worked on some of the most brilliant of his paintings, such as his study of the showy Carolina parroquets that had tempted him more than once, now at last appearing in a magnificent free pattern of green and orange, soft pinkish red and gray-brown. He painted a pair of summer redbirds on a spray of wild muscadine.

The summer was lush, full. The tall silver meadow rue rose in the fields. Giant yellow ladyslippers came into flower. On the low pinelands were tall flame-lilies whose slender petals and tall anthers broke in airy bright-colored fountains. Audubon still went to the swamps and waterways. On glassy ponds he found the pale wide yellow flowers of the water chinquapin lifted high—flower after tall flower. Their seeds were favorites with wild ducks, and the Indians still sought these for food. In autumn he often saw them silently shoving pirogues or canoes into the coverage of leaves. He was seeking the water thrush and the rain crow, as the yellow-billed cuckoo was called, a bird of secretive habits living on the edge of woodlands.

If he had ever doubted the worth of his painting he had few doubts now. He was bringing the work of years into fluent and natural forms. That yeasty "compound of ideas" of which he had been aware in New Orleans was becoming clear. He not only painted, he made hundreds of small sketches—a storehouse for future use. A story has it that at this time he learned from the Choctaws the use of the Indian blowgun, a very long tapering pipe of cane, polished as smooth as glass inside, polished outside until it looked like cherry or mahogany, with a feathered arrow of dried pithy weed which with skill and a perfect aim could be used to stun small birds without injury. Hunters often used candles at night to draw them into range. It may be that Audubon made his captures by this means; certainly he could work best and most rapidly from living birds, which he could later set free. He was painting in a fury of fresh accomplishment which left him no time for anything but his duties as a teacher, none at all for entries in his journal, which was now blank for months, though he continued to make notes on his observations in the woods.

The downward-pointing leaves of the sweet gum were red, brilliant green, yellow, when his long season at Oakley was over. He had come to think of Feliciana as home; so he was to call it for the rest of his days. But he could contrive no way of bringing Lucy and the boys there, and see them he must. He had

had few expenses during the summer except for paper and colors, powder and shot. He had saved most of his earnings, and he was certain that with his new achievements he could find pupils in New Orleans and further commissions for portraits. He sent a sizable draft to Lucy and begged her to take the next steamer down the rivers.

"I have *finished* sixty-two drawings of birds and plants, three quadrupeds, two snakes, fifty portraits of all sorts," he wrote her exultantly, "and I started, as thou knowest, my Lucy, without a dollar."

It was hardly surprising that Lucy was reluctant to join him after so many uncertainties, but Audubon insisted. With forty-two dollars in his pocket and a warm sense of accomplishment he rented a little house in Dauphine Street, and at last she came with Victor and John. The family was reunited, and this was happiness. Audubon quickly secured a few pupils and began to experiment freely in oils with the purpose of obtaining more lucrative returns from his portraits. Almost at once he was commissioned to paint Father Antonio, a popular priest, and the portrait, which was exhibited, made a considerable stir.

Under other circumstances, with greater freedom for all his work, Audubon might have become a portrait painter, though his mode would not have been the popular mode of the day. He had a genius for observing character, and the few portraits known with fair certainty to be his show his gift for decorative arrangement. He never signed his oils. He never truly considered him-

BLUE GROSBEAK. *PLATE NO. CXXII*

self a painter of portraits. At times he did not think of himself as an artist at all, but wholly as a naturalist. Apparently he experimented with many styles of portraiture out of curiosity or in the hope of hitting upon effects which might prove popular and bring him useful sums of money. It was transitory, difficult business. He still had plenty of successful rivals in New Orleans. He had no reputation made in Europe or in the East with which to dazzle prospective sitters. Vanderlyn and Sully and others came there with well-established names. And he was hardly more successful in securing pupils, for there was a growing number of teachers and schools.

If he had known it—and perhaps he did—he was attempting the impossible. His true work was of a highly original order, and it was still incomplete. With some of it he was even more dissatisfied than he had thought. He had asked Lucy to bring to New Orleans all the paintings which he had sent to her, all those he had left behind in Cincinnati. When he looked at them he "found them," as he frankly said, "not so good as I expected them to be when compared with those drawn since last winter"—that is, at Oakley. Perhaps he undervalued some of them.

He walked down to the river and out to the swamps, his head whirling with plans. Absorbed as he was he could still notice a small flock of white-bellied swallows—tree swallows—which he had known in the Ohio Valley, now settling for the winter glistening blue-black or green as they skimmed over watery sedge-grass.

Some way he must continue painting birds without too much conflict with the means of making a living. He set himself a stint, which he followed closely. He employed a hunter to bring him a new bird every day for ninety-nine days, excluding certain birds which he had already painted. For these he would pay one dollar apiece. If the hunter failed him in any respect he would be paid only fifty cents for each bird. These he would paint, thus accomplishing something each day toward his major plans. And difficulties or no difficulties, he resolved to paint again in a fresh style every bird of his earlier collection with which he was now dissatisfied.

He hit upon a further idea which seemed a happy solution. He would make bird paintings to sell. Birds were not in vogue, and some of his showed a boldness of design which may have startled beholders—that of his water turkeys or snake birds, among them. He had painted a pair, one behind the other, on a thick branch of dark yellow green, and their strange curves, the angles at which the long necks and narrowing green-black heads were set, made a double, flowing design of striking power. It turned out that nobody wanted these paintings.

"I suffered some mortification this morning in a house where I showed my birds," he wrote in his journal.

These were anxious times, for he was earning barely enough by teaching and portrait painting to keep his family together. He could not afford to buy water color paper or a daybook in which to write. Yet the Audubons were not too poor to give hospitality to a French friend until he could find work, and they were sorry when he left. "We shall miss his beautiful music on the flute," said Audubon.

At last Lucy found a place as governess, and the boys were placed in a school. Audubon decided to see what Natchez had to offer. Young Mason, who had returned with him to New Orleans, traveled with him but soon went northward. Having no money, Audubon gave him a gun, some paper, and chalks as a parting gift.

At first, in Natchez, he had the usual bright glimmerings of success, and he took every sort of commission that came to him. Someone wanted a picture of Natchez. He painted a view of the town from the river in oils, faithfully, without an ugly spot blurred over or omitted. He worked at odd moments with a wandering artist, John Steen, who undertook to give him formal instruction in oils. In turn he taught Steen the use of water colors and pastels. In the midst of this he made his study of the chuck-will's-widow with a harlequin snake wound around a gray branch like a small, slender, flexible totem pole. And he seems to have made some sort of excursion up the Arkansas for birds. Returning, he picked up a few more commissions, taught in a school, and earned hardly enough to pay his way. "I am in despair," he wrote in his journal. "I fear my hopes of becoming known in Europe as a naturalist are to be blasted. Daily the hope of completing my work seems less clear."

With faint expectations he showed his bird paintings to an

English traveler who claimed to be a naturalist. "You should take them to England," said this gentleman with an air of authority. "But of course you will have to spend a number of years to perfect your work, and also to make yourself known." Audubon closed his portfolio and resolved to forget his ambition.

At about this time he painted a portrait of himself in oils, in which his head is sunken upon his shoulders, his whole figure set low on the canvas, his eyes uncommonly wide, dark and enigmatic. It was not a great portrait, but it was a decisive revelation of feeling. At this moment he was bitter. But no one can read the statement on the canvas without perceiving that he was also stubborn. At the moment he was Gil Blas without humor.

A grandiose plan finally was hatched by Steen and Audubon, to travel through the southern states painting portraits. But New Orleans was not the only hunting ground for portrait painters. Men of considerable talent had been flocking for some years into the Mississippi Valley from Europe and from the East. Audubon and Steen may have found the walls of plantation houses or even of log cabins covered by admirable portraits. In any event their adventure was brief and came to nothing.

Audubon returned to Natchez with a solid resolution: "I shall break through. After this I shall follow only the birds of America." In a warmly responsive letter Lucy agreed with him, though she was having discouragements of her own. Her engagement in New Orleans had come to an end, and she was unable to collect her salary.

What followed seems to have come from the fullness of Audubon's enjoyment of Feliciana and the special ways in which he had felt at home there. Undoubtedly it was through acquaintances he had made at Oakley that Lucy was offered a position as governess at the home of the Percy family, Weyanoke on Little Bayou Sara. There and at the neighboring Beechwoods were a number of young people of all ages whom she could teach.

Audubon was invited to Weyanoke for a visit, which resulted in a brief flurry of misunderstanding with the Percys. Perhaps he was in a prickly mood because of his many failures. His temper was often easily stirred, and the bitterness with which he had painted his own portrait had not yet vanished. But this gradually passed, and he settled down to teach the young ladies music and drawing, with dancing lessons for the younger children. Victor and John were included in the household, so his family was again united. As at Oakley he was to have a margin of time for his own work. Pleasant ways had opened for the Audubons.

"Pucker your mouths and whistle!" he would cry to the children when he taught them dancing in the old gin house; he wanted to get into their heads and into their feet the tune which he had played for them on the flute. They puckered and puffed and blew, and went sliding around the floor with laughter.

The water in the spring house could be deepened at will, and here with Lucy he taught the smaller ones swimming. Then they would all be off to swim in Little Bayou Sara where a pool had been hollowed by the river as it carved its way to the Mississippi.

Some of these children Audubon loved as if they were his own, and they were often at his heels when he went into the neighboring Sleepy Hollow Woods. Like the boys at Henderson they had noticed birds and their ways; they could tell him where nests might be found, and they had a store of odd tales which they had heard from the Negroes.

"Chuck-will's-widow will roll her eggs away over the ground at night if you touch them and hide them somewhere," said one of the boys.

"Who told you that?" asked Audubon.

"Pomp."

Audubon talked with Pomp. "He roll 'em with his bill," declared the Negro. "One night I seen him. He mosquito eater. Sometime he swallow little birds whole."

This near relative of the whippoorwill was a favorite with Audubon because of its light gambols through the air at dusk. He liked the clear strong call, heard as soon as the sun was set, *Chuck will's widow, chuck will's widow*. At last he found one of their nests, which was hardly a nest at all but a well-concealed slight hollow on the ground, cunningly placed among leaves at the foot of a tree in a wooded ravine. He picked up the eggs and put them back; next day they were gone. He succeeded in discovering another nest, repeated the procedure, and then lay down in a moist gully to see what followed. But the night was dark; these birds were as quiet as owls in their flight. The nest was empty in the morning. It took Audubon many hours of searching and equal hours of waiting with a dog motionless at his side to discover what happened when the chuck-will's-widow's eggs were touched. At last he saw a pair flying from the nest through a misty half light before dawn; again the nest was empty; they carried their eggs in their bills, but though he searched the brush almost inch by inch with his dog for more than a hundred yards in radius he found no trace of them. Accomplishing the difficult feat, they had removed the eggs to a still greater distance.

With almost no guide in ornithology he thought such stories worth considering; at least they sent him off on one or another search which yielded something new. Sometimes on his longer expeditions he was accompanied by a Negro who had been a sailor and could go up a tall cypress as he would climb a mast, gathering eggs and nests, bringing down young birds to let Audubon examine them.

Most often he went to the swamps alone, taking a pirogue at some bayou landing across the river, pushing his way through pale water lettuce up one of the small dark streams, through tangles of muscadine and drooping gray moss. Water turkeys—anhingas—roosted in the feathery cypress tops, their long snake-like necks undulating black against blue sky, their tails like fans. They might drop like a plummet into the water if he were still long enough, yet leave hardly a ripple in diving. They would swim submerged, or with only their thin sleek heads showing, or they might disappear altogether and walk on the bottom of the stream.

Long afternoons went to hunting the white ibis; its slightly overdressed look, its neatly placed orange-scarlet legs, the long curve of its black bill, made this great bird an irresistible subject. These ibises were said to be prophets, building their nests high when high water could be expected, low when the lakes would be shallow. Now they seemed prankish teases, always beyond close sight or the reach of a gun when he sought them out at the heronries beyond Point Coupée. He saw the rare scarlet ibis but did not succeed in bringing this bird into range. Odd-looking storks, hunched and drooping, their heads covered by blue scales, their plumage white with black wing tips—these came to his hand more luckily, and he carried them home for hard sessions of painting. But the white ibis continued to elude him. Once he broke through thickets and waded to his middle to find one of the nests, discovered one, stayed all night in mud and water, cramped, hungry, tired, hoping he might bring down one of the birds at dawn. The ibis flew off as he had hoped, and he fired, but the bird, a fine male, had veered from the expected course and he lost him.

If he faced disappointments and sometimes downright bewilderment as to names and classifications, at least new birds were never lacking in these woods and along the waterways. He found the shy mourning ground warbler, whose migrations seemed secret, and the cerulean wood warbler whose nests were often in dogwood trees, and watched them feed on the dense red whorls of the Spanish mulberry. His portfolio grew heavier. The number of his finished paintings was mounting, and his journals were packed with new notes.

Once after a long day of hunting and drawing in a swamp he came upon a trapper's small hut and decided to spend the night there since the sky threatened a storm. A sudden crash of thunder, and the hurricane was upon him in a moment, sweeping into the thin shelter, with water falling in gusts without a pause as if it came from some great open funnel above the treetops. The hut was soon flooded; water came up to his knees and crept quickly higher. He held his portfolio of drawings over his head within the peak of the rooftree where a patch of long shingles was unbroken. Lightning flashed to the ground in red streaks. A great cypress split and fell within a few feet of the hut. His stretched arms and hands grew numb, and the storm seemed to increase rather than to slacken. He began to think with that clearness which is said to come to drowning persons, of his past life, of the improbable future. Once more his work might be swept away and he might have to begin again by slow stages. How slowly all of it had moved! Years had passed—twenty of them—since he had begun at Mill Grove. In the whirring of tossed branches and the pounding of the rain he reached the blackest discouragement. Then thought itself seemed to stop in the havoc.

Slowly the storm slackened. With the first glimpse of light he heard the music of the wood thrush, a song of a few clear, mellow, flute-like notes with a trill and a final high E, falling in gentle cadences. No instrument, no song could be so sweet, he thought, so gentle in its last, almost inaudible phrases. He had heard it many times before, in the Alleghenies, on the Green, along the prairies of Illinois, but never so sweetly; this was the song he loved best, perhaps because it was closest to the mood of untroubled happiness which had so often been his, against reason.

With a genius for discovering such pleasures he might have been content with them. Everything he loved most was here. In this fertile region he could have spent a lifetime, making such journeys, rewarded by fresh experiences, new discoveries. His passion for exquisite detail—for the precise curve of a bird's feather or the pattern of a harlequin snake—might have led him into sinking himself in the most minute pleasures. He was still the hunter, liking sport for its own sake; yet beneath the apparent unconcern of many of his movements still ran an implacable ambition.

What its whole substance was he still could not have said, though the plan of publication was well forward in his mind and in Lucy's. As he laid each new painting away in his portfolio it was with the idea of another distance traveled toward this goal. But he had never paused with birds; even when he knew his leisure was brief during these years in Louisiana he had stopped to sketch or paint whatever most brilliantly attracted him in the natural world. His notebooks and journals had steadily embraced experiences of many kinds, notes on people which were miniature portraits, notes on the look of the land, the ways of life in new places.

Were all these observations only glancing fragments which would come to nothing? Mixed and broken they surely were. Most of those who had known him best would have said that he lacked purpose, that above all he lacked a sense of order. His room was always in confusion; he found it hard to meet fixed engagements. It was only because his lessons at Weyanoke were given in the morning that his presence could be counted on, and then not always with security, for he might be up before daybreak and in the woods and forget to come back, or he might have spent the night in a swamp miles away. His haphazard ways would probably not have been tolerated except for the gayety and wit which went with them, and except for a further influence not so easy to define. The interest in natural history which he had encountered straightway in Louisville was in the air here too, floating in through philosophical articles, through new books; his pursuits possessed luster for cultivated people. And Lucy's dignity, her earnestness, were of assistance when Audubon forgot the exactions of lessons.

This apparent chaos had lasted for years. Even his prosperous period in Henderson had had only a slender and accidental framework. And he was still far from having completed all the paintings he had planned. He had counted on at least four hundred. He had hardly more than half that number which now pleased him. But he wanted to show what he had done, to obtain recognition, and if possible to secure the means of continuing his work. Philadelphia was a center of scientific and artistic endeavor. He decided to go to Philadelphia.

In October, 1822, he set out by steamboat with Victor for Shippingport. This older boy of his, who was now fourteen, had shown a talent for business and was to enter Nicholas Berthoud's establishment. Lucy and John were to remain at Weyanoke. How Audubon was to reach Philadelphia he did not know. His earnings had been small, and the steamer passages took a considerable sum. "But," said he, "I intend to proceed on my travels."

10 *An Artist Faces the World*

THE waters of the Ohio were so low that the steamer was obliged to stop at the mouth of the Cache. The drouth had been long and severe; no one could tell how long the boat would be delayed. Audubon decided to walk the two hundred and fifty miles to Louisville with Victor and two other passengers who were anxious to reach their destination.

They walked Indian file along the Illinois shore, cleaving their way through canebrakes, traveling through burnt forests, coming upon occasional orchards where they filled their pockets with October peaches. They found their lodgings for the night in whatever cabin seemed hospitable and clean toward the end of the day. Frost glittered over the fields in the early mornings, and the brilliance of autumn had come. Again, as on so many of Audubon's journeys, music was in the air, not his own this time, but that of one of his companions who played the flageolet.

After three days, when they had crossed the Ohio, this gentleman saved his wind. Victor began to limp "like a lame turkey," his father said. "It was a tough walk for a youth." When Audubon entered a cabin at the end of the fourth day to talk with the owner about sleeping accommodations for the night, he came outside again to find his son sunk in sleep on the grass. One of their fellow travelers was considering his sore toes. The other was "just finishing a jug of monongahela." But the next morning Victor had his second wind, and they crossed the Tradewater where a flock of wood ducks was feeding in the shallows on acorns, brilliant blue and tawny red and emerald in the clear stream.

On the whole their journey yielded only a small harvest of adventures. They stumbled into a cabin in the midst of heavy rain to inquire the way and saw a man lying on a dirty bed in the corner with a brass pistol on a nail over his head and a long Spanish dagger at his side. On a table was an open ledger or journal. "What do you want?" he asked in a surly tone. "The road to a better place!" said Audubon. The man shouted directions without stirring, and afforded them no further clew as to his character or his way of living.

They passed a salt lick where great kettles hung over blazing fires, and finally tired feet halted the two strangers. They decided to break the journey. Audubon and Victor continued until they reached a ferry on the Green, where the dark waters fringed by cane and willows looked like a mossy subterranean lake. Here at a cabin they found sparkling cider, a good meal, a clean bed, and the next morning they decided to drive the remaining distance in a hired conveyance.

Audubon entered Shippingport with his handsome, well-grown son at his side and thirteen dollars in his pocket. He was proud of Victor; and the long walk through regions which he had known well, in a beautiful season, had been a delight. He particularly remembered the warmth with which the little party had been received at cabins along the way, and he wrote down an account of the journey which still has a bright luster.

The sum with which he arrived in Shippingport told a different story. Philadelphia was a far-distant goal. He must have known when he left Feliciana that he could move there only by slow stages. He settled in Shippingport for the winter, taking whatever work was offered him as a painter—portraits, landscapes, scenes for interiors of river steamboats, and even shopkeepers' signs. He was finding that "delineations of American scenery" were now popular. With the influx of civilization the American landscape was rapidly changing, the wilderness was going, and there was a vogue for reminiscence. More than once Audubon was to speak of his regret at this change, and he bent his talents to this kind of painting with the same eagerness which had led him to write down in his journal all the odd circumstances of the day.

His plans widened. He would take a sheaf of these paintings with him to Philadelphia where they might prove him still more the artist, and where they might perhaps be sold. "Busy at work," he wrote two weeks after he reached Shippingport, "and resolved to paint one hundred views of American scenery. Shall not be surprised to find myself seated at the foot of Niagara." By spring he had earned enough money for his journey east, and he resolved to try to perfect himself while there in the use of oils by lessons with some excellent master.

At Philadelphia he received at the outset the kind of recognition which belonged to him, recognition as an artist, from one of the most popular artists of the day, Thomas Sully. It is possible to think lightly of Sully's work; much of it was hasty and facile; he was overwhelmed by commissions. But his taste cannot be discounted; he had great technical proficiency, and his generosity of spirit equaled the vogue which he enjoyed. The wonder was that he perceived the value of work so boldly at variance with anything that was being painted at this time, so radically different from his own. With a true instinct he saw that neither portraits nor landscapes belonged within the scope of Audubon's finest work, and he undoubtedly knew that oils were not his natural medium. He freely gave Audubon instruction in oils, but it was the bird paintings which captivated him.

To the end Sully persisted in regarding Audubon as an artist, in spite of the flurry of talk and argument which followed then and later as to his achievements in science. When he left Philadelphia for New York Sully pressed upon him introductions to three painters, Gilbert Stuart, Washington Alston, and John Trumbull. In one of these he said, "The inspection of one of his drawings of birds will be sufficient recommendation to your notice," in another that Audubon was preparing a work on ornithology "which for copiousness and talent bids fair in my estimation to surpass all that has yet been done, at least in this country," and he spoke of having "great esteem for the character of Mr. Audubon," whom he had then known for several months. Audubon wrote to Lucy that he was "overwhelmed by the goodness of Sully, who would receive no money for his instructions and gave me all possible encouragement which his affectionate heart could dictate."

But all this was far from meaning that he received primary recognition as an artist, or that his paintings or drawings of birds were accepted as works of art. There was in fact at the time no standard by which to gauge them. The known flower and bird paintings were those of the Flemish and French painters of the sixteenth and seventeenth centuries and others of their kind which had followed this tradition. These, in oils, were great opulent decorations, intended for castles or palaces, showing a few exotic birds, a mass of hothouse flowers; all was sheen, velvety textures, handsome fountains, ornate urns. In England, Bewick had created his woodcuts of British birds and animals, but the difference in medium would have distracted attention from a possible alliance. Both Audubon and Bewick were concerned with simple truth and with unstressed decorations.

Something akin to this might have been found elsewhere in this country if the critics of the day had cared to see it, in the primitive art of more than one native group. Pure decoration had occupied those Pennsylvania Germans with whom Audubon had lived as near neighbors at Mill Grove; on their slip ware and birth certificates and the paintings on their wedding chests they had used simple designs of birds and flowers. There is no indication that Audubon considered this work or that he was influenced by the Indian decoration with which he was familiar, yet in his own fashion he had come close to forms which were primary in this country. A difference was that he used naturalism in pure design, when these others used abstract forms.

What the critics and other observers in Philadelphia, even Sully, probably could not understand was his almost habitual lack of concern with backgrounds. His paintings and drawings at this time, even when they included abundant sprays of leaves and flowers, were upon white. Backgrounds were now being filled out by painters with the most studious logic. Still another element in his work would have met no answer. As this was laid out, sheet by sheet, a prevailing clear, grave, impersonal quality must have become plain. Its beauty had no pretensions. With all the wealth of color it was almost austere. But austerity was not a virtue of American painting at this time.

In the field of science some of the leading naturalists of the day in Philadelphia promptly declared themselves against Audubon. The center of a long-smoldering quarrel lay in the work of Alexander Wilson. Audubon had entertained the simple idea that since his own work was finer and more extensive than Wilson's—he had no doubts on this score—its importance would be recognized. But the last volumes of Wilson's work were now being published under the editorship of George Ord, who wanted no rivals. He objected to Audubon's portrayal of birds with plants. Audubon tried to make friends with Ord, who at best was a cold man. "Give it up," said one of his new acquaintances. "Ord has no heart for friendship."

Publishers who had a stake in Wilson's work brought their influence to bear. As to the publication of his paintings he said "not only cold water but ice was poured upon my undertaking." Charles Bonaparte would have commissioned him to make drawings for forthcoming books, but the engraver, who was allied with the Wilson camp, declined to undertake the work. "This gentleman's figure," said Audubon, "reached nearly to the roof, and his face was sympathetically long, and his tongue was so long that we obtained no opportunity of speaking in his company." With all his length the engraver was immovable. He said that Audubon's drawings were "too soft, too much like oil paintings."

Bringing up further guns, journalists and art critics began what was to prove a long warfare. Bonaparte had made much of the fact that Audubon was self-taught, but Audubon himself happened to speak of his few lessons under David as a boy in Paris. He was charged both with concealing the instruction which he had had and of boasting about it. He was accused of posing as a backwoodsman, when he was in fact a man of education. The truth was of course that he fitted both descriptions.

Yet even with this opposition both his genius and his character exercised their power. Charles Bonaparte stood by him, and he made friends with young Richard Harlan, a physician in Philadelphia, whom he thought "the very best among the naturalists" and to whom he gave some of his drawings. Edward Harris, an ornithologist and a man of means, helped him generously at the end of his stay when his hope of publication was gone and his money was exhausted. He had earned small sums giving lessons, but he had remained longer than he had planned and he lacked money to pay his bills and take him back to Louisiana. He tried to sell to Harris a painting which he had made of the Falls of the Ohio, asking an absurdly small price because his need was so great.

"Men like you should not want for money, Mr. Audubon," said Harris, and pressed a one hundred dollar bill into his hand. When he refused to take the painting, Audubon, who could rarely be outdone in generosity, gave him his whole collection of his drawings of French birds. Less finished than his later work, they were still of great interest to the student of natural history.

"I left Philadelphia yesterday at five o'clock, in good health, free from debt, and free from anxiety about the future," he wrote

Lucy from New York on the first day of August. He referred to the immediate future. In the warmth of this parting he seemed to have forgotten that his plans in coming to Philadelphia had come to nothing. He was not a step farther along the way toward publication. He had hoped to earn money; he had barely made his way. He had stirred animosities which he must have known would endure. He had for his pains only a new, distant, but glittering possibility to consider.

"Go to England. Go to France. The best engravers are in Europe. You must gain recognition there. You *must* go!" From many friendly sources he had received this urgent advice, and he already had a little packet of valuable introductions. Go he would! Uncertain how this would be accomplished he was positive about the event. In New York for a few hours he was carefree. "I felt happy and comfortable in the city and sauntered about admiring its streets and landings."

But the artists and scientists whom he had hoped to meet there were away because of the hot midsummer weather, and he stood for hours like a clotheshorse in Andrew Jackson's regimentals for Vanderlyn, now in New York, who was painting the General's portrait. Since Audubon's figure closely resembled Jackson's he pressed him into this service.

In New York he sounded out other chances of publication but with a marked lack of success. "I remember that I have done nothing," he wrote in his journal, "and fear I may die unknown." But after all there was Niagara, at whose feet he had thought of sitting a few months back. If he was to bury himself in obscurity he decided he might as well see Niagara on the way. He traveled up the Hudson and along the canal, and discovered a few new birds, and at last stood between two rainbows below the Falls, and forgot his discouragement marveling at the "verdigris green" of the water below white torrents of spray. He could not cross to Goat Island because his funds were too low. After a good dinner, for which he paid twelve cents, he went to bed in excellent spirits, thinking of Franklin, Goldsmith, and others "who had worked their way through hardships to fame."

Sleeping under the sky on the deck of a schooner from Buffalo to Erie, he was wakened by a violent gale which broke off Presque Isle, and was certain that his drawings would be destroyed. But a safe landing was made, and he started with a chance companion on a little journey to which he was often to refer. The two hired a cart to carry their luggage to Meadville. What followed was nothing but a long walk through unfamiliar country, but on these mellow late August evenings they heard the serenade of the rose-breasted grosbeak, and as they passed "old fields" or Indian burying grounds the notes of the hermit thrush fell sweetly. On the way Audubon filled his journals and sketchbooks, and paid for his own lodging and that of his companion at night by use of the familiar black chalk, drawing portraits. The little journey was full of tranquillity.

At Meadville he faced a familiar situation. The jaunt to Niagara had been reckless. He was again without money. "I walked up the main street, looking to the right and left, examining the different *heads* which occurred until I fixed my eyes upon a gentleman in a store who looked as if he might want a sketch." The gentleman was persuaded; he was also pleased, and Audubon went to an inn, where he was taken for a missionary priest because of his long hair.

A brisk little trade in portrait painting followed. He set up a studio in a dusty attic over a store, hung blankets at the windows to secure a painter's light, and there among old toys and worn musical instruments, fur caps and hogsheads of oats, he painted and drew whoever came to him, earning enough to continue the journey. With his nameless companion he set out in a few days by boat down the French Creek and the Allegheny for Pittsburgh.

There he spent two or more months. The river waters were high, making travel difficult, and he found plenty to engage him. After so many journeys east and west he had a wide circle of acquaintances in Pittsburgh, particularly in the French colony. They applauded his work; new plans for publication began to take shape; a considerable number of persons even put down their names as subscribers. At the same time he scoured the country for birds and continued his drawings. One of the finest of these was made there, his passenger pigeons, a fluent design in blues and rose which used a branch of his favorite old wood, whose texture caught the salient colors. Almost surely his magnificent painting of the American raven with shell bark hickory was done in Pittsburgh, with its bold use of horizontals, its sweeping sprays of leaves, its severe yet delicate grays, greens, and blacks.

Here he met the Bashams, who had a little school and were interested in natural science. Mrs. Charles Basham was a serious student of botany; she knew Sully and perhaps some of his other friends and acquaintances in Philadelphia. When Lafayette came to Pittsburgh, Audubon saw him and brought him to meet her. Naturally enough some of Audubon's talk at this time ran on the French Revolution. Mrs. Basham remembered his many recollections of that period. A Dr. La Motte was in Pittsburgh, who as a boy had been hidden in a clock case for a number of days in the midst of the storm. With him too Audubon seems to have talked about the past. The visit was full of reminiscences. He spoke of Captain Audubon's acquaintance with Lafayette, and he drew Lafayette's portrait. But no glow of sentiment overspreads this firm wash drawing; not the hero but the old man looks forth, his head a little stiff, the mouth sunken and crooked, the eyes full and wide beneath wrinkled lids, the hair straggling. Crookedness is faintly suggested in the pleating of the shirt frill, by the folds of the neckcloth, and the figure is set well to one side of the page. Overhead the rays of a small misty sun are spread obliquely. Conscience speaks in every line of this casual drawing, the conscience of the artist, with a touch of humor and fantasy.

Mrs. Basham spoke afterward of Audubon's popularity and his persistence in following his vocation. She had been charming; the

Bashams' home had been open to him; when he left he gave her a little notebook filled with exquisite minute paintings of insects, butterflies, lizards, magnolia blossoms, blue morning glories, a lily.

Still lacking funds, he had some lithographs made of his portrait of Lafayette to sell along the way, and started out in an open skiff with a few other wayfarers of fortune for Cincinnati. But heavy rains fell, and the inhabitants of waterside villages failed to buy the lithographs. When he reached Cincinnati at the end of October he was without funds and was forced to borrow a small sum from an old acquaintance. For some time he paced up and down before the house, unable to make up his mind to ask the favor.

"I got the loan cheerfully," he told Lucy, "and took deck passage to Louisville." He slept on a pile of shavings and meditated on the future, and was filled with an unaccountable elation. "The contentment which I now feel is strange. It borders on the sublime. Enthusiast or lunatic, I am glad to possess such a spirit."

On a wet sultry night of early December he reached Bayou Sara and arrived in the early morning at Weyanoke with torn and ragged clothes, hair longer than ever, and a pirate's beard. Lucy was giving a lesson to one of her pupils when he burst into the room and in a torrent of talk began to pour forth his happiness in seeing her, the events of his long journey, his new plans. He would go to England and publish his work there.

The idea had magnificence, which commended it to Audubon, and Lucy had faith in it, in part because of her English birth perhaps, more because Audubon was Audubon, with most persuasive arguments. He intended to complete a further large number of drawings and to earn money for the undertaking.

Perhaps because of the praise he had received in Philadelphia, particularly from Sully, perhaps because his enterprise seemed a daring one, he had no difficulty in obtaining a considerable number of new pupils in drawing, music, French, dancing. He rode over distant parts of the parish on these errands and even went back and forth to Woodville for a dancing class of sixty young ladies and gentlemen, teaching intricate steps and figures and providing the music on his fiddle at the same time. When he had to put his instrument down to teach the dances by example he would sing the tunes. He made a little show of the affair, and some spectators, enjoying it, asked him to dance to his own fiddle music, which he did, skipping lightly enough and perhaps reflecting that all his life he had in one way or another danced to his own tunes.

The months, lengthening out, brought their pleasures. Up before dawn he would ride the many miles to Wakefield to see his friend Dr. Hereford, who more than once had a bird for him which he had greatly desired, and with whom he could talk about natural history and new books. He had odd cronies at the inns in St. Francisville, where he liked to visit because of the meetings with travelers they afforded. French planters for miles around on both sides of the Mississippi were his friends; he hunted with them, eating broiled ducks or fish or turtles' eggs roasted in the sand by the shores of Thompson's Creek, and turning such trips to advantage for his notes and paintings.

When her own many tasks were finished Lucy often joined him for rides before sundown when the red roads were brilliant against dark foliage. They would often ride far into the evening, hearing the last call of birds, seeing gray foxes slide into the brush with bodies as close to the ground as a lizard's. When the moon was up they would gallop far up the river and come out in drenching silver light on bare spaces toward the Tunica Hills. A small shadow might fall on the pale road before them and they would look up to see a barred owl overhead, so quiet that they heard no faint rustle of wings.

They talked endlessly—of plans for the future, plans for Victor and John, and of "a happy old life," as Audubon called it, for themselves.

At last he could watch the four seasons wheel round in this beloved region. Before this he had not known the early onset of spring there, with wild wistaria and redbud and dogwood, wood violets and the yellow jasmine which Lucy loved more than any other flower. He made paintings and drawings of the wild olive or snowdrop—the silver bell, he called it—and watched for birds in the lemony fragrance of the spreading cucumber trees. In a warm February the yellow warblers came, throwing themselves by the thousands into the cypress woods and canebrakes, moving up and down in spirals through the air, among the thick branches, singing a long season through. In early summer there were long days when the shade of the live oaks lay so deep that it seemed like a black pool which the hand could stir within the yellow sunlight, and Audubon stole every moment which he could take from his lessons to spend in the woods and swamps.

The beauty of these months was their spaciousness. His work was at its best, his happiness at full tide. He had never had so wide a freedom. What came to him, what his own special gifts brought, was no narrow path toward an ambition, but a whole generous way of living in which all his talents came into play. He found time to learn from the neighboring Houma Indians how to fashion shoes from rattlesnakes' skins. He painted portraits, sometimes for pleasure, sometimes for useful rewards, and gave lessons in drawing to John. He still played his flute or flageolet or fiddle. He seemed tireless. He could still work from candlelight to daybreak and beyond, or sleep the night through in wet clothes in the woods when the day's tramping and wading were over.

With all this easy amplitude his painting of birds steadily went forward. Finally he painted the wild turkey cock. Many times he had attempted to portray this great bird, so magnificent in his iridescence, so stately of stride. More than one lady in Henderson had held a wild turkey in position for him for his early sketches, and nearly every plantation in Feliciana where he visited was later said to be the place where this bird was painted. The hen he had painted earlier. The true place where he painted the cock seems to have been the Sleepy Hollow Woods near Weyanoke, and the portrait in life-like sheen and color, bold, wild gait, was one of the finest of his bird portraits, though not one of the finest of his designs. Within the limits he had set himself he lacked space for its decorative completion.

A large body of his surest work seems to belong to this period, among this the pileated woodpeckers with raccoon grapes, a glorious leafy pattern of spotted brown-green leaves, clusters of tiny blue grapes, tendrils, and twisting stems with the variegated plumage of the birds breaking and joining this. He was showing wide command of color and a great variety of fresh designs. He used pure pattern in his portrayal of ruby-throated hummingbirds with rioting trumpet flowers; and a special conquest lies in the blue-green, pale gray, and yellow-green of the leaves, those beneath the larger sprays falling like a breath, like shadows. In his study of black-billed cuckoos every touch is integrated within a complex pattern, from the flirting upright tail of the female to the stripped fragment of a leaf which falls in balance, and the disposal of the pure white spaces is particularly beautiful, as is the severe placement of the flowers, and the curves of the breasts, and the line of the sleek heads.

By the spring of 1826 Audubon had accumulated upward of four hundred paintings of birds which he knew had excellence, and he had earned in rather more than a year over fifteen hundred dollars. He engaged passage on the *Delos*, sailing from New Orleans for Liverpool, and said good-by to Lucy and John in mid-April.

The *Delos* did not sail on time. Miserably depressed, Audubon walked the streets of New Orleans. Who could know what this adventure abroad might bring—if indeed he ever succeeded in going? The whole idea might be madness; after all he had formed this plan only because of the more or less casual suggestion of persons whom he hardly knew, who did not know him or his difficulties.

He seems also to have been beset by queries as to his birth and parentage. Though the lines have been lost, it is known that in the following months he mentioned these to Lucy in letters more than once, or made an allusion in his journal. Madame Audubon was now dead, but he was going abroad again; this was enough to bring back to him recollections of his youth. Perhaps such questions had always been evoked to some extent in New Orleans, since at one time or another he had met there persons who had known Captain Audubon.

It was a time of upheaval; his thoughts were in chaos. Still his ship was delayed. He returned to Bayou Sara and said farewell to Lucy again two days later at sunrise after a ride through the magnolia woods.

On the eighteenth of May the *Delos* set sail, slowly warping her way down the winding breadth of the Mississippi, through the delta, out into the blue Gulf. The voyage was a long one, more than nine weeks, and after the dolphins had left and a pirate ship failed to overtake them, a tedious routine of many slow days followed. Audubon read every book on board, some of them more than once, drew portraits of every interesting character, made many notes on his fellow passengers and the officers. He philosophized very little. Facing momentous decisions, he had almost nothing to say about them.

At last a whale was sighted, they smelled land, and passed the shining coast of Ireland. As the ship neared Liverpool he was beset by a wave of homesickness, but the many ships and the green misty hills in the distance as she drew near port, altered his dark mood, and he strode down the plank and into the noisy streets with a familiar elation.

11 *Wild Turkeys Abroad*

ALL his life Audubon was to speak with pleasure and gratitude of the "family Rathbone," as he called them, Quakers in Liverpool to whom he had been given a letter of introduction before he left New Orleans by Vincent Nolte, his traveling companion of many years earlier when he was riding Barro from Pennsylvania to Kentucky.

In the friendliest fashion the Rathbones invited him to visit them at Green Bank, their house in the country, and they introduced him to both men and women in Liverpool who were interested in painting and in natural history. "My heart is filled with hope," he wrote to Lucy. "These kind people praise my *birds*, and I feel the praise to be honest." This was the main thing.

"The ladies of Liverpool are ladies indeed," he continued gayly, saying that they were remarkable for "*their plainness of manners and superior acquirements*." Besides, they were "*fresh as roses!*" And Mr. Roscoe, to whom he had been introduced, "is a *come-at-able* person, who makes me feel at home immediately, and we have much in common."

Soon he was receiving invitations to many country houses. "I have taken to fine dressing again, silk stockings and pumps, and I shave every morning." His unfashionable coat failed to trouble him. Most people, as he quickly guessed, took him for a backwoodsman, and he saw that this was no disadvantage.

They liked the novelty of meeting this strange handsome artist out of the wilds who spoke with a strong French accent, who had candid eyes, an upward tilt of the head, fresh coloring, and a stalwart figure. He was still wearing the flowing locks of the western hunter, and he let them flow. "I assure thee that they do as much for me as my talent for painting," he wrote Lucy shrewdly. He was urged to imitate the notes of American birds, and in many drawing rooms he freely whistled like a mockingbird or a cardinal and gave the call of the chuck-will's-widow. Everyone asked him about Indians. "You would think our country contained nothing else. They seem surprised that I have not been devoured at least six times by *tigers*, bears, wolves, or foxes."

"No," he told them solemnly, "I was never troubled by any animals larger than ticks."

Europeans had their own notions as to what western Americans were like, and he tried to play his part well. But when his work was under consideration, that was another matter; acting was put aside. Shyness overwhelmed him. He wrote Lucy he was certain that his head, if closely looked at, would have been seen to resemble the body of a porcupine at bay, so stiffly did his hair stand on end when he met Lord Stanley.

But "Fine!" said Lord Stanley. "Beautiful!" He spread the paintings on the floor and got down on his hands and knees to look at them.

There was a sudden clamor of interest and Audubon was overwhelmed by courtesies in Liverpool. The newspapers wrote such flattering notices that "I no longer dare look into them." His paintings were exhibited at the Royal Institution, and he was obliged to spend part of each day there. The exhibition brought him more than one hundred pounds, but he discovered that he disliked to take money for showing his birds, and he was oppressed by Liverpool because the city was old and crowded. He was asked to paint flowers and birds—particularly wild turkeys—and he gave away many such paintings to his new friends and sold a few others. But "I feel quite too much cramped and confined," he wrote to Victor. In the garden pools at Green Bank he found no water moccasins; no white ibises rose from a dark swamp. He was homesick.

Yet he seemed to see everything. "I don't know why it is," he told Lucy, "but my *observatory nerves* never give way no matter how much I'm overcome." His long letters to Lucy were filled with close descriptions of people he was meeting. His journals were also letters to Lucy, beginning each day with a greeting, ending with a farewell; and their pages were crowded with further happenings, the look of people, their actions, the appearance of servants in a great house "moving quietly as kildeer," and of the waiters in a hotel who "were kept skipping about with the nimbleness of squirrels."

On all sides he was told that he must make himself and his work known in England before he attempted publication.

Armed with introductions he went to Manchester, only to encounter discouragement. "Only twenty people to see my birds," he wrote after a few days. "Sad work, this!"

The next morning as he stood waiting near the exhibition rooms two men drew near. "Have you seen Mr. Audubon's collection of birds?" said one. "I'm told it's well worth a shilling. Suppose we go in."

"Pah! it's all a hoax," said the other. "Save your shilling. I *have* seen them. The fellow ought to be drummed out of town."

But, as he wrote in his journal, a Quaker came "with four very pretty little daughters in gray satin bonnets, gray silk spencers, and white petticoats," and word of the exhibition spread among other Quakers. A group of them "praised my drawings so much that I truly blushed."

Then he received discouraging advice from a well known bookseller from London. Audubon had always planned on life-size reproductions of his paintings.

"Be governed, Mr. Audubon, by this," said the bookseller pompously. "At present productions of taste are purchased by persons who receive much company. They will wish to have your book laid on the table as a pastime, or an evening's entertainment. This will be the principal use made of it, and if it needs so much room as to crowd out other things or encumber the table, it will not be purchased by the very people who are the life of the trade. If large, only public institutions and a few noblemen will purchase it. If small, it may sell a thousand copies. The size must be suitable for the English *market*."

When they entered the exhibition rooms together Audubon slyly noticed that his new acquaintance was startled. He began to talk, he was enthusiastic. He cried, "They *must* be published the full size of life, Mr. Audubon!"

Edinburgh was next. He must conquer Edinburgh. Many of the foremost naturalists of the day were assembled there. Before the journey he returned to Liverpool for a short stay, and Mrs. Rathbone gave him a gold seal that she had had made with the imprint of a wild turkey and the motto, "America, my country." Perhaps the Rathbones had found him not unlike the shy, handsome bird which they regarded as a symbol of the American wilderness.

In Edinburgh he discovered keen eyes, clever voices, sharp wits, minds whetted on controversy. There the great Jeffrey wielded his vitriolic pen. Christopher North, naturalist and man of the world, occupied a powerful place as editor of "Blackwood's." Audubon realized that these personages might not welcome him, and indeed he was quickly snubbed by a professor when he said he hoped to meet Sir Walter Scott. The chilly reply was that Sir Walter had become something of a recluse, that he was greatly occupied with a new work, indeed that Audubon would not at all be likely to see him. "Not see Sir Walter Scott?" he said to himself. "I *shall*, if I have to crawl on all fours for a mile!"

Resolutely he went about the business of making himself known, presenting the "crowd of letters" which had been given him. "I unpacked my birds and looked at them with pleasure," he wrote Lucy, "yet with the fear that they would never be published." He was obliged to show them, to carry them under his arm to houses or offices, hoping for encouragement, and this made him feel like a beggar. But after the first rebuffs and a few experiences in finding great men too much occupied to see him or not at home, the importance of his work was recognized with generous warmth.

His paintings were put on exhibition, and made a profound impression. Christopher North of "Blackwood's" was dazzled. " 'Twas a wild and poetical vision of the heart of the new world," he wrote. Audubon thought these lines "a little queer," but there could be no doubt that they were intended as praise. He began to receive invitations by the dozen. "It is Mr. Audubon here, and

Mr. Audubon there. I only hope they will not make a conceited fool of Mr. Audubon at last," he said. He met the devastating Jeffrey, a tiny man who came into a drawing room, he said, with a hat under one arm and a woman under the other. They eyed one another. Audubon survived. Christopher North became his friend, and the strong influence of "Blackwood's" was brought to bear in his favor. And it proved natural enough for him to meet Sir Walter Scott, who thought him "acute, handsome, interesting," and who found "simplicity" dominant in his character. Perhaps Audubon's character was not altogether simple, but Scott meant this as praise and invited him to bring his paintings to his house where they might talk; and there Audubon was more comfortable than on the first occasion. With his birds before him he slipped into recollections of "our woods" and of his visits among the Choctaws and Osages.

Honors were soon heaped upon him. He was elected to the great societies established for the furtherance of art and the sciences in Edinburgh. "My situation borders on the miraculous!" he wrote Lucy.

Alas! some of these honors carried penalties. He was obliged to make public appearances, answer toasts before large gatherings, and read addresses. After his long seclusion in the woods his shyness was deep-seated, and he had never attempted anything of the sort before.

Toasted handsomely at the Antiquarians, he was dizzy when he rose to respond before the large assembly; his hands were wet with perspiration. He read a paper on his manner of drawing birds before the Society of Arts, "and I positively shook so that I feared I could not proceed to the end." He was to read another paper before the Wernerian Society, on rattlesnakes, and he found the rooms "as full as an egg"—a terrifying sight. He had been unable to finish the paper because of the pressure of engagements and was obliged to say so. He read it at a later meeting—"a job of three quarters of an hour." Though he was cheered roundly, "my cheeks burned." He handed the manuscript to the presiding officer and fled.

For another address he chose the habits of the wild pigeon as his subject. "If it were not for the *facts* it contains I wouldn't give a cent for it," he told Lucy, "and positively I brought myself so much among the pigeons and in the woods of America that my ears were as if filled with the noise of their wings!"

"So full is my mind of birds and their habits that in my sleep I continually dream of birds," he wrote later.

He sometimes forgot dinner engagements and on one occasion arrived the evening before he was expected. His hostess tried to persuade him to stay, but "I marched home as much ashamed as a fox who has lost his tail in a trap." After long official dinners lasting far into the night his head felt "like an immense hornets' nest . . . yet it all has to be done. Those who have my interests at heart say I must not refuse a single invitation." He never learned to enjoy the "smoky Scotch whiskey" as he called it; he disliked the custom of drinking toasts, and he was accustomed to far more sleep than he could snatch.

After a convivial affair lasting into the early morning hours he would be up at six, writing letters to the numberless persons who had assisted him, to others whom he must meet, to old friends in America, to Johnny, to Victor, to Lucy—besides the closely packed accounts of his days which he set down as journals—pages on end, rapidly written, telling every detail of the day, every small adventure, his visits to the theater, his walks about the city, to Arthur's Seat and Edinburgh Castle.

These narratives sometimes aroused memories of quite different scenes. "My breakfast came in, but my pen carried me along the Arkansas River."

The winter days in Scotland were so short that he was obliged to begin painting by candlelight. He painted to make money to meet his expenses, to repay favors. Offered by a dealer a hundred guineas for a large painting of wild turkeys, he presented it to the Royal Institution because of the kindness he had received there—but he sorely needed the hundred guineas. How was he to pay for the publication of his birds? He worked feverishly at commissions—for paintings of wild turkeys, pheasants, ducks, hawks, squirrels, foxes, an otter in a trap—a favorite subject—and even fighting cats. He was constantly interrupted by visitors. He was continually being asked to set up birds and animals and display his "method," and often painted in the midst of a crowd, when he had worked only in solitude.

The most serious obstacle was that he could not bring himself to dash off these paintings and let them go without further thought. Everyone wanted oils, and he had never felt at home in this medium. He still puzzled over questions of technique, and couldn't decide whether to "finish highly" and perhaps destroy the broad effect or to give up finishing and preserve the look of a swift sketch. He was uncertain whether to use a glaze over the painting or under it. "I have labored hard," he wrote at the end of a day, "but my work is bad. Some inward feeling tells me when it is good. Sometimes I like a picture, and then a heat rises to my face and I think it a miserable daub."

He was partially consoled when he saw a painting by Landseer because he knew that his own observation was more truthful. "The stag has his tongue out and his mouth shut!" he wrote gayly. "The principal dog—a greyhound!—holds the stag by one ear as if he were a loving friend. The young hunter is in the attitude of a ballet dancer and laces the deer very prettily by one horn; he is about to cast a noose over his head. What a farce!"

Since his own portrait was eagerly sought, he sat, or rather stood, for hours in his wolfskin coat and hunting dress. "I make a strange-looking figure," he wrote Lucy when one of these paintings was finished. "The eyes are more like those of an enraged eagle than mine."

At the moment phrenology was highly fashionable, and what could be more interesting than to examine the bumps of this backwoodsman-artist from America? The bumps were examined. He declared that his skull was measured as minutely and accurately as he would measure the bill or legs of a new bird, and he was persuaded to exhibit his head at a phrenological party, where another naturalist showed *his*. But this was not the end. "My eyes will have to be closed, my face and hair oiled, quills will be put in each nostril, and plaster poured over all. A bust will then be made." He consented to this operation, but he was disgusted; he had lost "a most precious day—a vast deal in a man's life-glass." Walking home with the other naturalist, he was glad to feel the frosty air and see the stars, and was suddenly homesick again for "our rich magnolia woods, the mellow mockingbird, the wood thrush."

Some days later he returned to his rooms to find, as he said, "his face lying on the table."

All this was trumpery, and he knew it. "It is mere wind, but still valuable in my situation." The question burning in his mind was that of publishing his birds. Nearly six months had passed since he had left Louisiana. He had discussed the question with his new friends in Edinburgh more than once and had been advised to offer his paintings to some well-known British naturalist who might lend his name to the publication. It would then appear as a joint work.

In meeting strangers or appearing before public assemblies Audubon could be shy enough, but he had no hesitation as to this suggestion. He flatly declined to consider it. "If my work deserves public attention it must stand on its own legs, not on the reputation of men superior in education and literary acquirements, but possibly not superior in the actual observation of nature in the wilds."

At last a Mr. Lizars, an engraver, came to see his paintings. Audubon did not clearly understand the man. "He had a look quite above my reach," he said. But there seemed to be no doubt as to Lizars' enthusiasm. When he saw the paintings of the mockingbirds attacked by a rattlesnake, of the wild turkeys, of the great-footed hawks, he declared that they must be published—life-size—and that he would undertake this work. Audubon was convinced of the excellence of Lizars' engraving, and the advantages were very great of beginning publication without further loss of time in the midst of the furor he was creating. A bargain was struck which Audubon later discovered was highly favorable to Mr. Lizars.

Audubon was to supervise the engraving, which was to be on copper, and the coloring of the plates, which was to be done by skilled craftsmen who were expected to reproduce the coloring of the originals exactly. Five plates were to be published at one time, as a single number, bound in paper. Each number would sell for two guineas. Five numbers would be published each year. It would take at least ten years to publish the four hundred paintings in Audubon's portfolios. These would finally make four great volumes. The size was that known as "double elephant," forty inches by twenty-six.

Slow publication was necessary to ensure excellence of coloring and engraving, and also to distribute the cost to subscribers. The whole amount, one hundred and sixty guineas, or nearly a thousand dollars, must not seem too heavy.

Three or four plates were finished at once for exhibition so that the subscription books could be opened. The great turkey cock led off—life-size! The Rathbones obtained a few subscriptions in Liverpool. A few institutions subscribed. But to obtain enough to publish the whole work: this labor would be stupendous, and Audubon knew it. He had enough money on hand to pay Lizars for the first numbers, but he would be obliged to sell his "Birds" in advance of publication if future numbers were to appear, obtaining separate subscriptions for single numbers or as many as he could for the whole work. He saw plainly what this effort would cost him, not alone in money. He had peddled his talents before, as a portrait painter; he was peddling them now, as he painted turkeys and pheasants, foxes and fighting cats. No one else could sell his "Birds." He would have to do this himself, and it would mean that through years he would have to give up the life he loved most.

Audubon was not much given to reflection; he had lived too completely outside himself for that, in the color and beauty of the external world. He possessed a deep and natural insight as to the life of wild creatures, and often as to people. But insight is not foresight. He had rarely looked ahead. Now he did so as he faced the uncertain years that lay before him.

"I must abandon my life to make my success," he said.

It was impossible to turn back, not only because of his hope to obtain a competence for Lucy and his boys, but for another reason quite as clear. He had painted his birds and flowers to please himself, yet not quite for himself. He had the pride of conquest that the artist and the scientist always feel in some measure; he knew well enough that his paintings had beauty and originality, and he knew that they must be published—must have permanent form—must be seen! They now made their own demands. In a fashion they were beyond himself.

Some of his friends in Edinburgh warned him against life-size plates; he was unshaken. His birds and flowers must appear as he had seen and had painted them. Against further advice he issued a general prospectus for the whole work while the second number was in preparation. Suppose the enterprise failed, his friends said. He could then draw in his horns if he had not pledged too much. Audubon was certain that his work would be completed, and he wished to make clear from the beginning the splendid scale on which it was planned. "I can't conceive of failure," he wrote to Lucy. When he saw a young American girl handling her set of the first plates carelessly he was sorry—on her account. He was sure that in fifty years they would become a rarity—as in truth they have—and he set down this conviction in his journal.

Selling his birds—selling his birds—that was the immediate task. For slow weeks, which became months, he went about Edinburgh trying to obtain further subscriptions; he made trips into the country, presenting himself to rich people who might, as the London bookseller had said, like to have his numbers on their drawing room tables, to look at occasionally as a pastime. He followed up every possible clew, every introduction, met refusals, and went on.

The "observatory nerves" were still sensitive. In an anxious whirl he could still be amused by passing glimpses of people—by an oddly matched man and woman in the street. "She was like a great round of beef, he was like a farthing dip."

Obliged to spend a few days in a castle in the country in order to obtain a subscription, he noted everything—the weak old earl with watery eyes who could hardly stand up, "weaker than a new hatched partridge," and the sofa whose down was so deep he thought it would swallow him whole, and the monstrously long high purple drawing room hung with paintings and crammed with expensive objects. The countess, in the midst of this gaudy splendor, wore a crimson gown with a yellow turban. His bedroom was yellow, his bathroom crimson. The servants, in powdered wigs, wore maroon liveries.

The names on his subscription books increased in number, five, ten, twenty, thirty, forty. If he could obtain three hundred names for the whole series he would have a goodly sum above the cost of publication. He decided to canvass the principal cities of Britain, and then to go to London.

When his departure was in prospect he began to receive advice from his friends as to his appearance, particularly as to his long locks which were now considered much too wild, and the color of his coat. "Why I cannot dine in my blue coat as well as my black I cannot say, but so it seems." It was hinted that even the black coat was not altogether suitable. He did nothing about the coats but he sacrificed the locks. More than once he had been accused of vanity in regard to them, and in fact they were thick and handsome. In his youth he had written a description of himself, noting his thick hair, his clear eyes, his sound white teeth, his straight nose; but this might have been a phrenologists' catalogue of bumps or one of his own close and careful scientific notes.

Shearing his locks amused him. "I sent for a barber and my hair was mowed off in a trice!" And in his journal he set aside a page for a memorial notice bordered in black. But he soon let his hair grow again.

At Newcastle he was disappointed as to subscriptions, but he had a friendly visit with the great Bewick, now an old man, whose wood engravings of birds and quadrupeds he had long admired. "He talked of my drawings and I of his woodcuts until we liked each other very much." When Audubon spoke, Bewick would take off his cotton cap and pull up his socks, but on went the cap again—or almost on—as he himself picked up the conversation, and the socks "would then resume their downward tendency." Bewick was astonished by the boldness of Audubon's undertaking, and thought that such painting and engraving must be immensely difficult. On the other hand he tried to show how simple it was to engrave on wood. Audubon for his part thought wood engraving no simple matter. "Yet he did it with as much ease as I could feather a bird. And he made all his own tools, which are delicate and very beautiful." Before he left the two had a cup of tea together, and Bewick gave him a letter of praise which he could use in any way he saw fit as he went on his travels.

At Leeds he was so disgusted by the whole business of begging people to buy his birds that he walked straight out of town and in a sheltered place by a small stream quickly undressed and in the icy water "took a dive smack across." This was at least a taste of the life he loved! Then once more he sought out possible subscribers and obtained a few names. In York and Manchester and Shrewsbury he gained a number, and at last he went to London.

"London," he said, "is like the mouth of an immense monster, guarded by millions of teeth." But he was welcomed by the American minister, Mr. Gallatin; his paintings were exhibited under favorable conditions, and as at Edinburgh, honors of all kinds were showered upon him. Almost immediately he obtained a few subscriptions, mainly from public institutions, without effort on his own part.

But a letter from Lizars contained the plain intimation that he was about to throw over the whole work of engraving; why, he did not say. On the whole Audubon had not been pleased by Lizars' plates. The colors were sometimes muddy; the engraving

STANLEY HAWK. *PLATE NO. XXXVI*

lacked real freshness; it seemed to have been laboriously worked over.

For a few days he was anxiously depressed; but he had heard of a London engraver, Havell, whose shop he now visited, leaving his painting of Baltimore orioles to be engraved and colored. When he returned, Havell set before him the painting and the engraving side by side on a broad easel. Audubon looked at them in silence for a moment. Then he began to coast around the room with a rapid dancing step, crying aloud, "The jig is up, the jig is up!"

Havell could hardly know that Audubon was likely to twist English sayings to suit himself. "What is it you do not like, Mr. Audubon?" he asked solemnly.

"I can't tell the one from the other! I can't tell the one from the other!" Audubon shouted. His words poured over each other; he could hardly express his delight.

Of his own accord Lizars withdrew and arrangements were completed by which Havell was to finish the work. His prices were less than those of Lizars, but the initial cost of producing the many succeeding plates was steadily mounting.

Audubon harnessed himself to his task again after the first pleasant flurry in London. Subscriptions—he must have still more subscriptions! The notices of the first numbers had been highly favorable but he had far less than a hundred names. He made long trips into the country to talk with possible subscribers and showed his bird paintings to artists whose praise might be useful.

Harried by the recollection of his failure at Henderson, he had determined to meet his obligations to Havell with absolute punctuality, and he kept this resolution throughout their long relationship though his pockets were often nearly empty. Once he had only a sovereign left and was obliged to take the first offer he could get for one of his oil paintings. His trips to obtain subscribers were constantly interrupted by his need to raise a considerable sum immediately for copper, colors, paper, and for the engraving. Ready money was nearly always to be had from his oils—bad though he thought them.

At times he resolved never to use oils again, whatever happened. "My birds in water colors have plumage and soft colors but in oils—alas!" He still obstinately wanted to learn all that could be learned about oils in spite of all the pressure to which he was being subjected. "How hard it is for me not to have another life to spend to acquire a talent that needs a whole life to reach any moderate degree of perfection. My hand does not manage the oil brush properly—neither the composition nor the effect are good. The pictures I sell are only purchased by my friends, and my heart and natural pride revolt at this, therefore I am very likely to abandon this style forever; yet it is with a considerable amount of regret, if it does not amount to sorrow. *Man*," he wrote Lucy, "and *particularly thy husband*, cannot bear to be outdone."

He was often in despair over all his undertakings, yet in the streets or during his interviews with possible subscribers "the observatory nerve" could still keep him amused. At Oxford he saw a venerable judge in an enormous curled wig—"a wig that might make a capital bed for an Osage Indian during the whole of a cold winter in Arkansas!"

A glinting wit could possess him even in the midst of disappointment. The Earl of Kinnoul summoned him for an interview. "He said he had sent for me to tell me my birds were all *alike*, and he considered my work a swindle!" Audubon bowed himself out without a word. "A small young man with a face like a caricature of an owl," he said.

But George IV and the Duchess of Clarence put down their names on his list of subscribers. That would cause a buzz-buzz of talk! And the disappointments of weeks were forgotten when he saw his painting of the Carolina parroquets beautifully engraved and colored. He was exultant! He now willingly battered the pavements of Cambridge until he was footsore, seeking a few subscribers.

Next he decided to storm Paris, and there he received a warm welcome, saw all the notabilities of science, met famous painters and engravers of the day, and was presented to the Duc d'Orléans and other members of the nobility, some of whom gave him their names for subscriptions. He attended the Royal Academy of Sciences where more than a hundred well-known individuals examined his plates.

"Fine! Very fine! What a work!" they cried.

"What a price!" they also whispered.

In Paris Audubon obtained fourteen subscriptions, six of them from the government, and he was officially praised by the Royal Academy both as a naturalist and as an artist.

He wound up his visit by going to Issy where French troops were to be reviewed by the King. He walked the eight miles alone and clambered to the top of a high wall, where he perched for a clear view. A lady in a carriage pointed at him with her parasol.

"Doubtless she took me for a large black crow. But I felt like an eagle on a rock!"

12 *In the Golden Age*

IN Paris he had remembered the American rivers he had known—the Hudson, the Roanoke, the Missouri, "the gentle Ohio," the Mississippi, which in imagination led him to Lucy. A sudden rainstorm had brought him memories of the great tropical rains in Louisiana.

He had expected to send for Lucy and young Johnny and perhaps Victor a few months after he reached England but the risks had been too great. A year passed, another was going. His expenses were never lightened; his ready money was always being drained away for his "Birds." He had sent Lucy a gold watch as soon as he had landed in Liverpool—a gift which had taken a good part of his funds—and a little later he had sent her six dresses that "are quite the fashion" and "warranted to wash," with handkerchiefs because he thought she might need them, and gloves that were "French and fashionable." When his surplus of money was enlarged in London he shipped a handsome piano to Bayou Sara so that she might have an instrument for her own use. Johnny soon received a fine hunting dog, his friend Bourgeat at St. Francisville a pair of them. Having a hundred guineas to spare he offered to send a piano to Victor, who was at Shippingport.

"Do you still continue music on the piano?" he wrote Victor. "Are you fond of it? And would you be pleased to possess an instrument of my own choice? I will send it with all my heart's good wishes. Say if it's to be a grand or a square one." In the meantime he was sending a fine new flageolet.

These were extravagances, but he could not resist them.

He wrote to Lucy as though he had seen her the day before, as though she were only a few miles away, wrote everything that came into his head. "I regret exceedingly not having brought barrels of reptiles with me." This message went winging across six thousand miles. "I could get fine prices for them, I assure thee, and also for rare birdskins and seeds of plants." Wouldn't she send him seeds? She did. He wanted rattlesnake skins to make shoes in the Indian fashion for some ladies who had befriended him. The rattlesnake skins were sped to England. Wouldn't John send birdskins? "Do, my Lucy, ask John to skin all kinds of birds for me, hawks, anything, even to the humblest-looking sparrow, and if he would make me a large drawing of a fine cotton plant in bloom and pods I would be very glad—also drawings of branches of hickory, black walnuts and other trees whilst in fruit, and also the different oaks when the acorns were on, because I could redraw them and make good paintings." He was accustomed to draw from nature, and now he could rely only on old sketches or memory. Another time he asked a *large* box of *old* branches of trees, magnolias and the like, covered with lichens or moss for the same purpose. Some of Lucy's pupils collected the branches and Johnny procured the birdskins, which reached him in due season.

He was always urging Lucy to have John draw and to observe birds. At times he was beset by the fear that he would not live to complete his great enterprise, and he wanted this son of his, who was gifted, to be prepared to go on with it. Victor, with his aptitude for business, might assist him later with the management of the subscriptions. He began to speak of "our work," "our stupendous work."

The work soon became still more stupendous. He decided that at least fifty of his paintings, made in earlier years, were not good enough for publication. They must all be as good as the best. And he was now convinced that he must have more water birds; he must also show a wider representation from different regions. A continent of birds! That journey to the far West which had captivated his imagination from the time he had known Boone in Kentucky still danced before him, and the Florida Keys—he had always planned to visit the Florida Keys!

With his subscription list far short of what he had hoped and with only a small surplus of funds, he sailed for New York in the spring of 1829, leaving his affairs in charge of Havell and of Mr. John G. Children, Secretary of the Royal Society, a naturalist on whose judgment he could rely. He was obliged to postpone the happiness of seeing Lucy since she could not come from Feliciana to meet him in New York or Philadelphia, and he dared not, for his part, spend any of the rich summer season in travel. "I *must draw hard* from nature every day that I am in America," he wrote her, insisting that she return to England with him when this work was finished.

He struck out at once for thick woods which he had seen near Camden and painted there for several weeks, choosing warblers for the most part, filling out his notes on their many variations in flight and nest-building. He then set out for Great Egg Harbor on the Jersey Coast, joining a caravan of hunters and fishermen, driving all one night along dim white sandy roads that wound through a forest, hearing the soft creak of wheels, coming closer and closer to the sea. The wild country, drenched in cool moist salt air, was intoxicating. Here were water boundaries once more, and he was free again to explore them.

He stayed at the hut of a fisherman who was also a hunter and "a tough walker, who laughed at difficulties and could pull an oar with any man, and had eyes like a sea eagle." His wife was pleasant and his little girl "wild as a sea gull." At night they all sat down to a clean table set with fat oysters, sound white fish, and other simple food.

According to his old custom Audubon was always up before daybreak and saw the sea glimmer gray and green with a sheen of foam in the breaking light. Terns danced silver and black before him. He searched salt marshes where many herons bred, watched marsh hens there, studied sea gulls. He redrew many of his earlier water birds and made new paintings in that free rich style which had seemed to flower for him in Louisiana. He painted the seaside finch with wild roses, the yellow-breasted chat, the black poll warbler. The thin crescent of white shore, a fringed island—he rapidly sketched or painted whatever seemed fresh and clear. Often the day's work was severely hard as he poled along inlets through the marshes. Then a sudden beautiful flight of herons, blue, green, white, some in young plumage, would break before him, and drudgery was forgotten. He must work—he worked furiously. Yet peace was here.

In a few weeks he completed thirteen large paintings and made many sketches: but he must have more—he lacked some of the shyer finches, larks, creepers; some of his thrushes must be painted again. Off to Philadelphia for a day to procure more colors and paper, he was away again at four the next morning by coach and reached Mauch Chunk as dark fell, with the huge shadow of the mountain above him, and went on at once by cart to the heart of the Great Pine Swamp or the Great Pine

Forest—both names were common—in Northumberland County. Through darkness the cart rattled down steep stony inclines, crossed the Lehigh more than once, curled around slopes, and at length in the scent of pines drew up before a woodsman's house.

Small things could always please Audubon. He went to bed in good spirits because a stranger staying there said good night pleasantly.

He waked to find himself in the heart of logging country. All winter, woodsmen had been cutting timber. Now in June the rivers were high and rafts of logs were ready; river drivers in bright shirts and colored sashes were riding rafts of logs, running from one to another, forcing stray timber out of shallows with pikes, working the boom downstream. These raftsmen prided themselves on their skill in riding swift waters. A slip of caulked boots would send them underneath the pounding heavy welter to certain death. They sang and even danced jigs on the floating logs, coming to camp at night drenched to the skin but ready to frolic and play their fiddles and tell stories. Their camp was not far from the cabin where Audubon was staying, and he heard some of the tales they liked to tell—not always of their exploits on the water.

Once a few of them went off to Mauch Chunk for huckleberries and were down on their knees in a rich patch, scooping in the fragrant berries, when they were startled by loud snuffings. Some large bears loomed up. Raftsmen carried hatchets in their sashes, Indian fashion, and they came eagerly "to the scratch."

"Scratch was the word," said one of them, "with a banging of them big paws and a gnashing of teeth. We went a-tumbling over each other down the mountain, *I* tell you. We got to our camp and went back to the mountain with something more'n hatchets, but there was no bears in sight and nary a huckleberry. A few bears can eat a sight of huckleberries."

Down in the valleys, sawmills hummed and Audubon was obliged to go far into the deep green of the forest, beyond cut-over land, to find the birds he was seeking: but he confirmed old surmises as to the nesting habits of birds, made fresh discoveries, collected eggs, nests, plants, flowers, made many sketches in the woods, and came back again and again to the cabin to paint. Its owner was Jedidiah Irish, a foreman in the camp, who knew these woods well; the two became great companions. At night as Audubon drew birds and flowers and leaves in outline Irish would read aloud to him from the poems of Burns.

As a boy Audubon had heard somewhere of the golden age but he had never been sure whether this existed, or could exist. Now he was sure. If he remembered rightly, the golden age was supposed to be a time when men worked and lived without hardship or envy or strife, happily concerned with poetry and music and the beauty of the world about them. Irish, the skillful woodsman, working at his craft all day and reading Burns at night, seemed to him an embodiment of this ancient idea. The simple comfort of the cabin, the plain good fare, the beauty of the great forest with its birds were a further part of it.

Autumn had come when he left, and he had some forty new paintings. He left for Philadelphia, and "had as my sole companion a sharp frosty breeze." There he encountered frosty breezes of another sort. After all the honors he had received abroad and with his plates to show he had hoped for many subscriptions. He obtained not one. In his few days in New York he had obtained none. On the voyage a fellow passenger had put down his name. This was the only recognition he had had as yet in America.

But he had work to do in Philadelphia, completing some of his many sketches. "I live alone," he wrote Lucy, "see almost nobody, rise before day, take a walk, return and set to my work until nightfall, take another walk equally short; hot water time comes on, I drink my grog, read some, think of thee and of tomorrow, and lay my head to rest with the hopes of rendering thee happy forever hereafter."

For months he had been urging Lucy to return with him when he went back to England. He wanted her to come to him now. But she would not promise; she would not come. She gave many reasons, one of them wholly unlike her. She said she could not travel alone from Bayou Sara to Philadelphia or even to Louisville. Lucy had traveled alone more than once. Her real reasons she did not wholly state. She still felt insecure as to the future, and she could not bring herself to give up a post which paid her well. She was now at Beech Grove, the Garrett Johnson plantation, where she had a fairly large class of children who came to her from several miles around.

Finally Audubon went to Feliciana, stopping at Louisville on the way to see Victor and John who were at work there in Nicholas Berthoud's offices, then journeying down the rivers again, this time by steamboat. The meeting with Lucy was joyous. Lucy was—Lucy: there was no one like her; this he had tried to tell her again and again in letters. "The older I grow the more I feel thy worth and need thy company," he had said. And happiness was topped by happiness because he was once more in Feliciana.

For a time he had no need to think of decisions. To be with Lucy, to receive warm praise from old friends, to work again in his beloved woods and swamps: these were enough. His portfolios of paintings and sketches grew heavier; he was filling out still more of those gaps in his great undertaking which he had seen when he had observed it as a whole. A burgeoning, fruitful season this was for him. He painted deer and squirrels as well as birds—perhaps to sell when he returned to England, or was another great work already taking shape?

From Louisiana he intended to make the long-intended journey to Florida, and another westward into the Arkansas Territory, perhaps to the Rockies. In the full flood of fresh work he had dozens of plans. He was brought up short by a letter from Havell, saying that a considerable number of subscriptions had been withdrawn during his absence and that other withdrawals were threatened. Audubon knew that he alone could unravel the difficulties and obtain new names to take the place of those lost. He would have to return to England with his work unfinished—with no certainty as to when he could study the birds and complete the paintings which he wanted for his full number.

Would Lucy go with him? She needed no arguments as to the beauty of his work. Stage by stage she had watched it develop, from their youthful days at Mill Grove onward. He had always given her the full harvest of his genius. One by one she had seen his paintings emerge in their splendor or delicacy of coloring, their beauty of design. The array of plates was only the outward proof of what she had always known. What had held her resolutely to her tasks was the conviction that his adventure was large, immensely difficult, and beyond calculation. Lucy kept her practical strain. She had rejoiced in the honors which had come to him but she knew as well as he did that these might be "mere wind" so far as successful publication was concerned. Now the adventure was again precarious; yet Audubon begged her to go with him.

Her decision must have been doubly hard to make because for twenty years, since she had first taken a position as governess at the Rankins' in Henderson, she had been in a measure independent; whatever happened she had known that she could make a livelihood by her own efforts. Now Audubon was asking her to throw this independence away, to cast in her lot with his as recklessly as she had done at the time of her marriage. Under the most favorable conditions eight years, perhaps more, lay ahead before publication of the "Birds" could be finished. They both felt the need of security for their later years. Audubon had written continually of his hope that they would have together what he called "a happy old life." As yet they had no security of any kind.

Lucy decided to go. What moved her was certainly not the prospect of ease or success, since at the moment this prospect was far from bright. Perhaps she was not even moved by the wish to be with this gay, always interesting, unaccountable genius who was her husband. She had that wish, without doubt, but she had often resolutely denied herself what she wanted. It was plain that he needed her; he had written her this a thousand times, but now as she heard at first hand of all the complex routine of publication, of his accounts, his lists, his letters, his engagements, she was not thinking of sentiment; she could be of definite assistance. The practical strain came out as she made her impractical decision.

On a slow journey to the eastern states they stopped for a brief visit with Victor and John, who were to remain in Louisville. There Audubon collected a barrel of Ohio River shells. "Send me a barrel full of shells," a fellow naturalist in England had commanded casually. He had collected over a thousand insects for his friend Mr. Children; and he was laden with boxes of furs and birdskins for other friends. He also had furs and birdskins which he hoped to sell.

At the end of his stay in this country he received a fillip of encouragement. When he ventured to Washington in the hope of obtaining support he succeeded in adding the Library of Congress to his list of subscribers, and he was invited to dine with President Jackson. At Baltimore, after tedious visiting, he obtained three names, and four finally in Philadelphia.

He had written Havell that he was bringing with him new paintings which would "make the engraver and his acids grin!" In London, he set to work with energy to put his affairs in good motion.

More than once he traveled on foot into the country with a packet of his big plates under his arm only to be rebuffed when he tried to obtain a new name. "I feel rather low in spirits," he wrote to Lucy on one of his more distant journeys, "but it is merely a cloud in the sky, and I daresay the buzz of the day will drive this off." On he went—and heard complaints as to the coloring of certain plates. Some of these seemed justified and he wrote sharply to Havell, "Should I find the same complaints as I proceed from one large town to another, I must candidly tell you that I will abandon the publication and return *to my own woods*."

"My own woods!" This phrase echoed through many of his letters.

But he could not, would not, return. Instead he inspected every plate before it was sent out, often working with the colorists.

He was slowly gaining enough new names to make up for most of those that had been lost. Within a few months his list included about one hundred and twenty-five subscribers, still not the three hundred for which he hoped, but enough to ensure continuance of publication. Again he painted show pieces of birds and animals in oils. Lucy helped him with important details of accounting and other business and it was a comfort to have her in England: but the heavy work of the day he still had to do himself.

Then as he again seemed on rising ground a fusillade of attacks began from both sides of the water.

In the paper on rattlesnakes which he had read before the Wernerian Society in Edinburgh soon after his first arrival he had drawn upon an episode recorded in his journal, written during his stay in Louisiana. He was lying on the ground watching a bird when he heard "a smart rustling" and saw a gray squirrel bounce from a thicket. The squirrel ran up a tree with the snake in close pursuit and out on a branch. The snake had followed, coiling and quickly uncoiling to slide after the squirrel, which then ran in and out of several holes and out over other branches with the snake still only a few feet behind. The squirrel took a long terrified leap to the ground. The snake also dropped, and before the squirrel could reach another tree the snake had him by the back, had rolled him over and around so fast that Audubon could hardly see the furry body. Slowly the snake uncoiled and began to swallow the suffocated squirrel, tail first, expanding his jaws for the rump, easily completing the remainder of his meal.

When this paper was published in England an American journal had stolen it, printing it in full without permission or payment. In the following issue the editor snorted with indignation; he declared righteously that he had been imposed upon. Audubon's paper was, he announced, "a tissue of the grossest falsehoods ever palmed upon the credulity of mankind." He said he had recently learned this from noted authorities.

The noted authorities were not slow in speaking for themselves. Those followers of Wilson in Philadelphia who had thrown "ice-water" on Audubon's undertaking four or five years earlier now eagerly came forward, led by the always unfriendly George Ord. Naturalists in England who favored Wilson's work also took up the quarrel, particularly the contentious Waterton. When after a time Audubon's painting of the rattlesnake invading the nest of mockingbirds was published, a clamor arose on both sides of the water. This painting was said to be a flight of pure fancy. A considerable number of naturalists announced that rattlesnakes never climbed trees, and further that a rattlesnake's fangs were not recurved as he had shown them. The snake was declared to be "a fabulous hydra," and Audubon was denounced as worse than a charlatan, he was an impostor.

"Sir," said one somber critic who had given both the paper and the plate his measured study, "this is too much for us Englishmen to swallow, whose gullets are known to be the largest, the widest, and the most elastic in the world!"

Heavy guns were soon drawn up over another question. This time a war was waged over the smelling power of vultures. Audubon had asserted that vultures found their food by the sense of sight, not smell, that they were in fact almost totally lacking in the sense of smell. But the ability of these birds to discover their food by its unpleasant scent had become proverbial; and besides, many of the attackers had publicly mentioned this in works of their own. Therefore it must be true.

Then Waterton roared that Audubon was absurd in saying that the ruby-throated hummingbird glued bits of lichen to its nest with saliva since it was obvious that a bird's saliva would be instantly dissolved by rain. Later a yellow water lily in Audubon's painting of the American swan was declared to be sheer invention.

Recklessly he furnished his enemies with more gunpowder when he published a sketch in which he described the visit of Rafinesque in Henderson and the chase through the canebrake. He used another name but the disguise was transparent. In a serious work Rafinesque had included a reference to the fabulous scarlet-headed swallow of which Audubon had told him. The hoax had long since been discovered; this bird with the mythical Devil Jack Diamond Fish had already been exposed to the public view. Now, with the sketch, they were used to prove that Audubon was another Munchausen, nothing more, nothing less.

It was incautious of him to publish the sketch, but Rafinesque himself seems to have enjoyed it, and spoke publicly of "my friend, Mr. Audubon." If caution had been uppermost in Audubon he would not have been in England at that moment; he would never have attempted any of his difficult tasks, much less have carried them through. As he looked back he had enjoyed the pranks he had played, and saw no reason why he shouldn't publish the story of them.

He was never wholly a scientist; he was what he claimed to be, an artist, a woodsman, even a backwoodsman, with more than a touch of the broad humor that had sprung up on the frontier. But he would have been incapable of playing a prank when he was expected to give a serious paper before learned men who had received him generously. In the Edinburgh addresses, as in his paintings, he had invented nothing. His story of the rattlesnake chasing the squirrel was too circumstantial to have been invented, but he had given his enemies a loophole by an unfortunate error. It was true that he had taken the story from rough notes in his journal, made at the end of the day of the episode, but he had probably written the word "snake" in haste throughout without designating the kind of snake. The address had been prepared in distress and confusion. Since rattlesnakes had loomed large in his experience he doubtless believed the snake in question was a rattlesnake. From the details which he so closely described the snake would seem to have been a blacksnake; and the blacksnake is known to vibrate its tail. If this strikes dry leaves the noise can easily be confused with that of a rattler.

As to the other questions time seems to have vindicated Audubon. The fangs of one species of rattlesnake have proved to be recurved, as he painted them with the mockingbirds. As to the rattlesnake's climbing habits he received, during the public furor, a large number of letters asserting that he was right. Abundant testimony was offered that rattlesnakes often climbed trees and fences. By what he regarded as a good authority he was given a sworn certificate, which he prized, declaring that a rattlesnake had been found twisted around the top of a mahogany bedpost in the chamber of a most venerable lady living in Florida.

As to the noses of vultures, he had probably first learned from the Osages that vultures rely upon their keen sight rather than upon the sense of smell to discover food, and a series of experiments later undertaken by some of his friends and by himself bore this out.

In England during all this warfare he was not left undefended. Admirers came forward, foremost among them Christopher North, who warmly praised the succeeding numbers of the "Birds," praised Audubon himself, and gave all his powerful influence toward his vindication. Gradually other support for his declarations has appeared. It was shown that the hummingbird fastens its nest to a twig by a salivary wafer which the rain does not melt. But it was only after Audubon's death that his lily, a rare one, was rediscovered.

These attacks were kept up for years. Audubon maintained a dignified silence. Privately he said, "Let those laugh who are winners!" Once he remarked he had received "a scrubby letter from Waterton." "Scrubby" was one of the most unpleasant epithets he could bestow unless it was to call an enemy a "beetle." Later, as the attacks continued he spoke to a friend about Waterton and Ord as "those beetles of darkness." Occasionally he called someone he disliked "a poor shoat." A few years later when Victor, then in England, wished to make a sharp answer to a new attack, he wrote, "Pay no regard to anything written against me. These things are mere vapors."

Even if he had wished to reply he was soon too deeply plunged into new labors to take time for such digressions. From the first he had planned a volume or set of volumes describing the habits of the birds pictured in his great plates; at intervals he had worked on these descriptions, drawing materials from his notes and journals. Now, while under attack, while still harnessed to the task of maintaining his subscription list, realizing as clearly as ever that he needed more paintings to complete his "Birds," he calmly expanded the plan for this text.

He realized that he needed assistance on the purely scientific side, in technical descriptions and classifications, though it is a mistake to say that Audubon had not learned the scientific names for his birds. His manuscript journals prove the contrary. Standing in bookstores, looking at scientific works wherever he could find them, he had copied classifications or had learned them by

ZENAIDA DOVE. *PLATE NO. CLXII*

heart. In his best days he had had a few scientific works of his own. But his text must be perfect! Besides, he wanted to free himself for other writing. He settled in Edinburgh with Lucy for a solid season, and engaged a gifted young naturalist named William MacGillivray to work with him on ornithological details.

The bulk of the writing he did himself for the "Ornithological Biography," and he pushed forward with his further plan, that of interspersing the scientific descriptions with small, clear adventures of his own in many a remote swamp or forest--his first sight of what he had thought to be a sea eagle at the Grand Tower in the Mississippi, that dark night in a Louisiana swamp, followed by a clear dawn when the wood thrush sang, his pleasure in the notes of the rose-breasted grosbeak on the way to Meadville. He was weaving with the accuracy of his observation the delight of years. And since his adventures among birds had been linked with many other adventures, he decided to scatter these wider narratives through the five volumes, calling them "Episodes." There were to be fifty-seven of these "Episodes."

To the sensible MacGillivray the scale of this work seemed nothing short of "imperial." He warned Audubon that his "Birds" might be only for the few, and that he was probably wrong in planning still another work which might find only a limited audience. Whom could he count for readers? The men of pure science might scoff at the story of Barro. Those who would enjoy his winter at the Great Bend of the Mississippi might care nothing for the nesting habits of hemlock warblers.

No matter! He had his idea—an idea as broad as the frontier—and he had never been balked by impossibilities. This was his book, and though he was not prepared to write it, much less to publish it, he plunged into both undertakings.

He had never mastered English; he had never even mastered French as a written language, but his journals show that he made new and rapid progress in the command of English when he undertook this new work. He was always frank enough in saying that MacGillivray helped him with matters of grammar, and Lucy, who copied the manuscript, almost certainly smoothed down some of his livelier expressions. The salty dash of the notes made in his journals was often lacking—more's the pity! But Audubon was bent upon the large scheme of things, quickly adapting himself to what he thought must be a suitable style and hurrying on. Manuscript piled up around him; the sheets were like the Mississippi in flood, he thought. He had learned that three editions of Wilson's "Ornithology" were to appear. "This only has a good effect on me," he said, and worked faster, determined to publish at least one volume of his own work before these came out. Rivalry with Wilson, which was none of his making, had dogged him all his life. Now he might as well grapple with it.

When his first volume was finished and he could find no publisher, he decided to launch the whole work himself, and did so, spending a substantial share of his surplus. Elated by the fine notices which the book immediately received, he made another decision. He was already well ahead with his manuscript. He gave the second volume to the printer and made preparations to go to America again.

The summer season at Great Egg Harbor and in the Great Pine Swamp had been only a whiff of what he had wanted. The last of the paintings which he thought good enough for the "Birds" would be reached within another year or two. MacGillivray and Havell could keep things going during his absence. Lucy, who would make the voyage with him, would visit their sons in Louisville. They sailed in August, 1831.

"I may yet come out at the broad end of the horn," Audubon wrote to a friend. "At all events I will *break it or make a spoon!*" The great horn spoon—the buffalo horn of the West, so hard to cut: he had slipped into the lingo of the frontier, and he meant to seek frontiers again, "away from white man's tracks and manners."

13 *Top and Bottom of a Continent*

A LONG white beach, a curving bay, an old fort at the scant little village of St. Augustine—Audubon was impatiently anchored there for weeks. "Little more in sight than the breaking sea surf in our front and orange groves in our rear," he wrote Lucy.

For a short time he had been able to plunge deeply into work. Drawing from nature once more acted upon him "like an electric fluid. . . . Last Sunday I certainly drew faster than ever I have done in my life." He spoke of "the fine flow of spirits I have." He had wanted particularly to study birds of the sea beaches and lagoons and mudflats—pelicans, plovers, terns, sandpipers. Many of these he had seen and painted during his stay in New Orleans, but he was dissatisfied with some of his portrayals and he meant to make others, to study seasonal changes in plumages, take notes on habits, and collect as many birdskins and rare shells as possible; he believed he could sell these when he returned to London.

With him was a young Swiss artist named George Lehman, whom he had met and liked during one of his visits to Pittsburgh. Audubon had always been interested in the American landscape as a painter's subject; he now decided that landscapes or water scenes would give variety to his work. In the midst of continual study he could not be certain of painting these; he employed Lehman, a landscape painter, to assist him with backgrounds, to make sketches, and to hunt with him. Another assistant, Henry Ward, was to prepare birdskins.

From accounts of travelers Audubon had supposed that Florida would be thronged with singing birds and bright with flowers; but he was well to the north, in the winter season; the weather was wet, cold, stormy, and he found the water and shore birds unaccountably shy. The *pill will willy* of the willet on the mud-flats sounded loudly, but procuring specimens was another matter. Crouching in sawgrass he watched stilts and yellowlegs, cranes, pelicans, curlews, and companies of wood ibises feeding in lagoons along the Indian River. Comical birds pleased him, like the little spotted sandpiper with its delicate teetering back and forth as if too elegant for its surroundings; the creole hunters in Louisiana had called it *chevalier de batture*, "gentleman of the shore." Gulls that looked like awkward but finely dressed dowagers when walking, rose and sailed against the sky in innumerable bold, beautiful outlines which he sketched. He painted a tall sandhill crane which he took for a young whooping or "hooping" crane, finding a posture that displayed the rich luminous gray feathers, the suggestion of a strong rapid gait, the stately curve of the back. Tirelessly he worked on studies of the great white heron and completed two of these, wholly different in pattern, equally bold in effect. In these first weeks he accomplished more than he was willing to say. He was impatient mainly because he wanted still wilder, stranger lands after the cramping efforts of years in cities.

The government schooner *Spark* was to take him up the St. Johns, but it had hardly entered the mouth of the river when a hurricane came up and the little ship lay to "like a duck." At daybreak the next morning thousands of snowy pelicans rose from the beaches as they made another start, and they found the shores of the river covered by Florida cormorants with green silky breasts and necks and tawny orange faces. Herons skimmed over the waters, the little green-black "fly-up-the-creek," the great blue, the black-crowned night heron. Water turkeys perched on the feathery tips of cypresses. Occasionally a Seminole would row out to them with fish or game to sell, and alligators slid into the water. These wild moss-hung shores had something he had hoped for.

Yet they offered him little about birds that he did not already know, and he was oppressed by the overhanging weight of what he had still to accomplish. Letters from London were constantly being forwarded to him; he had to consider questions of shipping, insurance, plans for the continuance of all his work, plans for joining Lucy. He couldn't hear from her often enough. "I am on thorns when without news of thee," he wrote. Ahead lay a projected voyage to the Keys for which he had been promised a government schooner, but the ship had failed to put in an appearance.

Up the St. Johns they met a party of "live-oakers," another of the many wandering bands of workers whom he had known. The "live-oakers" were woodsmen, coming down from the North for the winter season to cut timber in the monotonous labyrinth of the barrens. He heard their stories and from the river caught the song of Negro raftsmen–

> I pole dis raft way down de ribber
> O-h-o! O-oo-o! A-h-a! A-h-aa!
> De sharks and de sawfish make me shibber
> O-ho-o! O-ho-o! A-h-a! A-h-a!
> De fish hawk kotch'd a big fat mullet
> O-h-o! O-ho-o! A-h-a! A-h-a!
> But it found its way down de eagle's gullet
> O-ho-o! O-ho-o! A-ha! A-ha!

Notes on some of the adventures which he heard went into his journal to join the sketches of the "Ornithological Biography" and to enlarge his picture of American frontiers.

On the way back, following an ancient Seminole path with a dog, they encountered the sudden black vapor of a tempest which lay so thickly among the trees and hanging moss as to make it possible to see only a few steps ahead. The air was hot, breathless; lightning flashed and rain fell heavily, blindingly, and at last the dog, now their only guide, lay down and refused to move. Audubon got down on his hands and knees, found the trail with his hands, discovered that it branched off in several directions, chose the one which he thought to be right, and coaxed the dog to lead again. Pine trees that had been struck by lightning blazed high before them. They forded swollen streams in the dark, taking their chances against alligators. Suddenly the storm was over, the stars came out, they smelled the salt marshes and walked toward them "like pointers advancing on a covey of partridges," and at last saw the bright pinpoint of the St. Augustine lighthouse.

Still waiting for the schooner to the Keys, Audubon decided to visit one of the sugar plantations near the sources of the St. Johns which had been established in the back country by a few hardy settlers from Georgia and the Carolinas. In a skiff with Lehman and a pair of oarsmen he started on a skirmishing trip. "We meandered down a creek for about eleven miles." The sky was a rich blue, and they found sprays of fall grapes, rich colored marsh grass, high palms. When they reached that arm of the sea which is the Halifax they moved into a narrow shallow bay where the fish were so thick, he said, that they nearly obstructed the progress of the skiff. Finally they were grounded in mud, and had to spend the night on board. Stiff with cold the next morning, all hands had to get out and push in the midst of a northeaster; they were soon up to their waists; it took them more than two hours to traverse a few hundred yards to a salt marsh. When they scanned it for a way out they found that the nearest waterways had been blown empty by the wind. They had to leave the skiff and walk through mud for miles to a planter's house. During the brighter hours of the first day they had seen a colony of pelicans asleep in a mangrove tree, and Audubon was exultant; but his fingers slipped, for once his sure aim failed him, and he brought down only two of the "reverend sirs."

In a few days the party set out on another journey still deeper into the interior, following the old Camino Reale which the Spaniards had cut long before, now a faint trail. They saw only a few birds, which they knew. They reached rolling ground covered with live oaks, magnolias, red oaks, and passed clear small blue lakes framed in brilliant green; but this region—sweet to the eye—offered genuine pitfalls, for it was the home of armies of gophers who had undermined the ground. They had to lead their horses.

At a distant plantation they were shown a whirlpool of coppery water that cast up quantities of tiny shells as from subterranean regions. This spring poured into a broad cypress-bordered channel and then into a little lake, whose water, smelling of sulphur, was dark green. Audubon took a boat, and discovered that one lake led to another. He shot a pair of ibises which were new to him. Now at last he had a treasure! But the ibises tumbled into so deep and so muddy a hole that even he could not follow, and when he landed on a small island planted with orange trees whose fruit proved to be sour he felt that the fates were solidly set against him. "A garden," he said with unaccustomed bitterness, "where all that is not mud, mud, mud, is sand, sand, sand, where the fruit is so sour that it is not eatable, and where in the place of singing birds and golden fishes you have a species of ibis that you cannot get when you have shot it, and alligators, snakes, and scorpions!"

Back they went to St. Augustine and still the schooner failed to come. Coastwise vessels were infrequent; there was no other way that Audubon could make the trip to the Keys. These delays were grueling. It seemed that he might be stranded on this coast for years. He wrote to Havell about plates, to Lucy about everything. But in all this mixed turmoil and vacancy his letters to her were confident as to the ultimate future.

"My name is now ranging high and our name will stand still higher should I live through my present travels," he wrote her. "I have great confidence in what I have undertaken and am willing to follow all my plans to the last. I pray only for your health and comfort. Keep up a good heart, my Lucy—be gay, be happy." He still spoke of ascending the Arkansas to its headwaters in the summer months and of going on to the Rocky Mountains. "I cannot think of returning until my *journey* is completed, and with me it is *Neck* or *Nothing!*"

He added that his socks were wearing out. Socks, he must have more and more socks. Would Lucy knit them? Would she have them ready for him when he finally reached Louisiana? He also wanted a good partridge net "with long wings." And—"I long for thee every moment. It is such a comfort to speak to each other on all subjects and to have immediate answers when together."

In April, after four months, he had more than a thousand bird-skins, a large collection of rare Florida shells, a sheaf of new paintings and drawings—not as many as he had expected but still a comfortable number. And friends in Washington succeeded in having him picked up by the *Marion*, a revenue cutter headed for the Keys.

By smugglers and wreckers on the Florida coasts the *Marion* was called *The Lady of the Green Mantle*. Like a water witch rising from a fountain she would appear suddenly among the shoals and small green islands of the Keys to cast a spell upon their pursuits.

Men all over the world had learned long ago that the wealth of the Indies might be brought to their shores by the wreck of unwary ships. False lights were set near hidden shoals, and boats were kept in readiness to shove off for the cargo, but not for the passengers and crew. As the traffic of ships in the Carribean and through the Gulf had increased, the Florida Keys had made excellent hiding places from which to steal forth on such errands. Behind those palms had lurked captains and sailors who knew every shoal, with fast clippers which easily descended upon ships in distress; they would take off silks, tea, sugar, molasses, tobacco, cotton, and slide these into some sorry looking schooner which would idle its way to Mobile or Galveston or northward to some hidden port on the Atlantic, there to sell and unload the spoils.

Ships in the government service had succeeded in routing out most of these stealthy wreckers, preying on distress, who had their nests in the Keys. A miracle had in fact been accomplished. Wreckers could perform valuable services in these bright treacherous waters, where almost any ship might be driven suddenly upon shoals by a hurricane. They could be life savers, salvaging cargoes instead of stealing them. They still kept their old piratical name, but they now were licensed. It was the business of *The Lady of the Green Mantle* and of others like her to make sure that no unlicensed ships or men plied this trade.

As *The Lady* neared the Indian Key Audubon's discouragement vanished. Here at last was the magical strange world on an outermost boundary which he had hoped to discover. The great coral reef beneath the blue waters seemed to him like a wall reared by an army of giants, and the Key was covered by brilliant flowers, plants with strange leaf-forms, palms and mangroves and sea-grapes. The shallow lagoons were purple, gold. In the deeper waters were parrot fish, changing bright green and blue, yellow angel fish with feathery plumes, butterfly fish, sea anemones, sea cucumbers. He never ceased to marvel at the numbers of birds, thousands upon thousands on every shore. For a moment they all seemed unknown to him.

He had hardly landed when a small boat was put at his disposal with a pilot and some fishermen who knew these waters. They skirted the shore of Indian Key and were off to one of smaller, wilder islets where they found multitudes of flamingoes, egrets, white herons, pelicans, and a little city of Florida cormorants. "The air was darkened by whistling wings." The shelly beaches were covered by birds. Purple herons flew up swiftly, and nests of the white ibis showed among gray cactuses. Rose-colored curlews stalked gracefully beneath the spreading mangroves. Florida gallinules floated and dived, and a frigate pelican chased a jaeger that had just robbed a gull of its prize. The pilot, who had been a conch diver, stripped and searched the bottom for curious shells. Audubon declared that "he knew the Keys and the waters about them the way some dandies know what's in their pockets."

Back before sunset on Indian Key he set up his drawing materials in the pilot's house and began outlining some of the new birds, working through the long evening without interruption even though the sailors had a dance in the next room and though screeching tunes were played on fiddles strung with silk instead of catgut. He swung himself for the night in a hammock under the eaves of the piazza and was up before sunrise for another expedition, and out on the water when the sun came up.

"A gentle sea breeze glided over the flowery isle, the long

breakers rushed over distant reefs. As we proceeded toward some distant Keys seldom visited by men, the sun rose from the waters in a burst of glory, the waters shone in tremulous smoothness, and the deep blue of the heavens was as pure as the world that lies beyond them. A heron flew heavily toward the land like a glutton with well-lined paunch retiring at daybreak from the house of some wealthy patron. Gulls and terns gamboled over the water."

Many such days followed, as *The Lady* went about these waters on her affairs. On a distant Key he watched Zenaida doves feeding on grass seeds and the leaves of aromatic plants, and listened to their soft, shy notes, and made studies which showed the tawny rose and blue, with something formal in their grace. On the mudflats, hunting shells and crabs, he saw crowds of birds walking, fluttering, flying inshore, driven by the tide, driven too by a knowledge which even Audubon's skillful pilot did not have. A little later when the tide was in and they had started back to Indian Key and were drawing toward a tiny islet where the pilot knew flamingo nests could be found, the bright light of day was suddenly gone; a black cloud had covered the sun. "We're going to get it," cried the pilot. The sails were quickly reefed. Sharp yellow lightning flashed and flashed again. A pair of night hawks whirling through the air were struck and fell into the sea. "A furious cloud now approached," Audubon wrote later, "like an eagle with outstretched wings in haste to destroy us."

SANDHILL CRANE. *PLATE NO. CCLXI*

"Sit still," said the pilot calmly. "I don't want to lose any of you overboard. The boat can't upset if you will sit still. Here we have it!" The boat shivered. In an instant she was blown ashore.

Audubon and the crew, crouched in a wind-blown thicket, watched huge waves drifting fast and the mangroves bending their tops to their roots. Wild scattered flocks of belated gulls and terns were driven into the sea or beaten down upon the shore. Masses of green water flew toward the little group of men striking them blow after blow, circling away in tossed waves.

In half an hour the storm was over, the sky was pure blue again. Only the tattered gray of leaves, broken branches, and the strewn bodies of birds showed the weight of the storm.

When *The Lady* went to the Tortugas, Audubon went with her. Bales of cotton were floating in the coves of the Keys far out on the Gulf, and beyond a palm-covered reef was the dismantled hull of a ship which had been driven there by the hurricane. A strange vessel came toward them, leaping "like a dolphin in eager pursuit of its prey." "How trim," thought Audubon, "how clean-rigged! She swims like a duck!" She came closer, rolling, dancing, tumbling, until her copper sheathing glittered in the sun. She was a Florida wrecker, and after an exchange of news with *The Lady* she slid away again. At the Tortugas more wreckers were anchored.

Audubon had expected to see them manned by black-whiskered piratical fellows in ragged shirts with cutlasses, but they were hearty Yankee sailors. The captain of one of the ships had long been a collector of birds' eggs, and he begged Audubon to accept his whole collection, with some rare marine shells. The mate of another ship thought his visit to the Tortugas in search of birds "rather a curious fancy," but invited him on board for an excellent meal. The next day he went with some of the officers to Booby Island.

By way of a frolic a pair of boats raced, and Audubon found that these sailors knew more about noddies and boobies than nine-tenths of the naturalists he had met. Like woodsmen and boatmen they had their songs—

> When daylight comes a ship's on shore
> Among the rocks where the breakers roar.
>
> When daylight dawns we're under way,
> And every sail is set,
> And if the wind it should prove light,
> Why, then our sails we wet.
>
> To gain her first each eager strives
> To save the cargo and the people's lives,
> Amongst the rocks where the breakers roar,
> The wreckers on the Florida shore.

Another day they took him on a search for marine shells. Stripped, up to their waists, they would suddenly tip downward into the smooth water like feeding ducks and come up with a smooth pink spiral or clusters of ivory white grotesques, or purple or red wedge shells. Sea grass, sponges, sea feathers, corals —he had a great harvest of all these for sketches or notes, or to carry away.

The motion of the wary hawk-billed turtles reminded him of that of a bird, so easily, swiftly did they move over the shelly beaches, and he made a drawing of one of them; he would willingly have spent days on the subject of turtles—green turtles, trunk turtles, the great loggerheads, which often weighed nearly half a ton. It took the strength of several men to upset them. The wreckers would swim up to them as they lay asleep on the surface of the water and turn them over, when they could be secured if a boat was at hand. Their flesh as well as their eggs was greatly relished.

In the end Audubon could not resist devoting some days to turtles and turtlers, hunting for eggs, watching the men stalk their strange big prey, jotting down what he could learn and adding the whole picture to the wide-flung "Episodes" with which he was portraying many frontiers in his "Ornithological Biography."

Though he was feeling the pressure of time he still could take these days as he had always taken his adventures, with an easy spaciousness. Even now, his special ambition did not claim him altogether. The strange growth of the lofty mangroves—he could have spent days drawing them, with their arched red roots beneath the water and aerial branches streaming downward to make fast and join the contorted net where colored fishes swam. He explored the jungles of tamarind and bamboo and satinwood, looking for snowy herons' nests but pausing over whatever exquisite bending branch or cluster of sawgrass or custard bushes pleased him.

Out of this long-delayed journey, perhaps even from his tedious wait in St. Augustine, came something more than further paintings for his "Birds" or even notes for more extended writings. He had recaptured something of his youthful delight in the whole natural world, and with this sharpened awareness came a fresh expression of his genius. What he had known of watery shores took a heightened form. Light occupied him more than heretofore. The soft watery light from a wet beach was reflected on the soft pale breast, the tips of wings, the head of the red-backed sandpiper. Light gave transparency to his snowy herons, and shone on the green silky breast and neck, the deep rusty feathers of his Florida cormorant.

But he could not linger; when the work of *The Lady* was finished he was obliged to leave the Keys. On his way north he stopped at Savannah to seek subscribers, gained six new names, and traveled to Charleston by coach. He was brown as a Seminole with the comical beard like a pirate's which he had often worn before—a beard now "as gray as a badger's," his new friend John Bachman said. "A grizzly bear might have claimed him as a brother when he leapt down from the top of the coach."

In Charleston he received a hearty welcome. On the way down he had halted there to seek out subscribers; his stay had lengthened because he was obliged to make the trip to St. Augustine in a government cutter, and this had been delayed. He had met Bachman, a minister and a naturalist, and the two at once had become fast friends. Bachman called him "Old Jostle," and when the two were not hunting or studying birds, they played chess.

"Mr. Bachman!! Why, my Lucy, Mr. Bachman would have us all to stay at his house—he would have us make free there as if we were at our own encampment at the head waters of some unknown rivers—he would not suffer us to proceed farther south for three weeks—he talked—he looked as if his heart had been purposely made of the most benevolent materials granted to man by the Creator to render all about him most happy— Could I have refused his kind invitation? No!—It would have pained him as much as if grossly insulted. We removed to his house in a crack—found a room already for Henry to skin our birds—another for me & Lehman to draw in and a third for thy husband to rest his bones in on an excellent bed! An amiable wife and sister-in-law, two fine young daughters and three pairs more of cherubs, all of whom I already look upon as if brought up among them.

"Out shooting every day—skinning, drawing, talking ornithology the whole evening, noon, and morning." He next had written of hunting shells with Dr. Ravenel. "Dr. R. a great conchologist and *will* give me a fine mess of shells." He wanted Victor to send a box of Ohio shells as soon as possible which he would give this benefactor in return.

On his journey north from the Keys he was tempted to remain among these congenial friends, but more than nine months had passed since he had left England, and the broad scope of the continent still lay before him. He went on to Washington almost at once, hoping for government support of an expedition to the Rockies, but he was disappointed. He could not finance this himself with all the necessary guides, runners, and assistants. Well, he would go far north along the Atlantic, seeking the nesting places of birds he had known in Louisiana or Florida in winter, and perhaps finding new species.

Audubon had long had the hope of bringing his family together. From St. Augustine he had written to Lucy, "I feel fully decided that we should all go to Europe together and work as if an established partnership for life consisting of husband, wife, and children." Now they all met and went to Boston, where Audubon received so discerning and hearty an appreciation of his work that they were all cheered, and finally took a holiday, setting off by carriage and coach along the coast of Maine to Eastport; there the boys—now young men—helped Audubon scour the woods for birds, and he made a number of new drawings. They even went up the St. John in New Brunswick, towed in a flatboat by mules. Only a few late birds were seen, for autumn had come; the trip remained a pleasure jaunt, though Audubon managed to collect material for added "Episodes" on this northern frontier, about lumbermen in Maine, log jams, booms, and moose hunting along the lakes.

Back in Boston he worked so hard painting a fine specimen of the golden eagle that he fell into a severe illness. When he recovered the family partnership began in earnest. Victor went to England with a sheaf of the new bird paintings and was to supervise the further engraving of the plates, assuming the routine of business details at the same time. Audubon now planned a trip to Labrador on which John was to accompany him as assistant. "I hope to return with such a cargo as I brought from the Floridas—I mean in bulk and novelty," he said. "If God grants us success and a safe return no man living will be able to compete with me in knowledge of the birds of our country."

At Eastport he encountered the familiar experience of delays. It was now more than a year since he had left the Keys. But at last they were off in the *Ripley*, a small schooner which he had chartered, with an eager company of four other young men interested in natural science.

The voyage was hard. The schooner was obliged to beat off to sea in order to avoid the broken rocky Canadian coast. The small ship was crowded by the party and all their gear for hunting, drawing, preparing birdskins, and camping. When the weather permitted Audubon was up at an early hour—and routed John out—to work on paintings of birds he had seen at Grand Manan on an excursion he had managed to take while waiting at Eastport. The space was cramped, in an open pit under the main hatch, but the light was fair, and he could not keep from working.

At the Magdalen Islands they saw Bird Rock, which seemed covered with snow and ice, but this white covering lifted and was shattered and broke into clouds and spirals of flying gannets as they drew near. Thirteen days out they neared the mouth of the Natashquan, where they were met by a whirl of foolish guillemots "rising like spirits," and the *Ripley* was anchored well inside a small bay.

They had found a land where there was "not one square foot of *earth*," Audubon declared; all was rock. He thought the trees were "like small wiry mops." But he was positively charmed by the "wonderful dreariness" of the country, with mossy gray-clad rocks heaped and thrown together in huge masses, bays without end sprinkled with thousands of rocky inlets, and wild birds everywhere. "The peculiar cast of the uncertain sky"—gray and lowering—was a strange delight, "with butterflies flitting over snowbanks, and probing the flowerets of many hues which push their tender stems through thick beds of moss."

In the morasses he plunged with John and his young companions up to the knees; every step was hard going over a spongy moss where the feet sank as into a deep cushion and had to be pulled out again. Thickly growing scrubby bushes intercepted them. But they found fresh water lakes where red and black divers swam, and eider ducks, and little ring plovers. Snow larks were here, which he had sometimes seen in Kentucky on their brief migrations south, and the Lapland lark buntings that had been casual visitors, and the little winter wrens that spend more than half the year in travel from the far north to Louisiana and Florida, that live shyly, and have a song of fine cadences and unwearied strength. He found the bay-breasted warbler which he had known only briefly in migration. This bleak country was full of warblers.

The ship moved from harbor to rocky harbor along the Labrabor coast, making hard roundabout trips into open water since the captain did not know the narrow waterways among the rocky islands. On shore they encountered trappers, fishermen, seal-catchers, whalers, Indians, "eggers," who despoiled the nests of the game birds; Audubon made notes of everything he saw, filling pages for more "Episodes," and working steadily at his drawing table though it was often so cold that he couldn't hold his pencil in his fingers.

"The fact is," he mourned, "I am growing old too fast. Alas! I feel it." But he was able to tire the five young men of his company on the hunt any day and to work at his drawings out of doors from fourteen to seventeen hours almost without a break, often in the midst of dirty weather and an east wind. He kept them all enlivened by his flute. He felt the burden of advancing age mainly because he found that he could no longer sleep in wet clothes as he had done, when he chose, all his life.

Rain, driven in sheets, sometimes stopped his work. "No, I cannot call it rain, it is a thick cloud of water." He worked on his drawings incessantly by candlelight, saving daylight for the coloring. He had caught the richness of tone belonging to this strange landscape, which seemed so dull to the casual view; his work took on a somber brilliance which it had not had before.

He painted puffins, a cock ptarmigan, a razor-billed auk, and was gay when he could draw three young shore larks, "the first young shore larks ever portrayed by man!" With unflagging ambition he chose difficult subjects, such as eider ducks in fluttering action. He made a superb simple painting of the large-billed guillemot, blacks and whites and grays against a white background, dwelling only upon the firm markings, the beautiful taut lines of breast and wing and back. His red-throated loons made one of his finest works, sure and clear among rushes on green water, exquisite yet bold, with the gray stripes and mottlings, the long necks and sharp beaks, all handsomely brought together. And as if he wished to prove that he could return at will to the leafy delicate patterns on which he had first lavished his gifts, he made a few paintings of that order, among them a portrayal of Hudson Bay titmice in lacy sprays of pale gray-green leaves and small red berries, with the gray-brown and white birds lightly placed and subtly shaded.

He was still responsive to fresh arrangements, new clear tones, though he was pressed by a sense of obligation and might have sunk into mere repetition or routine. He still possessed that many-sided responsiveness which had always made him more than the artist or the ornithologist. The young men of his company became his devoted friends. In spite of hard hunting and his many hours at the drawing board, in spite of the bending dark sky and the inconveniences of a crowded life on a small ship, the voyage went with a broad flourish. He had completed twenty-three new paintings of birds, had seen nearly a hundred species, and brought back a wealth of fine birdskins and a large collection of plants. But he was delighted to hear crickets again when they reached Nova Scotia on the way back, and to catch in the dampness of a summer evening the fresh odor of newly cut hay.

14 *The Making of an Epic*

CHRISTOPHER NORTH, alone by the fire, heard a bold knocking at his door.

"Not loud but resolute," he thought. "The man may be expecting to see my nightcap, which I never wear, popped out the window. No doubt he believes I will scold him for breaking my slumbers."

He lay back in his easy chair and began pondering the affairs of the nation. The knocking continued, followed by the "rustling thrill" of the bell-wire and a tinkling far below. "That is the fist of a friend," he decided, and gathering his slippered feet off the rug he took a lamp in hand and stalked down the stairs and through the halls to the door, which he unlocked, unbarred, unchained. A tall figure in a great furry cloak stepped inside, held out both hands, and blessed him with a strong French accent.

"Audubon! My dear friend Audubon—fresh from the Floridas and breathing the pure air of Labrador!" cried North gustily.

Three years earlier these two had said farewell on the same spot, at the same hour. There were few men in Britain whom Audubon had found so congenial as John Wilson who masqueraded under the name of Christopher North, the author of "Noctes Ambrosianae" and editor of "Blackwood's." It was not only that North had been one of his strongest supporters or even that North was a naturalist; he liked the man. "He is as free from the detestable stiffness of ceremonies as I am when I can help myself," he wrote in his journal. "No cravat, no waistcoat, but a fine *frill* of his own profuse beard, his hair flowing uncontrolled, and his speech dashing at once at the subject in view—that is Christopher North."

Coals were heaped on the grate. The bright brass kettle began to sing, and a hundred Scotch oysters—North said there were a hundred—turned languishing eyes at the pair of friends. A Scotch grace was said, and one by one the oysters began to disappear, slowly since they were greatly relished.

"You've never looked better," said Audubon. "The eagle is renewing his youth." North's eyes had always seemed to him like those of the eagle he had first seen at the Grand Tower in the Mississippi.

"I know bold bright birds of passage that wing their way through worlds," North answered.

"But I can see the crow's-feet in the corners of our eyes more plainly than when we parted." Audubon pretended to be sad about it.

"I will not deny that I find in you an image of the white-headed falcon. The top of your head is brown but the lower parts—you must admit it!—are fringed with gray or white."

"My dear friend, I know I am an old bird. But that is not the description of him in my first volume!"

Each speared another oyster, and North lifted a bottle. "This," he declared, "is the mildest, the meekest, the very Moses of ales. Down each of our gullets it shall graciously descend with a gurgle!"

The fire blazed higher and the long night was spent in talk, as Audubon related his newest adventures and told stories of men he had lately met "in this boisterous world of ours."

"It was quite a *noctes*," said North. "Ambrosial!"

Perhaps Audubon did explain how boisterous the world had been for him during these last months. After his expedition to Labrador he had gone to Philadelphia, and had been arrested for debt; his failure at Henderson still haunted him though he was legally free of it. Friends came to his assistance, and the charge was lifted, but the experience was humiliating, and he had not been able to complete the further journeys he had planned for lack of money. Washington Irving and others had tried to obtain government support of the trip he had long hoped to take to the Rockies but nothing had come of this. He wanted to stay in America for further study and painting. "After another year," he wrote Victor, "I could go to London full-headed and full-handed." But the Labrador trip had proved expensive, and he dared not dip deeper into his funds.

Back in London with his harvest of rare birdskins from Florida and Labrador, he found the market for these glutted; everyone seemed to have American birdskins to sell; prices had fallen to almost nothing. And a fickle public now seemed absorbed in stones, or beetles. "The world is all agog—for what?" he wrote Bachman. "For *bugs* the size of *watermelons!* Two hundred and fifty dollars for a beetle—as large as my fist, it is true, yet nought but a beetle after all. I almost wish I could be turned into a *beetle* myself! I fear the world will cease to think that such beings as birds exist under Heaven's canopy."

"Friend Bachman" for one was not permitted to forget that birds existed. Audubon, at work on his "Ornithological Biography," constantly urged him to send fresh notes. "Study our *dear herons* as much as you can," he commanded. "Write what you know of the whooping crane, kildeer, plover, wood ibis, yellow-breasted rail, great and least terns, dabchicks, grebe, solitary sandpipers, sandwich terns, roseate terns, long-billed curlews, pied oyster catchers—send me several skins!" He urged Bachman to hunt and to climb trees for nests and eggs, to spend as many hours as he could in the woods, and to send him specimens pickled in spirits. "Go to the woods and to the shores! Take your gun at all your leisure hours. Have barrels, or jars, or gallipots prepared of all sorts and sizes, and then have them filled to the brim with common whiskey or rum." He wanted specimens to verify certain of his measurements; with MacGillivray he would examine bony structures.

And would his friend kindly raise a pair of anhingas for him which could be sent later? "Anhingas are very easily raised when taken young," he insisted. "They feed on all sorts of small fry and even eat corn meal mush!" He declared that he had once seen a pair raised by some squatters in a remote part of Mississippi—fine anhingas! "And birds' eggs! birds' eggs!! I long for. Don't mind the expense." And Bachman could set to work some of the officers on the revenue cutters which frequently came into Charleston harbor. Surely they would hunt birds' eggs.

"Do, my friend, exert yourself kindly for me as soon as you get this letter. Write to many of your friends in the country—spur them up on the sea islands, beg the collector of the custom house to assist you. I am growing old fast and must work at a double-quick time now. You will see that though old I am as ardent as ever in my life if not more so."

He was asking for heavy contributions, but they were no more than he himself would freely have given to friends, hardly more than his barrel of Ohio River shells, the thousand insects, the exquisite birdskins which he had brought to England as gifts. On this last trip he had even transported a few live raccoons and some

SWAINSON'S WARBLER. *PLATE NO. CXCVIII*

painted finches, mockingbirds, and grosbeaks because his friends had asked for them, though he still disliked to see birds and animals in cages. And he now sent Bachman a pointer of the "finest English blood."

"Yours up to the hub!" he signed himself.

A printer's devil was constantly at his elbow, and he was never satisfied with what he had written. The "Episodes" were all done in haste and he considered them only "so so." The information about birds in these volumes he regarded as "pretty fair." His expenses were still heavy, and he had upon him again the dull labor of coaxing subscribers, but he was exhilarated when new plates came from Havell, whose work, he thought, had grown steadily finer.

The engraving and coloring of the water scenes for his new water and shore birds enchanted him. As for the plate showing his crow, "I am delighted. Never was a *crow* represented in print before now!" He scrutinized every detail. "Have the edges of the little grouse softened," he wrote Havell after seeing one of the first of these plates, explaining that the outer primary should be pure white instead of a dirty white as in his own painting, whose tone had changed as result of poor colors. And "the little black-capped titmouse is not dark enough on the back, and in my drawing there must be *a white spot at the lower end of the black cap* near the shoulders."

He begged Havell to take special care with the plate of the great white heron. When the first plate arrived a month later,

"*The bird* is perfect!" he wrote, but he asked for changes in the background. "The terminations of the darker portions of the sky are too harsh, and I should like you to have these extremities or *outer edges* SCRAPED and the purplish tint about those parts rendered darker by the colorer. Subdue the little figures in the distance somewhat."

In the midst of other labors he worked at his main task, to complete his paintings of new birds from the sketches he had made on his expeditions. "What do you think!" he wrote Bachman at the end of a year. "I have positively finished thirty-three drawings of birds!" He was exhilarated, then cast into the depths. Sometimes he feared he might not live to complete all his undertakings. Then he would proclaim his courage, even with a touch of bravado. "Should death stare me in the face I shall laugh at her, as being quite too late to hurt *my feelings!!* I shall go on to the last just as I began, and my work shall be not a *beacon* but a tremendous *lighthouse!*" Evidently someone had referred to it as a beacon, which he thought an insufficient comparison. "My work, I feel assured, will be a standard for ages to come, for I feel certain that with the exception of some few errors, the truths and facts contained in my writings and in my figures of birds will become more apparent to every student of nature *out* of his *closet!*"

Again the months spun out; a year passed, and more than half of another. Early in 1836 he began to see that completion was in sight for his great "Birds." Three volumes had been published, containing more than three hundred plates. "The *first number* of the *last* volume of the 'Birds of America' is now under the graver, and my friend Robert Havell tells me that unless I keep him back, the enormous work will be finished and complete in twenty-two months from this date!!" he wrote to Bachman. "How delicious is the idea, and how comfortable should I feel at this moment were I able fully to say to Havell *you shall not be detained a moment!*"

He knew that these last stages would not be easy. Certain birds must still be found, and he must achieve the balance and the scale which he had first planned—the scale of the American continent. Again he must cross the Atlantic—"go, and ransack the wildest portions of our southern country." With John as an assistant to help in preparing skins and with sketching he would "take a tremendous concluding journey, the Lord knows where—but I shall certainly go to the Everglades of Florida, then to the mouth of the Sabine—and up into the broad prairies. I love the prairies!" And he still hoped to visit the Rockies.

With John he sailed in August, 1836, and not long after he landed had a great stroke of luck. He wrote to Bachman in excitement, "Now, good friend, open your eyes! Aye, open them tight!! Nay, place specs on your proboscis if you choose. Read aloud!! Quite aloud!!! I have purchased *ninety-three birdskins!* Nought less than ninety-three birdskins sent from the Rocky Mountains and the Columbia River by Nuttall and Townsend! Yes, ninety-three birdskins—cheap as dirt too—only $184 for the whole of them, and hang me if you do not echo my saying so when *you see them!!* Such beauties! Such varieties! Such novelties! Ah, my friend, how we will laugh and talk over them! So do you see how lucky the old man is yet!"

He had encountered delays and difficulties in attempting to make the purchase, but he had been "wrapt up" in the desire to see these skins since the trip to the Rockies was uncertain; from them he could extend his descriptions and perhaps his paintings. Nuttall and Townsend were also to furnish him with notes on habitats. He confided in Bachman what may have been the truth, that he had obtained the skins because he was thought "a—a—a—(I dislike to write it but here goes) a Great Naturalist!!! That's all! Oh! what a strange world we do live in!" He was sure that it was his reputation rather than his ability which had tipped the scales, but in any event he now had the birds, and he went almost at once to Bachman's home in Charleston to work on them while his applications were pending in Washington for assistance on the ambitious journeys he still hoped to make.

The expedition to the Everglades had to be abandoned because the Seminoles had begun their final warfare with the United States. Again nothing came of the expedition to the Rockies, but he at last received the promise of a government cutter which would take his party to the coast of Texas. Edward Harris was to join the party, who had befriended him long ago in Philadelphia when he had come there from Louisiana unknown. After waiting at Charleston for the cutter they went overland to Mobile where they waited again.

But there were no blank spaces in Audubon's life: in these months of disheartening delay he packed more observation than many men would have achieved in a long period of deliberate study, and as always, he saw far more than birds. He watched the miraculous beauty of changing light and color over the marsh grasses and waters of Mobile Bay. He found time to write a few bitter, brilliantly descriptive pages in his journal on the plight of the Creeks, numbers of whom he saw in irons in the city, on their way to the new lands of the West to which they were being unjustly exiled. And at last, after a visit to Pensacola and many more weeks of waiting, he sailed with his party from New Orleans in April, 1837, in a government cutter, the *Campbell*, whose captain proved to be Napoleon Coste, commander of the *Marion* on Audubon's voyage to the Florida Keys. They were accompanied part of the way by another cutter, painted black like a pirate. The long delays were forgotten. Audubon was once more in the highest spirits.

Slowly they cruised in and out of the wide-mouthed bayous of southern Louisiana, where he fell into his old ways, taking a skiff or a pirogue to explore hidden channels. The time was auspicious, that of the great spring migrations, and he was able to watch old favorites in new ways, fill out his notes, and consider changing plumages. They followed the Texas shore and ranged over Galveston island where the pirate Lafitte had found a final hiding place, and watched terns and noddies and laughing gulls along its narrow beaches. In Barataria Bay they came upon Audubon's old favorites, the brown pelicans, and were able to observe the feeding habits of many shore and water birds. Inland the many-colored Texas spring had come, and little clouds of warblers, flycatchers, larks, buntings, were in the air. He was enchanted by the fork-tailed flycatcher, so awkward on the ground, so graceful on the wing, and sketched a pair in the midst of the white flowers of the loblolly bay.

"Mr. Audubon makes no more of tracking it in all directions than a shot star does in crossing the heavens," an acquaintance had said of him. It seemed inevitable that he should have come to this far frontier at a significant time. The Alamo had fallen the year before; the battle of San Jacinto had been fought. At the new muddy little capital of Houston he met Sam Houston, and wrote a short sketch from which the man emerges without embellishments—anxious, tired, angry, forced into a false pomp, disliking his tawdry regalia. As the party traveled inland Audubon talked with Texan soldiers, Mexican prisoners, Indians, squatters, planters, and heard their stories. Once they had a rough encounter with surly planters. A group came up to them with guns, believing that they were a set of rascals who had been plundering fields and stables in this region; the piratical-looking cutter offshore perhaps had given them the idea, though Audubon thought their appearance was enough: unshaven and plastered with mud up to their thighs, he said they looked like a crew of freebooters.

But they convinced the Texans of their innocence and they went back to the ship laden with gifts of fresh butter and eggs.

The journey was of the sort that Audubon liked best; he was not seeking birds alone but discovering new landscapes, new flower forms, meeting lone adventurers in a country still only lightly brushed by civilization. The time had passed when he could expect to find many rarities among birds; he now knew them as no other American naturalist had known them. On these fresh watery shores, on the rich wide plains as he followed the Sabine, he was able to complete many useful pieces of scientific observation, discovering ducks which had been thought to breed only in the North, localizing birds whose habitat in Texas had not yet been determined, procuring eggs which he needed for some of his descriptions. If he had discovered no new species, he could write, "I feel myself now tolerably competent to give an essay on the geographical distribution of the birds of America." That wide spread of observation which he had always coveted seemed fairly achieved.

By slow stages he traveled east, stayed again with the Bachmans for a short time in Charleston and reached New York in midsummer of 1837 to face the full force of the great panic of that year. "Scarcely a dollar in silver is in circulation," he wrote with dismay. "Business of all descriptions is at a stand. Money is scarcer with me than I anticipated. No money, no credit, no likelihood of new subscribers." Not only that: many American subscribers withdrew, and he learned on returning to England that the financial disaster in the United States had had its reverberations there and that his list was badly cut.

The slavish work of painting in oils was resumed again in London, now with the assistance of John, who was becoming a successful portrait painter, sometimes with as many as five sitters a day. But John felt obliged to keep his prices low since his reputation was not established. Money was not abundant for any of them. Audubon was badly pressed because he had lent money to friends who were now not in a position to repay him. He kept all his mills grinding at once, painting small oils, completing his paintings of birds for the great work, writing the accounts for his "Ornithological Biography" and the last of the fifty-seven "Episodes."

At least, in the midst of new anxieties, the partnership within his own family of which he had once written Lucy had come about. Victor, who was also gifted as a portrait painter, worked with John and managed most of the financial details of publication. John had married one of Friend Bachman's daughters, of whom Audubon had become particularly fond during his visits in Charleston. This made a measure of happiness, though they were all oppressed, though none of them had leisure for its full realization. For the first time in fifteen or more years the family was living together.

Audubon was so deeply occupied that he could sit only in the evening, by gaslight, for a portrait by Healy. This painter spoke afterward of his eyes—"the most piercing eyes I ever saw—real eagle eyes." The painting shows him seated beside a table and resting his head against his hand. The whole posture is that of a tired man, yet the head has the characteristic lift; the glance seems to encompass the scene. The two seem to have talked little, but Healy recalled in later years that Audubon spoke of Lucy and said that "the only real happiness is a good marriage."

Panic or no panic, Audubon meant to finish all the paintings he had planned. When he learned that Townsend had come back from a second expedition to the West he was enviously stirred. "*I* may yet ransack the country," he cried. His friend Edward Harris promptly secured from Townsend many new birdskins and notes for him. As soon as these arrived he plunged into work on them with fresh ardor. "What!" he wrote, "shall the last volume of the 'Birds of America' be closed when new species are here in my hands?" Every American bird known to man must be included.

He worked, he was restless, he paced the streets of London for his accustomed walks, and was well remembered, a tall figure with hair that was now almost white. Some observers thought his eyes were angry, as if this long confinement in cities had been too much for him. The number of his plates was greatly exceeding that named in his original prospectus, and some of his subscribers were protesting. No matter! He persuaded them of the importance of this final work.

At last, in June, 1838, twelve years after he had set out from Louisiana, the last print of the great "Birds of America" was engraved and colored. Nearly five hundred species were represented, more than a thousand birds. Audubon never obtained the three hundred subscribers for whom he had hoped at the beginning. Not more than two hundred complete sets of the "Birds" were published; but with all the changes and disasters and interruptions in the course of these years, this represented an almost miraculous achievement. In the history of publishing the "Birds" was a landmark that has hardly been passed, and he completed the stout five volumes of his "Ornithological Biography" at almost the same time.

Perhaps he felt a wry humor in this achievement. His failure at Henderson had weighed so heavily upon him that he must have drawn the inevitable conclusion. He who had been called impractical, careless, without order in his ideas or his affairs, had completed an undertaking which was, among other things, a triumph of steady business management. Apparently aimless, he had kept a consistent aim, and had kept it without narrowness.

His "Ornithological Biography" was a partial measure of his scope. The frontier had been described by many naturalists, some of whom were artists; and a few, Le Sueur particularly, had recorded the look of people and places in ephemeral sketches. But who had thought of giving the life history of birds against the background of the wilderness and of men's life there? Audubon had drawn in words a wide picture of the scene from the Alleghenies to the Mississippi, from Cumberland Gap to the bayous of Louisiana, peopling this not only with birds but with animals, evoking the look of plants and trees, picturing something of the life of the Indian, portraying that strange species, the frontiersman, so many-sided and in the end so hard to know.

This immense study was imperfect because in it he was breaking new ground for the first time, because these volumes were done in haste, because he lacked time to learn the many disciplines of the writer. To the end he was unsure of his own strong, thrusting manner of speech and glossed this over or let others do so. But he created one of the most beautiful of all our descriptions of the Ohio as he saw it when he floated with Lucy in a skiff to Henderson in autumn weather. In his portrayal of the long wintry season at the Great Bend and the labors of the crew in moving the keelboat to Ste. Geneviève he revealed a rustic, heroic energy which has sometimes been called Greek; and his lesser pieces are full of unforgettable glimpses.

These narratives could never have been complete. No one knew better than Audubon how fragmentary were the records of that early life when men were pitting themselves against the wilderness. But the panorama remains, in the epical scale, achieved early in a period when the spirit of the epic was beginning to shape itself in this country in cycles of legends about the frontier, already centering upon such characters as Boone and Crockett, and reaching literary fruition two decades later in the work of Whitman and Melville and lesser others. Audubon's mode, like Whitman's, was largely personal; within this he communicated an immense zest. What he revealed, what he so amply experienced, was a way of living in the broad natural world, accepting its beauty, its ugliness, its savagery and destruction, enjoying the five senses to the full. Perhaps it was the element of pleasure, almost imperially accepted and expressed, which his enemies could not forgive.

During these years of final work on the "Birds" attacks had continued. James Hall complained of these personal narratives as intrusions. Ending a diatribe in the "Western Monthly" for May, 1834, he spoke of Audubon's talents as a painter, but he meant that he was nothing of an ornithologist. From Dunlap, the leading American critic of the arts at this time, he received only sneers. Dunlap mentioned "Mr. Audubon's account of himself, which may be considered as that of a friend." Well, some men are friends of their genius, some make war upon it. Audubon's relation happened to be that of a friend.

Probably neither Dunlap nor any other critic of this period at home or abroad could have measured him as an artist, even when the full abundance of his work had appeared. Science then seemed to belong to a separate compartment of knowledge, far removed from art, even at an opposite pole; and Audubon was like the men of the Middle Ages who were unaware of such divisions, who were skilled in the handicrafts as well as in the arts, who could consider and use the science of their day. He was as far removed from the artists of the studios in Philadelphia, New York, London, and Paris as he was from the museum naturalists. He had rarely had a studio, and his continual work out of doors or

RED-AND-BLACK-SHOULDERED MARSH BLACKBIRD. *PLATE NO. CCCCXX*

from nature must have seemed to them an affectation or an eccentricity. He had no gift for "easel pictures" though he struggled to create them.

An effort in that direction appeared in his association with Lehman in Florida, whom he employed to paint backgrounds for some of his shore and water birds. This was an unsuccessful experiment, though the scenes may have tended to popularize Audubon's work. In the main they are like old-fashioned photographer's backdrops, incongruous in line and quality. Their smooth erasure of graphic interest contrasts with the bold or grotesque or sheerly beautiful patterns which Audubon naturally used. A distant view of a rice plantation in the background of the painting of the great white heron was strange; graphically this bears no relation to the subject, though Audubon accepted it, perhaps because he was oppressed by the need of haste. His original intention is clear in the placement of the magnificent bird and the exotic leaves among which it is standing. His fine severities show how shallow were Lehman's pretty distances.

Within the large sequences of his work Audubon kept to the clear impersonal record. That settled the matter for the critics. He was a scientist, one of the opposing clan. What they failed to see was the constant pressure of his sense of design. Their failure may be forgiven, since design was not dominant in their era. They faltered again since his work appeared through the medium of the aquatint. Later this was to be considered an imperfect medium, and the way was open for the contention that, in any event, the beauty of the "Birds" was created by Havell.

There can be no doubt as to Havell's contribution as a transcriber. He remains one of the greatest artists in the difficult medium of aquatint. He lavished immense skill, conscience, even affection upon this work. Across one of his paintings Audubon wrote, "Amend this rascally sky and water!"–his own. In some of his later studies he only washed in the color of water or sky and let Havell develop this, often beautifully, sometimes within a convention. In a few instances Havell removed a leaf or spray, breaking the composition, sometimes for practical reasons because they would have fallen across the descriptive letterpress below. In a number of the prints the backgrounds are noticeably less daring in color than Audubon made them; the great blue heron, on which he had worked since his days at Mill Grove, is lower in key. In his paintings of rushes and sawgrass Audubon moved at times decisively into pure, almost abstract pattern, seeing colors which the painter's eye in his period seldom perceived, painting these green-blue that went into turquoise, answering colors in the plumage of birds. Havell reduced them to greenish brown. These alterations may be regretted, yet they are minor faults when the great body of his work is considered. Without Havell the full sequence of Audubon's paintings might never have been truly known.

The uncolored prints show the beauty of the graver's line. But the basic line, in great purity, was always present for Havell to follow. The large number of Audubon's originals, still existing, tells the final story. Many of these are signed and dated, showing sequences and progressions. Though there are occasional listless works, he made fresh discoveries to the end, in Labrador, in Texas, and in his studies of birds made from Nuttall and Townsend's collection. He could fill the entire space with an intricate design, as in his "Mockingbirds Attacked by a Rattlesnake," a work whose high decorative values have been obscured in the wave against story-telling in art. With no story at all he achieved the same effect in his meadow larks with their nest in a thicket of leaves. He knew equally the values of tranquil untouched spaces, which are never empty because they are so beautifully enclosed. He had learned early the possibilities of intermingled repetition and variation in the mere placing of a pair of birds, and could achieve by this studies that were spacious and fugue-like or as simple as a folk air.

Some of his boldest complete designs remain unpublished. He evidently thought his first study of water turkeys, made in New Orleans, too wild and strange for the ordinary observer, as perhaps it was; he made another in Florida, wholly different. In Florida, too, in the midst of his final work, he made a second study of the great white heron, which may be thought even finer than that included in the "Birds." It is simple, with only a dark cloudy gray for background; the great bird stands in a magnificent posture with the egrets luminously patterned.

There seemed to be no end to his invention and experiment. He made numbers of related studies, of birds, flowers, insects, leaves. During his whole career he tossed off literally hundreds of works outside his great sequence—landscapes, portraits in chalk, pastel, water colors, oils, some of which may never be known since he did not regard them as important and seldom signed them. He would make watercolors on scraps of paper to please children. He once painted a garland of the favorite flowers of a friend on the flyleaf of a book. He was lavish with such mementoes. The epical scope appeared fully in his painting. A flowing, uncalculating abundance belonged to him.

This proceeded from a temperament, and may have been difficult for niggling minds to understand. The warfare over rattlesnakes and vultures was honorable in comparison with much that followed in American magazines while Audubon's work on the "Birds" was being completed. James Hall's brother, Harrison Hall, had a financial interest in the publication of Wilson's work. But Hall had at least been willing to admit that Audubon was an artist. John Neal, a more persistent enemy, denied this on grounds that challenged the very structure of his art, and added personal questions which had no place in reputable journalism. Neal always delighted in controversy; his history shows him frequently in the midst of it, but the reason for so great an animus as he now displayed is difficult to discover. It may be trivial; he may only have sought to justify himself for his withdrawal of a subscription to the "Birds."

Neal was in Cincinnati in the winter of 1833-34, where he undoubtedly saw Hall, and where he also met young Mason, who had accompanied Audubon on his journey to New Orleans. He seems to have made further inquiries in Philadelphia, where Audubon had met something less than friendliness because of the old feeling about Wilson; but the substance of his attack was constructed from what Mason said or wrote. He had urged Mason to make his charges, telling him "not to falter or forbear" and he published the elaborated story in three numbers of his paper, "The New England Galaxy," beginning in January, 1835. Neal declared that during the entire period of some eighteen months Mason did "all the botanical drawings" for Audubon and "painted the feet, legs, eyes, and beaks of all the birds in water colors, the rest being done by Audubon, who rubbed the colors on dry. There are about two hundred and fifty pieces in all, every part of which, except the *bodies* of the birds, was done by this boy, *between the ages of twelve and fourteen.*"

Two hundred and fifty pieces would include half of Audubon's work. Allowing for a few holidays and a small amount of travel and the time necessary for the mere picking of flowers, this accomplishment would have entailed the steady completion of one flower painting every two days, many of them magnificent, besides the minute and delicate work on feet, legs, eyes, and beaks. Prodigious! And the boy was only thirteen or fourteen. Neal also declared that Audubon had known nothing of water colors until he traveled with Mason, who had instructed him in this medium, though he noted at the same time that Mason had been a pupil of Audubon's in Cincinnati.

Mason in a letter to Neal admitted that he had not seen the "Birds," and that if his drawings were used they "may have been copied, altered or rearranged by somebody." He referred somewhat hazily to a few flower and bird paintings which he said were his. He also said that "Mr. Audubon never shrinks from labor or expense, prosecuting his plans."

Now among the originals are two with the notation, "Plant by J. Mason," those of the red iris, with the blue yellow-backed warbler, and the pine spray with cones and the pine-creeping warbler. Both are extremely simple in execution. A few others, clearly belonging to this period and coarse in handling, may have been done by another hand, perhaps Mason's; they do not show Audubon's habitual concern with design, though in one or two of them shadings of stems or a shadow over flowers seem to have been added in an attempt to achieve it. If Audubon used any of Mason's paintings of flowers there is no reason to suppose that he did so dishonorably; as to this he may have had a complete understanding with Mason, or he perhaps decided not to stress the slight assistance of his pupil because he knew the work was poor, inviting criticism.

At all points Audubon was inclined to acknowledge help far more lavishly than the occasion required; the text of his "Ornithological Biography" is full of such hearty references. He thanked Maria Martin, his friend Bachman's sister-in-law, for helping him "on several occasions by adding beautiful and correct representations of plants and flowers." While he was in Charleston he had given Miss Martin lessons in drawing birds; she painted or drew a few flowers for him in return. It seems certain that he "re-arranged" them—to use Mason's word—according to his own ideas. In the study of Swainson's warbler with orange azaleas, of which he was writing, the original shows that a sure hand freely filled out the rising flowers at the top, added stamens that give drift to the pattern, and worked out a use of linear reds in these and in the veins of the leaves, making a rich underply of color. The alternating tones in the leaves are characteristic of Audubon, as is the pliant use of complex blues in the butterflies, and the interwoven browns and blacks. Such organization is not accidental; it cannot be contrived or pieced together; the shy brown warbler is perfectly placed and diminished within the whole.

Design is the answer to such charges as Neal's. Design marches through all of Audubon's work; in study after study his instinctive preoccupation is clear. In piece after piece there is an even flow of pattern; the originals show no break in technique or handling. Such a highly organized and evenly executed piece as his study of yellow-billed cuckoos with papaws could only have been achieved by an artist of the first rank, working alone; nothing could have been superadded, not the butterfly, or the woody stems, or the spirited broad diagonals into which birds and leaves and branches are massed. This study does not stand alone; in painting after painting the same close fluency appears. The black-billed cuckoo with magnolias, which Mason claimed, is one of the most complex and beautiful of his designs; it is painted without a break in form or technique. Whatever assistance Audubon had was inconsequential, or, as was true of Lehman's work, against the grain.

Neal buttressed these flimsy charges with a personal taunt. "I received life and light in the New World," Audubon had said in the introduction to the "Ornithological Biography." Neal made much of the fact that he had mentioned neither date nor place. "He was born *nowhere*," said Neal. Audubon was undoubtedly reticent now about his birth. Some eight years later Neal flung the same challenge, with a fusillade of smart abuse, in another of his periodicals, "Brother Jonathan." Audubon must have heard some of the buzz of talk on this question. He made no reply. "As to the lucubrations of Mr. Neal," he wrote Bachman, "I really care not a fig—all such stuff will soon evaporate, being mere smoke from a dunghill."

15 *The Old Hunter*

WHEN the "Birds of America" was finished Audubon closed his affairs with Havell as he had closed his brief association with Lizars, on the friendliest terms, and went with Lucy and Victor and John and John's wife on a tour of Scotland for a holiday. His farewells in England and Scotland were hard to say, so warm were the friendships he had made. His tall figure had become familiar in many streets, in many houses, in Liverpool and Edinburgh and London.

He had always intended to return to America when his work was finished. He meant to bring out a "miniature" edition of the "Birds" there. As soon as the Audubons landed in New York, late in 1839, he attacked this plan in earnest. Tedious months of labor followed. Selections of detail had to be made from his original drawings; many of these had to be redrawn or reduced, and the engraving supervised. The scope of the new edition did not permit inclusion of the "Episodes," but the text on the birds, made from his journals and including many of his personal adventures, went into the seven volume work, though not by an easy process of transcription. A few errors had crept into the "Ornithological Biography," which demanded revision, and Audubon set up what he thought to be a better arrangement throughout. For good measure he included engravings of many new flowers and shrubs which had not appeared in the "Birds," and he mentioned or described twelve species which were new to ornithology.

This edition was thus a fresh work, and it had to be sold, as the elephant edition had been sold, by subscription. Though Victor and John could assist him with many details, only Audubon could accomplish the persuasion by which buyers were found. For three years he made constant trips for this purpose and even went on a canvassing tour to Canada. No monetary rewards had been reaped from the elephant "Birds," only great recognition, but the "miniature" edition, usually called the octavo edition, was to bring the Audubons substantial sums and even a measure of prosperity. It lacked the splendor of the great folios, and since the compositions were broken for the smaller pages, artistic values were lost. The colored engravings did not compare with those by Havell; the process was mechanical. But the illustrations were greatly superior in accuracy and charm to those in other ornithological works of the time, and the volumes found their way into many private libraries.

When publication was well under way, early in 1843, Audubon left this to the supervision of John, and was off with Victor and Edward Harris and others on a long journey. He had another towering enterprise in view.

In the autumn of that year a traveler on the Pennsylvania Canal saw a bale of green blankets and fur on a bench on the canal boat, as Pittsburgh was being left behind. When the berths were given out, Audubon's name was called but he did not appear. It was called again. The bale stirred slightly, the furs moved, and turned over; the blankets sat up and from the top emerged a fur cap, a pair of keen eyes, a thick comical fringe of white beard. Audubon stood erect, in an Indian hunting dress. He was "feathered to the heel," said the traveler. The spoils of a far western trip were with him, furs, ceremonial costumes of the Blackfeet, beaded ornaments, bears' teeth, buffalo horns, and his portfolios of drawings and sketches and his notes. He also had on board a few live foxes, badgers, and Rocky Mountain deer.

He was alone; the party had divided on their return to St. Louis, but interested admirers surrounded him on the canal boat who wanted to hear stories of his journey up the Missouri, and considered it a privilege to spy out hidden birds or a fox squirrel with him as they walked along the towpaths. His far vision was still acute, and one traveler decided, yes, he was sure that he too could see a squirrel on a stone wall a quarter of a mile away.

In Philadelphia, tramping about in his leather hunting clothes, he enjoyed the attention which he attracted, but his pause there was short. He went on to the little estate, "Minnie's Land," on the Hudson not far above the village of Harlem, which he had bought when the success of the "miniature" edition of the "Birds" was assured. There he received a royal homecoming. Parties of his family and friends ran down each of the two roads leading to the house when carriage wheels were heard to give him a first welcome, but he took a short cut over a steep hill and came striding down through the woods, arriving before them, to greet Lucy on the piazza. The house and grounds were filled with friends. Captain Cumings was among them, with whom he had traveled down the Ohio and the Mississippi nearly twenty-five years before, making his decisive journey to New Orleans. Other newer friends were eager to see him after his six months' journey, and all his family had gathered, a growing number, for the marriages of Victor and John to the daughters of John Bachman had brought them children. "Minnie's Land" was dedicated to Lucy, taking its name from the Scotch word of endearment, "Minnie," which Audubon had learned to use when they had lived in Edinburgh.

For this last home Audubon had again sought out one of the great waterways. The wide blue prospect of the Hudson opened through tall elms and beeches. A pretty stream ran through the place with a dam and a pond and a waterfall. Deer and elk that had been captured as fawns, wandered among the trees, and foxes, badgers, and wolves were kept in large enclosures. Simple and square, comfortable without pretension, the house had high wide piazzas reminiscent of the galleries he had known in Louisiana, with the same slanting, downward glimpses of a landscape through trees. If this was not wild land, it offered a measure of freedom, a quiet place in which to work, and a prospect of that "happy old life" of which Audubon had written and spoken so often to Lucy.

Erect and slender as in her youth, Lucy had come at last into a measure of peace and pride after the uncertainties, hardships, and disappointments of many years. She herself was not venturesome; she had made her one great experiment when she had married the lively young Frenchman who was like no one she had ever known. "Write point-blank and plain," she once said in a letter, and it was thus she liked things, simple, orderly, clear; but on the surface at least nothing about Audubon could be called well-ordered. Perhaps in minor ways their relationship had been more chequered than has been supposed. Certain of his letters and journals suggest passing disagreements as to plans. Perhaps when he went to England he did not receive from Lucy the assistance on a large scale with which she has been credited. His mention in letters to her at that time of his expenditures and balances suggests that he left Louisiana with a comparatively small sum, most or all of which he might have earned by teaching in Feliciana after his return from Philadelphia; he certainly earned in England the considerable money required for the beginnings of his enterprise.

But if Lucy had never given him a penny her gifts would have been lavish. If misunderstandings had formed between them because of the alteration or expansion of his plans, because of his delays in returning to America when the "Birds" was first launched or his often blind regard for his work, these misunderstandings were transitory. She was not pliant; she was naturally frugal. With her consciousness of the position into which she had been born and her slight if enchanting touch of primness, she was not a mere embodiment of wifely virtues or of simple romance. It may be surmised that she could be stubborn or even obtuse. But she could betray a fluent, unexpected warmth, and she could hardly have held the lifelong devotion of the restless Audubon if she had not possessed an interesting character.

No revelation of buried circumstances can alter the fact that a fundamental identity existed between these two wholly different individuals. Its structural pattern is revealed as plainly as the basic design in any of Audubon's portrayals of flowers and leaves and birds. A symbol of it remains in one of these, a painting of swamp sparrows and May apples. Across the original Audubon wrote, "Drawn from nature by Lucy Audubon. Mr. Havell will please have Lucy Audubon's name on this plate instead of mine." Her name appears, but in this instance Havell's work fell below his usual excellence; the tones are a little flat. The original has an extraordinary beauty. If Lucy painted it she was highly accomplished in her own right. The sure use of white lights on the fresh silver green of the leaves and upright stalk has breadth as well as delicacy. The whole, with its simple harmony of browns and pale pinks and silvery white, falls into a free design, different in color and handling from any of Audubon's other work. Yet it seems to be his; Lucy may have made the pencil drawing. They had seen May apples in the woods near Mill Grove and perhaps elsewhere; these may have had associations which Audubon wished to commemorate, or he may have thought that the unobtrusive strength and delicate coloring of the plant were like Lucy, and so gave the painting her name.

She gave him great assistance, but more than that, happiness. His marriage explains in large part the fullness with which he achieved expression and the fortitude with which he buffeted disaster. His finest work shows a balance, a tranquillity, which could only have come because in a fundamental relationship he was secure. Everyone who saw them in these years spoke of the clarity of understanding which existed between these two who had faced their common life with radical differences of character but with a firm bond of feeling.

At "Minnie's Land" Audubon settled down with immense zest to paint American quadrupeds. Further study of these had taken him up the Missouri in a slow steamer filled with trappers going to the headwaters for their annual rendezvous. The stops for wood gave the party plenty of time to hunt and explore, and at

Fort Union they made wide hunting trips. Indian country, a Blackfoot princess, crowds of Riccarees, new birds, buffalo hunting, these made the diversions of the long days. He had drawn both birds and animals steadily, again in a cramped space on board a boat. His party was devoted to the substantial task of discovering new species of fox, wolves, antelopes, but on the whole it was a prosaic journey. Audubon did not reach the Rockies which had been his goal since he had first come into the West; but he had days of hunting in open country once more; and he came back with a harvest of new plans and with his eyes trained for fresh problems, ready to use new natural forms, new color arrangements, untried patternings on the page.

"Please forward to me a fine black bear and one or two wolves," he wrote in his old imperious manner to Friend Bachman, who was preparing the text for the new work and had problems of his own. "I must have them!" He bought another pair of elk and a buffalo calf, and a young friend at a distance promised him a live catamount—if possible. He must draw from nature whenever he could! The habit persisted: yet behind him lay a lifetime of observation. Through many years, even when time pressed, when it might have seemed that he should confine himself only to the study of birds, he had often turned aside to draw or paint otter or mink or squirrels; he had watched black bears swimming in the Ohio, catamounts or panthers stealthily moving through leafy branches, deer in their changing coats and winter colors, chipmunks, field mice, opossums and raccoons, all in a thousand swift attitudes. His old portfolios were full of animal drawings.

He used again the familiar medium of water colors and pastels, now with new ranges of color and tone, rich browns and blacks and reds, quiet grays, the many whites, and the texture of fur instead of down or feathers. He had always loved the feel of fur, and he suddenly made great strides in its portrayal. Nothing in his early drawings of animals had promised this full conquest of the technical problems involved. Here are soft pelts, exquisite to feel, many kinds of fur, many textures, many a different touch for the hand, mingled with movement and life. In his finest paintings of quadrupeds every tiny hair seems spun to tension by cold wind, or by fear, or by the lust for prey, and the small squirrels and prairie dogs and gray rats are shown in fleeting subtle movement. The structural problems were new. On the Missouri journey and at "Minnie's Land" he studied and drew skulls and skeletons to make these clear. He never knew animal forms as well as he knew bird forms, yet it may be that where structure seems to be missing he was painting slack lines as these existed, where the eye less richly trained cannot see them.

If he had been young, if he could have lived still another of those many lives which he had often longed for! To make the truth-telling record and to discover at the same time ways in which portrayals of wild creatures could persuade and lead the eye into interesting and beautiful patterns: that would have been a monumental achievement for any painter. For the most part he kept to the record. John and perhaps others filled in the backgrounds, not always fortunately, because the scope of the work was large, and the time, again, too short. They made concessions to popular interest in the picturesque. The mechanical process was still new; the colors were often crude, the perspectives faulty. Yet the large volumes represent another landmark in the study of natural history because of their brilliant, daring scale and the accuracy of their major effects, buttressed as these are by Bachman's careful scientific descriptions.

The work was in all ways a monument of friendship and family feeling, for Bachman gave his services freely, wishing profit only for the Audubons, often working under great difficulties. Victor undertook the ardous canvassing tours which had been a burden to his father in earlier years. Half of the originals were John's, with assistance from Victor. Time has made a true ascription as to Audubon's work in these folios. This does not as a whole match his "Birds" in beauty or achievement. Yet his mastery was often complete, and certain bold flashes of arrangement can be only his. The soft-haired squirrels with a few rusty brown oak leaves at the tips of bending gray branches make a fine free pattern which is natural history if you like, but also a decorative outline in which the dry leaves and twigs faintly suggest the springing bodies of the squirrels yet assert their own forms.

Magnitude in an undertaking always was a stimulus to Audubon. These were happy months, brief happy years, four or five of them. He enjoyed this close association with his sons, and declared more than once that he had no need to paint since Johnny's work surpassed his own. Lucy was always at his side, and he was constantly sought by friends—numbers of them. Before he went to the Missouri Samuel Morse had worked on his invention of the telegraph at "Minnie's Land," and the first telegraph message from Philadelphia had come there by wire strung across the Hudson. Audubon had much in common with Morse, who was gifted both as an artist and an inventor. He had always known men of new or strange or distinctive achievements, George Rogers Clark, William Clark, Daniel Boone, Captain Cumings, Christopher North, Bewick, with whom he had so readily made a tie, and many others unknown to fame—hunters, trappers, *voyageurs*, lumbermen, wreckers—responding to them as easily as to men of learning or knowledge of the great world, always responding to the life of young people and children. Many years later Shattuck, Ingalls, and Coolidge, who had joined him on the trip to Labrador, wrote of him with warm feeling. Jedidiah Irish, the woodsman who had read Burns aloud to him as he worked at his easel in the Great Pine Swamp, was still his friend. John Bachman and Edward Harris gave him years of unremitting devotion.

"I feel as though I had a world of talk for you," Audubon once wrote an acquaintance. This eager absorption in the affairs of others and his lively intensity in regard to his own, his broad humor, his odd twists of expression, the range of his interest had made him a coveted companion.

As he looked back Audubon concluded that his own life had

been "curious," but he had enjoyed "the *world*—a world which though wicked enough in all conscience is *perhaps* as good as worlds unknown." He was too intent upon the claims of the present to dwell deeply upon the past. "I have had an abundance of mortifications and vexations yet have rather rose above water," he had told Lucy during the final press of work in London on the "Birds," and he kept to the end this somewhat casual attitude toward the obstacles he had faced or passed. A friend said that in these years "he seemed to enjoy to the utmost each moment of time."

At the last, even his absorption in new birds or quadrupeds diminished before the mere pleasure of handling brush and colors and pencil. He was the artist rather than the naturalist, contented only at his easel. Then his eyesight failed; he could no longer command the sight necessary for painting, though his distant vision seemed almost as keen as in his youth. With his growing flock of grandchildren around him he sang old French airs or played his flute, and at night Victor's wife would sing a little Spanish song for him, *Buenas Noches*, which he loved.

The few quiet years wore away. In 1851 he was gone.

Nearly every measurable force had been set against recognition of Audubon's work in his own time. His communication had been with an extremely small audience, the limited group who had subscribed to the "Birds," with their friends, and those who had seen his paintings on exhibition. These individuals were not always interested in either science or art. Sets had often been bought as a private luxury, to be placed, as a bookseller had warned him, on a drawing room table as an expensive ornament. The bound folios were unwieldy since he had insisted upon a scale which would permit him to show the largest of his birds life-size; they could not—they still cannot—be easily scanned. Of the "miniature" edition, which only suggests his gifts as an artist, not more than a thousand copies were issued. The "Quadrupeds" appeared in small editions.

He had stumbled into an era of romanticism, and romanticism played almost no part in his work. His wrens peering from an old hat and his nesting barn swallows show a touch of sentimentality, but this was exceptional. In Europe, where he first was recognized, he had seemed the fulfillment of a prevailing romantic idea as to life on American frontiers. He appeared as the untaught genius, the "American woodsman," who had lived in free concord with nature, whose gifts had flowered in the wilderness. He looked the part, with his furred or leathern clothes, his fine stature, the free encompassment of his glance. The idea, given its main impetus by Rousseau, seemed to have evoked the man. Yet Audubon had exceeded this idea. The disciples of Rousseau have seldom been concerned with precision, with order, with any sort of design. Buffon and Linnaeus, upon whom he relied for scientific guidance, must be linked with Rousseau; they gave him a conviction as to "systems of nature." But he was not naturally a follower of abstract systems; he was nothing of a philosopher;

he mastered systems of scientific classification because he felt he must. His sense of order and design was that of the eye.

The sheer beauty of his work no doubt cast its spell upon many who saw it, yet there had been others who had distrusted it because of its beauty. He had confirmed certain expectations, but he had also stirred antagonisms. He had worked outside his period or beyond it. Even now his place in the sequences of American art has hardly been recognized.

Audubon was a great original, and the destiny which befalls such men in their own era is often disappointment or oblivion. Yet from the time of his early recognition in England his fame has never been in doubt. He obtained this on a great scale. The attacks upon him certainly widened this interest; yet it seems to have been his own character that created the primary momentum, the edge of his humor, his unexpected mimicries, his ardors, the warm persuasion of his everyday talk. But this too only raised a question which must have been in many minds. Who was he, this half-French figure from American frontiers? What accounted for him? Genius often stirs such questions, and sometimes they may be answered in part. The age will tell the story of certain elements. Youthful or personal influences may be shown as a force. Inheritance may have much to say. Audubon's inheritance remains puzzling.

The question of his birth played a considerable part in his life; this occupied him intermittently; at times it seems to have been a matter of deep concern. It aroused the curiosity of others. "I saw light and life in the New World." This statement, which Neal held up to scorn, remains as his sole public utterance on the subject. He never gave the date of his birth, or his age; when he referred to this it was to suggest at least once that he was older than he would have been if the date given in the papers of adoption, registered by Captain Audubon, were correct. In a private journal he said, "The precise period of my birth is yet an enigma to me, and I can only say what I have often heard my father repeat to me on this subject." Having made it clear that he was only repeating what he had been told, he went on to say he was born in Louisiana, that his mother was Spanish, that he had lived in his extreme youth in Santo Domingo, and that his mother had died there during the Negro insurrection. At times he spoke of Captain Audubon as his father; in private he indicated his belief that Audubon was not his own name, and that he was bound by an oath to the Captain not to reveal the mystery of his birth and early years. He once mentioned an Audubon of La Rochelle who had cheated him out of essential knowledge. According to one of his granddaughters Audubon was paid a large sum by an agent, which was said to have come from his mother's family.

A clear alliance raises questions, that with the Berthouds. Certainly this was long; it seemed unbreakable. The Berthouds were generally supposed to be royalists who had fled from France during the Revolution, as had others of the group whom the Audubons knew in Louisville and Shippingport. Nicholas Berthoud married Lucy's sister, but this was hardly enough to account for the enduring relationship. Audubon's papers are full of references to Berthoud, whose position seems to have been that of his agent or banker; but Audubon's finances were always too uncertain to make this an advantage, and if it were friendship alone which created the bond it is singular that he rarely mentioned Berthoud with much warmth, or as anyone but N. Berthoud.

His affection was given to the older Madame Berthoud, who had fled from France, about whom many stories have been told, that she was a noblewoman of the old *régime*, that she had been a lady in waiting to Marie Antoinette, and that Berthoud was a name assumed in exile. The steady usefulness of Nicholas Berthoud can be explained if his family felt themselves bound to Audubon by alliances that went back to their life in France, or if they believed in his high birth. Lucy seems to have believed in Audubon's high birth without question. When John died a few years after Audubon's death, Lucy, who was too late to reach him, exclaimed, "My son! my son! To think that you should have died without knowing the secret of your father's life!" She quickly covered this statement with a vague reference, which she refused to explain. Lucy was not credulous; her clear mind had a strong vein of common sense. Whatever she believed must have rested upon some sort of evidence; and among the French colony in Louisville and Shippingport she would have had ample opportunity to learn whether such convictions as she held were credible. From these people she may have received what she believed to be evidence. Apparently she kept them to the end.

A story—or a legend—is still current in places where Audubon lived in Kentucky and Louisiana, which Lucy must have known and may have accepted.

One of the great miracles of history would have occurred if Audubon were the lost Dauphin, but this is nothing against the idea. It must be said on behalf of those who entertain it, that any career of the Dauphin, if he survived, might have highly incongruous outlines. Historians generally agree that he did survive, and that he was spirited out of the Temple soon after the death of Louis XVI or even before, and that the little boy whom Marie saw in the courtyard waving the red flag and singing the *Marseillaise* as she looked down from the window on the staircase was not her son but another child.

There are some odd coincidences. Nearly every theory as to the escape of the Dauphin places his immediate destination as La Vendée, the province near which Audubon spent his boyhood, where Captain Audubon was born, where royalist sentiment ran high. The Dauphin's birthday varied by only a few weeks from that of Audubon as given in the papers of adoption. Captain Audubon's connections in both camps could have made possible an agreement to hide the small Louis XVII. If the escape was arranged by the Comte de Provence or the Comte d'Artois, who wished him removed from the succession, it would have been a bold stroke to place him in a region where the Revolution was raging; if he were recognized he might be killed; if not, his life among the revolutionary faction would be obscure.

According to this supposition, Captain Audubon gave the general history of the little boy born in Santo Domingo, then perhaps dead, as that of the Dauphin, who could be coaxed into a partial or entire forgetfulness of the confused events of his short life. This would not have been difficult since Marie had made an effort to keep from him full knowledge of his rank. It must be noted that the name Jean Rabin was not used by the Audubons until much later in legal documents, and that these were framed in 1816, after the accession of Louis XVIII to the throne of France.

If it seems unlikely that Marie Antoinette and Louis XVI produced a genius, there may also be a measure of doubt that Audubon was the son of the rough sea captain and an unknown woman living under his protection in Santo Domingo. When the appearance and temperament of the Dauphin are considered theory might lean rather more strongly toward the Capets. Audubon must have been a child much like the young Louis XVII. Marie said he was "born gay," that he was hot-tempered, imperious, willful, and that his only real fault was a tendency to embroider little episodes according to his fancy. He was excitable, vigorous, "a real peasant boy" who had his mother's high coloring and arched eyebrows; his hair curled naturally; his head was large, with a high, somewhat receding forehead and a strong modeling over the eyes; he had a dimple. His hearing was particularly acute. Audubon as a child could have filled this description. Curiously enough a portrait of his son John, painted by himself in later years, could be set beside those of the little Dauphin without incongruity. Portraits of his two sons in early manhood bear no possible relation to the portraits or descriptions of Captain Audubon; that of Victor, painted by Cruikshank, shows a slender figure, a delicately modeled head, definitely French in character, which might have been related to a highly distinctive ancestry. The Dauphin's eyes are said to have been blue; the account varies as to those of Audubon.

Those who wish may go still farther. Audubon's passion for hunting may be related to that of Louis XVI. His manual dexterity might have been developed as result of Louis's insistence that his small son begin to learn a trade, that of shoemaker. A cage of birds is said to have hung outside the Dauphin's apartment in the Tuileries, and the paintings of flowers and birds by Desportes and others which adorned the royal palaces might conceivably have had an influence, even though Audubon's work made wholly fresh departures. A portrait of Louis XVI in prison shows him with a globe in his hand and the Dauphin on his knee; he is giving the child instruction in geography, which might have created early an interest in far spaces and in travel. Apart from any of these possible threads of connection, there was a closer resemblance in temperament and ability between the Dauphin as he appeared in childhood, and Audubon as a growing boy and young man, than has existed for the formal pretenders, who seem on the whole to have been uninteresting and slow-witted.

Every theory may be answered. Every answer may provoke a

counter reply. Whether the explicit story came from Lucy may never be clearly known; she may have believed a similar narrative which made Audubon less than royal. Whether Audubon tossed off such an idea in a moment of high spirits or in despondency or dark irony, whether he believed it or merely played with it, or what led to the impingement of this idea upon his own mind or that of others will probably remain a mystery.

Consider, if you like, that Audubon believed himself to be the lost Dauphin, and that he had some reason, now unknown, for his conviction. Men have wasted their lives attempting to unravel such mysteries, and a considerable number have made careers out of their claims. Audubon, if he had it, was able to fit this belief into his scheme. It neither warped nor altered his purposes. The years went on, his ambitions increased; and he kept royalty, so to speak, up his sleeve. The magnificence of the idea he would not have found displeasing. To have invented the story little by little would not have taxed him. Unquestionably he possessed the legend-making faculty. To deny this is to deny one of the rich constituents of his mind. Yet steadily matched against this was the almost flawless integrity which ran through every phase of his work. And this strange conjunction of traits he kept in extraordinary balance.

It will be said that Audubon contrived the idea or others similar to it as a measure of self-justification, because of his early failures, because of the attacks upon him, or because he was unwilling to acknowledge to himself or to others that his birth was illegitimate. If this was true, the effort does not seem to have created in him the mental and emotional upheavals which modern theory would lead us to expect. Excitable Audubon certainly was, yet the main movements of his life were extraordinarily calm. He had at times a disarming humility about his work but no dark turmoil of doubt. His fits of shyness can be accounted for by his long seasons of work in comparative solitude; his shyness invariably wore off, and few men have had a freer enjoyment of social pleasures, or have expressed this more contagiously. Complexities and oddities and oppositions were woven together easily in his character. He seemed to possess that simplicity which many men, Scott among them, discovered in him.

His work is the final touchstone. He might be puzzled or troubled, he might indulge in masquerades or vagaries, but his painting was singularly undisturbed. Simplicity is at its core. His strong decorative sense might have carried him away; sometimes the balance was swung in that direction, but not greatly, not often. His errors in faithful portrayal were few when his scope is considered, and the conditions under which he worked. Dramatic his effects often are, but it would be difficult to prove that the drama was of his own making. It was to be found largely in the world outside himself, and appears because his vision was swift and true. A measure of his integrity lies in the fresh perceptions that may come to those who know his great sequences well.

As to the circumstances of his birth and lineage, there is no final reading of them. The spaces of his earliest years, where a clear picture might exist, remain unfilled.

"The first of my recollective powers placed me in the central portion of the city of Nantes," he said. This was at the time of the Revolution. His history, as we know it, begins then. In a fashion, he stepped from darkness; and it is strange that he found on American frontiers forms of life which were completely his own. There he received encouragement in the pursuit of science, and if the way toward artistic expression was not widely opened to him, neither was it closed. Magnitudes were there to which he felt akin, not least in humor. The frontiersman could also produce miraculous stories, and at the same time could note with intense precision the small trails of wild creatures through bending grass or the significant changes in the color of water or sky. He had found a natural place among such men.

No one knew better than he how swiftly that primary life was passing, even in his own day. The parroquets are no longer a cloud of green among leafless sycamores. The bold ivory-billed woodpecker can be found only in the deep swamps of the far South. The traveler in winter along the Mississippi will not see, as Audubon saw, a flock of trumpeter swans rising with a beating of white wings and a great clangor. Yet slowly the wilderness is stealing back upon this continent through the creation of refuges and sanctuaries. This was nothing that Audubon could have foreseen; he was a hunter, often a ruthless hunter, belonging to his time. But he had known the primal natural world as part of our inheritance, and he had enjoyed it more than most men. The sheer beauty of his work remains, of catbirds balanced on ripening blackberries, the summer redbird on wild muscadine, the banded cuckoo, the gay purple gallinule in spring plumage with red eye, blue crown, bright yellow bill, pale yellow legs. It is no accident that the light on these is always clear and cool, as though the world were seen in the early morning. These paintings have a fresh, impersonal air that belongs to an era of discovery.

NOTE

THIS biography had its more distant origin in a concern with American frontiers. Audubon's writings, imperfect as he knew them to be, are essential to a knowledge of frontier life along the Ohio and in Louisiana during a significant period, and his development has something to say as to the place of art and science there. But characters have a way of transcending the liveliest general questions. This book would not have been written except for a growing interest in character—Audubon's character. Materials relating to him gradually assembled themselves, tales about him, queries, apparent contradictions, remembered glimpses of his original work in portraiture and the painting of birds, and the recently published journals and letters. None of these told the whole story. It is a great misfortune that the originals of all but two of his long series of journals, probably beginning as early as 1802 and continuing for many years, should have been destroyed by members of his family. They would have yielded unparalleled reflections of places, people, and of his own temperament. Yet even with this loss the materials relating to Audubon are voluminous. The traditions about him have salience and strength, and though the wilderness which he knew has almost vanished, some of its look and contour may still be evoked.

By good fortune the more immediate work on this biography

began in the place which he finally called home, in West Feliciana. Leisurely conversations, rides through an enchanting country, permission to consider libraries which had their beginnings before Audubon's time, music with which he was certainly familiar and portraits of people whom he knew—these came through kindness which cannot be adequately acknowledged. To Miss Hélène Allain of Wakefield, Miss Louise Butler of The Cottage, Miss Lucy Matthews of Oakley, Mr. and Mrs. George M. Lester of Waverly, the Misses Bowman of Rosedown, warmest thanks are offered for such gifts and many more. Miss Mildred P. Harrington of Louisiana State University had much to do with the decision to write this book by suggesting possible new materials; she too was generous in all ways during this visit. Miss Alice Louise LeFèvre was a friendly guide and companion along many roads leading from Baton Rouge and St. Francisville. Through the interest of Miss Essae M. Culver and Miss Debora Abramson of the Louisiana Library Commission it was possible to use with great ease many materials relating to Louisiana in Audubon's time, and an equal courtesy was offered by Mr. Robert J. Usher of the Howard Memorial Library in New Orleans.

Since the literature of the Ohio River is abundant it was perhaps unnecessary to travel along its course, some of which was already familiar. But Audubon had liberal ideas about pleasure, taking this with or without excuse, and it seemed a plain duty to follow his example. The time was favorable, late spring; the rivers of the green, spacious valley were high, the journey full of fortunate accidents. Search for a portrait that had long since been transported elsewhere led across flooded Illinois prairies at dusk and over the Ohio at a time of the morning when Audubon habitually saw the world, at daybreak. It was easy to make digressions into country which he knew well.

Naturally Henderson was an objective. Many materials concerning Audubon have been assembled in the Henderson Public Library by Miss Susan Starling Towles, who courteously placed them at the author's disposal. The researches among court records by Mr. Spalding Trafton, seen in manuscript through the kindness of Miss Towles, show that Audubon's circumstances there were different from what has been supposed. For those who like figures it may be said that the deeds show some thirty-seven transactions in land on his part; he always sold for cash and at a greatly enhanced profit, and received nearly fifty thousand dollars through this sort of enterprise. The itemized bill of sale of the Audubons' household goods, made at the time of the failure in 1819, proves the comfort in which they were living; a piano, a parcel of music, one hundred and fifty books, four mirrors, twenty Windsor chairs, rugs, carpets, decanters, china, and silver make only a portion of the many articles listed.

These researches go far to dispel the idea that Audubon, a struggling artist and scientist, lived with hardship on a crude frontier; indeed this idea is not borne out by the essential record. Crudeness has often been attached to the frontier as by a stereotype, and the notion that men had no concern there with matters of the mind has had widespread currency. But Audubon's writings show that he enjoyed a many-sided companionship in these years with others who shared his interests. Crudeness was to be found in these places, but ways of living changed with great rapidity. A manuscript article read before the Filson Club on March 7, 1921, by Lily Ernestine Levi on "Traditions of Shippingport, Kentucky," indicates the pleasant character of life there in Audubon's time. Struggle he had in plenty from the time of the failure of the mill onward. Struggle was his even in his years of triumph abroad, when as he said, he gave up his life to make his success. But in Kentucky his life had an easy abundance; he had—and took—the best of the frontier.

The following works have been highly useful in amplifying the circumstances of Audubon's life in this period and later:

C. L. Bachman: John Bachman. Charleston, 1888.

Temple Bodley: George Rogers Clark. Boston, 1926.

Louise Butler: West Feliciana, A Glimpse of its History, Louisiana Historical Quarterly, Vol. VII, 1924.
The Louisiana Planter and his Home, Louisiana Historical Quarterly, Vol. X, 1927.

Ben Casseday: The History of Louisville from Its Earliest Settlement till the Year 1852. Louisville, 1852.

Fortescue Cuming: Sketches of a Tour to the Western Country. Pittsburgh, 1810.

NOTE

Samuel Cuming: The Western Navigator. Philadelphia, 1822.

W. D. Funkhouser and W. S. Webb: Ancient Life in Kentucky. Kentucky Geological Survey. Frankfort, Kentucky, 1928.

George P. A. Healy: Reminiscences of a Portrait Painter. Chicago, 1894.

Benjamin Henry Latrobe: The Journal of Latrobe, Being the Notes and Sketches of an Architect, Naturalist, and Traveler in the United States from 1796 to 1820, with an Introduction by J. H. B. Latrobe. New York, 1905.

Vincent Nolte: Fifty Years in Both Hemispheres. London, 1854.

Otto A. Rothert: The Outlaws of Cave-In-Rock. Cleveland, 1924.

Edmund L. Starling: History of Henderson County, Kentucky. Henderson, 1887.

Charles Wendell Townsend: In Audubon's Labrador. 1918.

Susan Starling Towles: John James Audubon in Henderson, Kentucky. Louisville, 1925.

Alexander Wilson: The American Ornithology, or the Natural History of the Birds of the United States, Edited by George Ord. 3 vols. Philadelphia, 1828-29.

It would not be profitable to enumerate books from the literature of early western travel from which only minor details have been drawn, or to name works of natural history relating to regions which Audubon knew well though these have been freely used, since they will be readily available to any student of these backgrounds.

The following works by Audubon, or containing his writings, have formed the basis of this biography:

The Birds of America, from Original Drawings by John James Audubon, Fellow of the Royal Societies of London & Edinburgh and of the Linnaean & Zoological Societies of London, Member of the Natural History Society of Paris, of the Lyceum of New York, &c., &c., &c. 4 vols. Colored plates, double elephant folio. Published by the Author. London, 1827-1838.

Ornithological Biography, or an account of the habits of the Birds of the United States of America; accompanied by descriptions of the objects represented in the work entitled "The Birds of America" and interspersed with delineations of American scenery and manners. 5 vols. Edinburgh, 1831-1839.

The Birds of America, from Drawings made in the United States and Its Territories. 7 vols. of text and plates. Published by the Author and J. B. Chevalier. New York and Philadelphia, 1840-1844.

The Viviparous Quadrupeds of North America. 2 vols. of 150 lithographic, colored plates. Published by J. J. Audubon. New York, 1845-1846.

NOTE

Audubon and His Journals, by Maria R. Audubon, with zoological and other notes by Elliott Coues. 2 vols. New York, 1898.

Journal of John James Audubon during his trip to New Orleans in 1820-1821. Edited by Howard Corning. Published by the Club of Odd Volumes. Boston, 1929.

Journal of John James Audubon, made while obtaining subscriptions to his "Birds of America," 1840-1843. Edited by Howard Corning. Published by the Club of Odd Volumes. Boston, 1929.

Letters of John James Audubon, 1826-1840. Edited by Howard Corning. Published by the Club of Odd Volumes. Boston, 1930.

Not only the "Episodes" but the descriptive pieces on birds in the "Ornithological Biography" are rich in small bits of personal narrative. These have been closely followed except for occasional inconsistencies as to dates. In spite of probable changes and omissions in the European, Labrador, and Missouri journals as edited by Maria R. Audubon, a granddaughter, these two volumes offer a wealth of essential material, including as they do Audubon's brief sketch, "Myself," and the notes drawn from family reminiscences. Apparently the originals of these journals have been destroyed. The "Journal of John James Audubon during his trip to New Orleans in 1820-21" and the "Letters of John James Audubon, 1826-1840" have been printed without alteration and contain significant evidences as to these crucial years. The later journal, of 1840-1843, is without special interest except as it shows the renewal of Audubon's energy at this time. He had learned to smooth out his style, and the racy notations of the earlier journal and the letters are lacking. Permission to quote from the volumes edited by Maria R. Audubon and the several volumes published by the Club of Odd Volumes has been most courteously given by Charles Scribner's Sons and the Library of Harvard University.

Four hundred or more original watercolors for the "Birds of America" are owned by the Library of the New York Historical Society, an unrivaled collection, which also includes a group of drawings for the "Quadrupeds." Others may be seen in the Library of Harvard University. The notebook filled with paintings of butterflies, dragonflies, lizards, and flowers, made by Audubon during the early part of his stay in Feliciana and given to Mrs. Charles Basham of Pittsburgh in 1824, is in the possession of her great granddaughter, Miss Bertha Bowen of Louisville. The little watercolor of a cardinal grosbeak, made in Louisville almost immediately after his arrival there with Lucy, a token of his early sense of design, hangs in the Filson Club. Among notable private collections of oils, watercolors, and memorabilia is that of Mrs. Frank Shafer of Cincinnati, whose interest in everything that concerns Audubon has been untiring.

Only a few of Havell's copper plates survive. Their later history has become known through the researches of Mr. Ruthven

Deane ("The Auk," Volume XXV, 1908), who discovered that a year before Lucy Audubon's death in 1874, these were sold for old copper. Mr. Charles A. Cowles of Ansonia, then a boy, who was greatly interested in ornithology, noticed the traced outlines of birds on the copper as they were being cast into a furnace. By importunity and a commendable guile, he succeeded in rescuing a number of them. Some of these have remained in private hands. A few may be seen at the American Museum of Natural History in New York, with portraits of Audubon, oil paintings by him or attributed to him, a few wash drawings for the "Quadrupeds," and interesting memorabilia. To the Librarians of the Museum of Natural History, to Mr. A. J. Wall and the assistants in the Library of the New York Historical Society, to Miss Ludie J. Kinkead, Curator of the Filson Club, to Miss Bowen, Dr. Florence Brandeis, Miss Anna Blanche McGill, Mrs. Charles Williams, Miss Mary Verhoeff, of Louisville, and Mrs. Shafer, most cordial appreciation is offered for their generosity and patience during the author's consideration of these and other related materials.

The portraits in black chalk which Audubon made for friendship or from necessity were usually small; for the most part they seem to have been signed; they were sometimes dated. An early drawing of J. B. Bossier of Ste. Geneviève has been seen in photographic reproduction for the purposes of this book through the courtesy of Mrs. Nettie H. Beauregard, Archivist of the Missouri Historical Society. Originals in the possession of Miss Susan Starling Towles of Henderson, Kentucky, of Mr. J. T. Rouse of Cincinnati, of Mr. Allan C. Bakewell and Mr. Erskine Hewitt of New York, have been considered through the courtesy of their owners. A drawing of Miss Jennett Benedict, made in Meadville in 1824, is reproduced in Francis Hobart Herrick's "Audubon the Naturalist." A hasty self-portrait made in Liverpool in 1826 may be seen in both "The Life and Adventures of John James Audubon" by Robert Buchanan, and in "Audubon and His Journals" by Maria R. Audubon. A drawing of Benjamin Page, owned by Mr. Howard Burgwin of Sewickley, appears in "Antiques" for August, 1932. Others are known by the description of Basil W. Duke in "Fetter's Southern Magazine" for August, 1893, which also offers interesting details as to the early French colony at Shippingport.

In Lucy Audubon's "Life" a reference is made to Audubon's first lessons in oils as given him in December, 1822, by John Steen, the wandering painter whom he met in Natchez. This has mistakenly been construed to mean that he had not used oils up to that time. More than a year before this, in a journal entry for October 20, 1821, he speaks of finding a box of oil colors at an importer's; and there is every reason to believe that he had experimented much earlier in this medium. The portrait of Daniel Boone was probably painted in 1819 or 1820. This was generously shown the author, with interesting commentaries, by Mrs. Daniel Russell of St. Louis, to whom it has descended by inheritance through the family of General William Clark. A portrait of James Pirrie, belonging to Miss Lucy Matthews of Oakley, that of Miss Eliza Pirrie, belonging to the Misses Bowman of Rosedown, West Feliciana, that of William Johnstone Bakewell, owned by Mr. Allan C. Bakewell of New York, have been seen by kind permission. These are authenticated by family tradition or history as having been painted by Audubon. A similar history has been traced for a portrait of Nathaniel Rochester, now in the Memorial Art Gallery at Rochester, New York. Portraits of John and Victor Audubon as boys are designated as the work of Audubon by Maria R. Audubon in her "Audubon and His Journals," where they are reproduced. A number of other portraits ascribed to Audubon have been seen by the present writer either as originals or in photographic reproduction.

When the group is considered certain questions inevitably arise. They are characteristically unsigned and wide differences in technique and style exist among them. Such differences prove nothing in themselves. More than one portrait painter of this period, particularly in the West, adopted different styles at different times. Matthew Harris Jouett is a conspicuous example of this fluency, who was told as a young man that he could not hope to make a living as a portrait painter in Louisville since Audubon had failed to do so. Portraits ascribed to Audubon are still coming to light. No full conclusions can be reached without a study of biographical materials relating to the subjects and to Audubon, and without comparative materials which are not as yet available, as to portrait painting in places where he is known to have worked.

NOTE

Three studies of Audubon, or more strictly speaking two, are indispensable:

Robert Buchanan: The Life and Adventures of John James Audubon, the Naturalist, edited from materials supplied by his widow. London, 1868.

Lucy Audubon: The Life of John James Audubon, the Naturalist, edited by his widow, with an introduction by James Grant Wilson. New York, 1869.

Francis Hobart Herrick: Audubon, the Naturalist. 2 vols. New York, 1917.

The first two are nearly identical. Each consists of a slender biographical sketch, frequently broken by quotations from the journals and filled out by a number of the "Episodes."

Professor Herrick's researches put all later writers under great obligation, particularly for his work on essential phases of Captain Audubon's life and on Audubon's youth in France. Grateful acknowledgment is made to the D. Appleton-Century Company for permission to quote briefly in one or two instances from personal material which he has assembled. It has seemed unnecessary to repeat here Professor Herrick's extensive bibliography of magazine and pamphlet materials having to do with Audubon, but it should be said that these have been seen and used at first hand for the purposes of this book.

From his discovery in France of papers revealing the birth of a son to Mademoiselle Rabin in Santo Domingo and because of the use of the name Jean Rabin much later by the Audubons, Professor Herrick has concluded that Audubon was her illegitimate son. This possibility cannot be dismissed, but the present writer, as perhaps is clear, submits the Scotch verdict "Not proven." Proof that Captain Audubon brought the small Jean Rabin with him to France and that this boy was the identical child later adopted by the Audubons would be difficult if not impossible to establish. The first eight or nine years of Audubon's life are still a blank. The fact remains that the name Jean Rabin was not used to designate Audubon in legal documents until he was past thirty years of age, and that all circumstances relating to his birth were concealed in the papers of adoption.

A few further notes may be added here. Various commentators have suggested that this concealment may have been due to the fact that Mademoiselle Rabin was of noble birth, that indeed a romance of unusual character existed between her and Captain Audubon. But the facts, as revealed by Professor Herrick's researches, do not suggest this. It would be difficult to explain why a woman of this station would join the Captain, who was already married, in a venture on a tropical island, under primitive conditions. Nothing is known of Mademoiselle Rabin except that her name was a common one, that she was sickly, and died within a year after the birth of a son. She was attended by a physician who also cared for slaves belonging to Captain Audubon, and the care of slaves was not of a superior order in Santo Domingo at that time. Almost immediately after Mademoiselle Rabin's death the Captain seems to have formed an alliance with the woman who became the mother of little Rosa. Since Captain Audubon lived with Mademoiselle Rabin for a number of years this circumstance would surely have been known among his friends and business connections in Nantes. These few facts suggest no reason for concealment of her name when the name of Rosa's mother was freely declared.

Professor Herrick has effectively disposed of the so-called "Marigny myth" as transmitted by the Reverend Gordon Bakewell, that Audubon was born on the Marigny plantation in Louisiana. From his analysis it is clear that this plantation, as it was described, did not exist at the time of Audubon's birth, and that the member of the Marigny family who said he remembered the occasion well, Bernard Marigny, was of about Audubon's own age. Yet there is a certain amount of smoke in this story which may indicate a small amount of fire. Gordon Bakewell was Lucy Audubon's nephew; he was with the Audubons in London for a time and at "Minnie's Land." He saw Lucy Audubon in her later years. He told this story as an old man, but he could hardly have invented it entirely.

Pierre Enguerrand Philippe de Mandeville, Ecuyer Sieur de Marigny, lived in New Orleans at the time Captain Audubon was a visitor there. His connections with the royal family of France were strong; in 1798 he entertained the Duc d'Orléans, afterwards Louis Philippe. There seems to be no evidence that

Captain Audubon knew Marigny, yet the probabilities are in that direction since business was the main concern of the French colony. In the much larger New Orleans of some thirty or more years later Audubon had no difficulty in making the acquaintance of Philippe de Marigny's son Bernard, who bought some of his drawings. He spoke of having met members of the Delafosse family, who had known Captain Audubon.

Perhaps the most that can be drawn from the Marigny story is that Captain Audubon had connections among royalists and that a trail of association with Audubon's birth seems to lead through Louisiana. It may be noted that Captain Audubon, once a good republican, signed his will in 1816 with a "Vive le Roi!" (Herrick, Vol. II, 362). It is probably a coincidence that this thread of connection through the Marignys should lead to the Duc d'Orléans, for whom the Dauphin was a stumbling-block and who has been accused of conniving in his disappearance. The judgment "Not proven" must of course be submitted in regard to the theory that Audubon was the lost Dauphin. The significance of the question of Audubon's birth remains in the fact that he greatly pondered and speculated over it, perhaps enjoyed some of his beliefs, and on the whole disregarded them.

The four articles by John Neal in "The New England Galaxy" for January 3, February 7, April 18, 1835, and in "Brother Jonathan" for September 30, 1843, not included in Professor Herrick's wide net, may be noted here for those who wish to follow closely the attacks to which Audubon was subject. Neal's claim that a large amount of Audubon's work was painted for the most part by Mason, and his taunting questions about Audubon's birth, made only a part of his bitter fulminations. Although he did not mention her by name he directed a slur against Lucy Audubon, as of low birth, looking up to her betters in England. He repeated a story which he said Mason had heard from Audubon about his escape as a boy from Santo Domingo during a rebellion, which may have been a garbled story of one of Captain Audubon's adventures. Neal lavished moral seriousness upon a bit of Audubon's humor about Labrador, and with James Hall charged that Audubon had never known Boone and that Boone never returned to Kentucky after his removal to Missouri. In particular he ridiculed the story of Boone's marking of a tree by a tomahawk, which was afterwards used in a land claim, yet in Neal's day the meaning of "tomahawk claims" was well understood. It is known now if it was not known then that Boone returned to Kentucky after he settled in Missouri, and the date to which Audubon referred in general terms, about 1810, is the date usually given for this journey. Boone's concern with an appeal to Congress at just this time is documented. (American State Papers, Public Lands: Washington, 1834.) Neal made much of Audubon's description of Boone's stature as approaching the gigantic, when in point of fact Boone was of medium height, and it would seem that Audubon yielded to his sense of the dramatic; but the malevolence of the articles is obvious. They are answered by their ignorance, inconsistencies, and bushwhacking style.

NOTE

Some of the research for this book has necessarily been done at long range. Appreciation for assistance of many kinds is due to Mr. C. Tefft Hewitt and Miss Blanche Robertson of the Hackley Public Library at Muskegon, Michigan, to Mr. Samuel H. Ranck of the Grand Rapids Public Library, to Miss Ethelwyn Manning of the Frick Art Reference Library, and to members of the always resourceful staffs of the New York Public Library and of the Library of Congress.

INDEX

INDEX